BRITISH VOICES

THE UK IN ITS OWN WORDS

BRITISH VOICES

THE UK IN ITS OWN WORDS

JOE HAYMAN

Matador
9 Priory Business Park,
Wistow Road, Kibworth Beauchamp,
Leicestershire. LE8 0RX
Tel: (+44) 116 279 2299
Fax: (+44) 116 279 2277
Email: books@troubador.co.uk
Web: www.troubador.co.uk/matador

ISBN 9781780883878

British Library Cataloguing in Publication Data.
A catalogue record for this book is available from the British Library.

Typeset by Troubador Publishing Ltd, Leicester, UK
Printed and bound in the UK by TJ International, Padstow, Cornwall

Matador is an imprint of Troubador Publishing Ltd

For the people of the United Kingdom

Contents

Introduction

"I'm not racist," Rose told me over a cup of tea, "but immigration has got too much."

"I go on the bus," she went on, her voice shaking a little, "and there are lots of coloured people not speaking English. I used to know every family in this street but now I hardly recognise anyone. People come and go and you don't know them – it's like a different country now."

It was the 27th of August 2011 and I was in Romford, Essex, on the first day of a three-month tour around the UK seeking the views of ordinary people about the state of British society. I hoped to speak to thousands of people as I travelled, planning to recount what they told me as close to word for word as possible, but the conversation with Rose, a widow in her nineties and my first interviewee that day, forced me to question my approach.

I had decided to undertake the journey because of my growing concern about the UK: in the wake of the global financial crisis and ongoing turbulence in the Eurozone, the national economic outlook was bleak and the Coalition Government's austerity programme included significant public spending cuts. Phone-hacking, MPs' expenses and the banking crisis had undermined confidence in those at the 'top' of British society, while the Scottish National Party's promise of an independence referendum by 2015 had called into question the very notion of a United Kingdom. For me, however, it was the way that ordinary people seemed to be feeling that gave the greatest cause for concern: opinion polls consistently showed that large numbers of Britons felt isolated and alienated, unclear about their place in a rapidly changing country and with little sense of belonging. Voter apathy was high while trust in the integrity and competence of politicians was low. While the Royal Wedding had brought great pleasure and pride for some, I felt that such events masked deeper problems and, when riots spread across English cities that summer, some of my worst fears seemed to be confirmed.

I was thirty-one at the time, working for an education charity in London and beginning to think about my future. I was keen to make my contribution to the country and seeking to get involved in national politics had always seemed the best way to try to do so. The more I thought about it, however, the more I was concerned that Britain's adversarial politics, so tainted by recent scandals, was not the answer to the questions I was asking, which were not so much about the state as about society itself.

The riots hardened my resolve to make a positive national contribution, but also left me less sure about what that could be. The sudden ferocity of the unrest had taken me by surprise and reinforced my sense that I didn't understand England very well, let alone the rest of the UK: I came from a middle-class family and had lived in an affluent part of London for all my life, apart from time spent in university bubbles in York and Warwick. I had spent only one day in Northern Ireland, in a Holiday Inn in Belfast city centre, and had never seen the Scottish Highlands or visited a Welsh-speaking town.

It all combined to leave me feeling uneasy: certain that something was wrong but not confident that I knew what the problem was; keen to help to improve things, but unclear about how best to do so. I decided that if I wanted to answer these questions, I needed to get out from behind my desk in London and explore the UK, visiting parts of the country I had never been to and talking to people directly about the way they saw British society. I was granted three months of unpaid leave, hoping in that time to catch a glimpse of what the country was really like, to identify the key issues facing the UK and to become clearer in my own mind about the contribution that I wanted to make.

I decided to set off at the end of August and began to sketch out where I wanted to go, planning to start in the South-East before heading west into south Wales, then north to Scotland – including the far reaches of the Shetland Isles – and then giving myself plenty of time to explore Northern Ireland. I planned to end the journey by heading back to London through northern England, north and mid Wales and the Midlands. I organised a few interviews in advance but for the most part I wanted to go to different parts of the country and just talk to people wherever I could find them: in their homes, at the shops, in cafes, restaurants and pubs, at sporting events and in local parks, hoping to capture how they were feeling about life in the UK at that moment in time. I knew this approach would mean I would not get a completely representative sample of the British population but I felt that hearing from people in the context of their own lives would give a unique, raw insight into life in the UK.

I knew that in order to get that insight, I would need to meet a wide range of people and recount their views faithfully and without judgement, even if what they said clashed with my own perspective. I was looking forward to hearing this range of views, but the conversation with Rose – and, in particular, her use of the term 'coloured' – brought the challenges of my approach into sharp focus. I had wanted to capture an honest picture but, if I chose to recount comments such as hers, I knew I might offend some and be seen by others to perpetuate stereotypes or to paint the UK in a negative light.

As Rose and I talked on, however, I felt that I should stick to my approach and recount what she had said in the words that she had used. The riots had hardened my view that failing to address the way that people were feeling – including the sense that ordinary people's voices often went unheard – would simply leave those feelings to fester. With that in mind, I promised myself that no matter what people said I would present their opinions as faithfully as I could, editing their comments for brevity and clarity but never censoring them.

The conversation with Rose also highlighted a separate challenge in the approach I had chosen: with so much ground to cover, I would not have time to explore the issues individual people raised in as much detail as I would have liked; neither would I be able to do justice to individual places, such as Romford, where I would spend only a couple of hours. I felt, however, that if I was seeking to learn lessons about the country as a whole, it was right to focus not on individual issues, people or places but rather on the themes that emerged through conversations with different people in different parts of the UK and how these themes linked together. Through this approach, I hoped to build up a patchwork picture of modern British society from the perspective of the people I met.

Rose and I talked on for a while, and she told me that she felt manners had changed across the country, giving the example of a teenager from a local family who had parked his car across her driveway and had threatened her when she had asked him to move it. As she spoke, I sensed not anger in her voice, but fear. I had more questions, but she had to get on with her day and, when I left, she wished me well and I felt she was glad to have had her say.

This book is the result of conversations with over a thousand ordinary people of all ages, backgrounds and perspectives across the UK, their views recounted in the same way as Rose's: in their own words and without judgement. Some details, such as names and places, have been altered, but the voices are real and deserve to be heard.

1

Immigration, Integration and Diversity in London, Essex and Suffolk

From Romford, I headed to Southend on the Saturday of the August bank holiday weekend. By the pier I asked a woman in her fifties what she thought about the state of British society. She looked around her, at people of all backgrounds enjoying a beautiful late summer's day.

"This isn't my England any more," she said.

I asked her what she meant.

"I just feel like we're being overtaken," she replied, "like there are more of them than there are of us. Some of them are alright – my boss is Asian and she's fine – but some you just can't trust. I work in benefits and I know the Sri Lankans are lying to me – one day they're married, the next day they're not."

"My grandson is disabled," she went on, "and my daughter has to work so hard to get any support for him while they just get benefits easily."

She wanted to move on, so I approached another woman by the entrance to an adventure playground.

"The country has gone downhill," she told me. "I'm not racist – my neighbours are Indian and they're really nice – but there are just too many immigrants. I walk down the seafront now and it's all foreign voices. This is supposed to be my country but *I* feel like the foreigner."

I walked away from the seafront and met Andy, a man in his thirties who worked at a local college. We got talking and he told me that, while he personally liked living in a multicultural society, he was aware that anti-immigrant feeling in Essex had been growing for some time.

"It's boiling," he said.

* * * * *

I left Southend and headed to Basildon. It was seven o'clock on a Saturday evening, and at the Festival Leisure Park, an out-of-town entertainment complex, the pubs were full as I looked around for people to talk to. By the bar in one pub, a busy chain packed with people enjoying a night out, I found Steve, an electrician from London who was waiting to meet a friend.

"There's no such thing as British society any more," he told me.

I asked him what he meant and he offered to buy me a drink and talk about it.

"You can't stand in the way of change," he said. "People will always come into other countries – just look at America – but I just want it to be a level playing field. Eastern European electricians can work for ten months a year, go home for two months, and get all of their taxes back. How am I supposed to compete?"

"Eastern Europeans get the same entitlements as British people," he went on, "even though they haven't paid into the same benefits pot. We could do the same in their countries, but who from England is going to go to Poland or Albania? How can it be fair that British pensioners can't afford to heat their homes but people who haven't paid anything in taxes get benefits from their first day here?"

We talked on, and he told me how he had seen a black man putting on a sling and neck brace and walking into a benefits office. He had taken photos of the man coming out, removing the sling and neck brace and driving away. He said he had shown the photos to the benefits office staff but they had done nothing.

"In fact," he said, "the Indian woman in there asked me if I would have reported him if he wasn't black. What the fuck does that matter? I like the different cultures, I take my kids to Notting Hill Carnival every year – I just want everyone to compete on a level playing field and I don't want to be called a racist for it."

His friend arrived and he wished me well with the book.

I looked around the pub for more people to talk to and, at a table nearby, I met two women in their twenties, Claire and Hayley. The conversation quickly moved to cultural integration.

"We built this country," said Claire, "people died for this country, but some people don't respect that history and our culture, or even bother to learn the language. My mum lives on the Costa del Sol and I tell her to make an effort – when you're in someone else's country you have to respect their customs and try to integrate."

"I'd wear a headscarf in a Muslim country," she continued, "and I only expect Muslim women to respect English customs when they're here. In our society women are equal to men and it's important to us to be able to see people's faces, so I think the burqa should be banned."

I said she seemed to have strong views on the issue.

"My boyfriend is in the BNP," she said, "and they do go too far sometimes, but they also make a lot of sense on education and social issues."

Hayley, who had been quiet until then, said they had to go. Claire wished me luck with the book and they left.

* * * * *

The next day, I headed to Thetford in Suffolk, and, on the train, I got talking to a group of young men, players in a local football team, who were sitting at the table opposite me. One said he had strong views on immigration and class and seemed keen to share them.

"It's not an immigration problem," he said. "If you're fucking English, and you're on the dole and getting your housing benefit, while a fucking Pakistani man next to you is running his shitty little corner shop, but he's paying his taxes because he's part of the system, I'd hate you more than I'd hate him."

"It's the mentality," he went on. "It's not working class, it's 'benefits class' – the little fuckers who go robbing because 'Oh, I've got a hard life.' Well, fuck off home then – if you got on the next boat to fucking Somalia and got your hands cut off, I wouldn't give a shit – you haven't worked a single day in your fucking life."

I said he seemed to feel that immigration and benefits fraud were closely linked.

"The reason that happens is because of the media," he said. "The people who are committing benefits fraud, supposedly the majority of them are immigrants – because they're illegals, they're not on the system. The chances are that you'd probably find as many people who are twentieth generation English who are causing as much grief to our system but when you say 'immigrant' I immediately think of someone who is over here, getting our money and doing fuck all for us. You see refugees from Kosovo walking around during the day with their flashy mobile phones – it's difficult to understand a new culture coming to the country and they're taking advantage."

"If someone is disabled and they've come here legally," he went on, "we should support him because we're not a Third World country. But why should he miss out because some scummer doesn't want to work? That absolutely makes my blood boil – people who don't work because they think someone owes them something – 'I'm English so I'm just going to go on the dole'."

"My mate's just finished university," he went on, "and I told him to go on the dole, but he wouldn't do it. It's a pride thing. It's supposed to be for normal people who are just looking for a job, but, if you asked us to draw a picture of a job-seeker, I guarantee we'd all do a picture of some fucking chav, smoking his weed, never done a day of work in his life. It doesn't matter if that fella is black, yellow or fucking Caucasian."

The conversation moved on to integration.

"They shouldn't cover their faces," he said. "We're in England, we're

English – if you don't like it then fuck off. The thing that got me was the air hostess and the teacher who got in trouble for wearing a crucifix – fuck that! We're a Christian country – most of us aren't actually Christian, but, still, if you gave me the choice between a burqa and a crucifix, I'd say 'Hello crucifix'."

"My brother lives down in London," he continued, "and when I visit him I see a load of burqas and I don't quite trust anyone. But it's the ultimate untouchable – religion. You can't question it – some fucker might put a jihad on you or something."

"And then the government is paying for the mosques," he went on. "If I went to fucking Baghdad and tried to build a cathedral there, I'd probably be lynched in the street. But our government still takes it up the arse from these people. We even give them priority planning because we feel they should fit in."

He was quiet for a moment.

"As long as you can see their face, I don't mind the burqa," he said finally, "but people take advantage of it. It's like your man on the July bombings, travelled on his sister's fucking passport. If I covered my face now, I could be arrested under the Terrorism Act for concealing my identity, but if you wear a fucking dishdasha with a fucking letterbox then no one can touch you because everyone's too scared."

"It's difficult for us to deal with religion," one of the others added, "because we're on the border of Christianity and nothing. Like national security, we're concerned with keeping everyone safe and on that basis you'd ban the burqa. This is the way we run our country and I can't understand why people can't say, 'Look, human life's at stake; that's above religion.' Keeping people safe has to come above offending people."

"No one minds about immigration," he added as the train pulled in. "It's when they don't integrate. They had a hard life, fair enough, but they still need to integrate."

They all wished me well as they stepped off the train.

* * * * *

5

On the Monday of the August bank holiday I returned to London to visit the Notting Hill Carnival. By Notting Hill station, the streets were packed full of people drinking, dancing and having fun. Next to a convenience store, I met two young women waving Jamaican flags and wearing Union Flag T-shirts and told them about the book.

"I'm proud to be British," one said. "I was brought up by Caribbean parents, but we had fish and chips on a Friday night."

"Britain is a mixing pot," she added. "It's not just straight British – we take bits from different cultures and make it our own."

"We love this country," her friend said, "and we love London."

Across the street, I visited a stall where flags and lanyards bearing the colours of almost every country on earth were on sale. Around me, people of all backgrounds were enjoying the fun, and it felt a long way from Essex and Suffolk. I wanted to get some perspectives from migrants to the UK, towards whom so much of the animosity I had heard had been directed, but I was also keen to try to understand the root causes of the anger I had encountered in Essex and Suffolk. First, though, I wanted to explore the issues raised by the recent riots.

2

Crime, Social Unrest and Attitudes Towards the State in London

The next day I headed to Hackney in East London, the scene of some of the worst trouble during the riots. I decided to conduct my interviews in London Fields, a park where I knew that people from many different backgrounds congregated, hoping to find a range of perspectives on what had happened.

Before starting, I went to buy a sandwich in a small grocery shop on the edge of a housing estate. Inside, I was surprised to find five staff.

"This is my cousin's shop," one of them, an Asian man in his thirties, explained, "and we always make sure there are lots of us around. We know anyone could attack the shop at any time."

I asked if this was something they felt every day, or just since the riots.

"Every day," he said.

Outside, it was a beautiful day just before the end of the school holidays and London Fields was full of people. By the main path, a man urinated against a tree; young children enjoyed themselves on the swings; two men played petanque; and drugs were dealt in plain view.

By the swings, I met a Slovakian nanny who told me about the six-year-old she looked after.

"This boy," she said, "he's brilliant on the computer, but he can't buckle his shoes."

"Kids don't know how lucky they are," she went on. "We grew up behind the Wall, my mother died and my father brought me and my brothers up. He was lucky if he slept three hours a night with travelling to work and looking after us."

We talked about the riots.

"Children need discipline," she said. "My father used to smack me, not to hurt me, just because I needed to learn."

She pointed to the dog she was walking.

"It's like hitting the dog so it knows black from white," she said. "Every child is brought up twenty years before they are born. In my town everyone knew everyone. There's a saying, 'It takes a village to raise a child,' and I think that's right."

The boy wanted an ice cream so they went on their way and a man in his twenties approached me. He told me he was an anarchist, so I asked him for his view of the riots.

"I'm not happy," he said. "People lost their homes, people with their own businesses got burnt down, and where was our Prime Minister? On fucking holiday in the fucking Caribbean or somewhere. I don't pay taxes, but I feel sorry for people who do. How many fucking thousands did he pay on that hotel while people felt they were so fucking poor that they had to bust a window to get a new TV or trainers?"

"Anarchists are against the violence," he continued. "Like, the people in yellow T-shirts who were sweeping up after the riots – that was us. I've been in a couple of squats recently where they said anyone involved in the riots had to leave, because anarchists are about bringing society together. We were out applauding the police, saying, 'Good job on bringing those louts down,' and then the news blamed us for a jewellery shop robbery. When's the last time you saw anarchists wearing diamonds?"

"There's just so much greed in this country," he went on, his voice breaking a little. "I don't know where it comes from but it's just, like, 'I'll take what I want.' If people just took what they actually needed to get by... People throw away so much food; our society is, like, 'Just chuck it away,' but then you have to get permits to feed the homeless..."

He walked on. I was conscious that I hadn't spoken to any young people, so, when I saw a group of young women in their late teens relaxing on the grass, I went over and asked them for their opinions on the riots.

"It was great how youths were united by the riots," said one. "Gangs you wouldn't expect to mix going up against the police together. It was great to see such spirit."

"People outside London had no right to do it," another said. "It wasn't about them. But people in London had the right because of the man who got shot."

It was the only mention I heard all day of the shooting in Tottenham that had triggered it all.

"The police are always late," she continued. "My brother is autistic and he was held at knifepoint, and they knew who did it but they didn't do anything. And now the government is cutting support to get people like him into flats – they're cutting youth clubs, too."

"It was wrong to burn people's houses and family businesses," she went on, "but the big shops all had insurance so what does it matter? It was opportunistic, but I don't see how it's different from MPs and their expenses."

I asked whether the expenses scandal justified violence and looting.

"No," she said, "but it sets a bad example."

"What I really hate," she added, "is when older generations scrutinise our generation when they put us in this situation through all the cuts."

"Besides," she went on, "adults don't understand. We're wiser than their generation. They have to respect our opinion, they have to understand that, while some people did it for no reason, some people did have a reason, and I commend those people."

I left them to it. Sitting alone on a bench nearby, I found Jordan, a slightly meek teenager.

"The police are just ignorant," he said. "I get stopped and searched the whole time and my friend was slammed on the ground by the police for no reason."

"But the gangs are getting out of hand, too," he added. "Two of my friends have been stabbed recently."

As he got up to leave, I couldn't help feeling that he seemed trapped, fearful of both the gangs and the police. Behind him, I saw a boy in a T-shirt bearing the name of a friend, with the words 'Rest in Perfect Peace – Put the Guns Down' underneath.

I walked on, and found four teenagers dealing drugs from a bench.

"They shouldn't blame it on the young," one told me. "They should blame it on the government. That's the truth. If people get along with us, we'll get along with them. It's simple. We're just here smoking a spliff, enjoying the sun, and they come and harass us. They should go get the real criminals – there's paedophiles out there."

"I'd love to see an officer shot in the head," another said.

I asked why.

"Because two of my friends got shot and they did nothing," he said, "and then, when my friend shot someone, they caught him. There was a cause for the riots. Everyone has a grudge against officers and this was an opportunity to fuck them up."

"They strip-search us," another said, "take us to police stations miles away, and then make us walk home just to fuck us off. They're taking the piss."

I asked why people would risk their futures by getting involved in the riots.

"Most people already have criminal records," one said, "or they just covered up their faces."

I asked about those who didn't cover their faces.

"They're just wallies," he said.

They started playing music on a mobile phone. 'Give the middle finger to the fucking cops' went the song. I decided to move on and they all shook my hand warmly, wishing me well.

Standing by a tree, I found a young man who said he would talk to me until his friends arrived. Given all the violence that was around, I asked whether he ever got scared in the area.

"There are places you can't go because of postcode wars," he said, "but it doesn't bother me. I don't fear attack anywhere – I'm a boss."

"Being a boss is about attitude," he explained. "If you walk around with confidence, people will believe it. If you believe you're a boss, you're a boss, and you're less likely to be attacked; if you believe you're a sissy, you're a sissy, and it's inevitable that you'll get attacked."

"If you're teenage," he continued, "you know that if you're seen in an area you're not from then there'll be an issue. But I don't get into that – I go to Peckham and don't get touched. I used to be scared and then I thought, 'That's moist – I'm not going to be that way any more.' It's like I don't wear a hood because that says you're scared to show your face – when I go out I want the world to see my beautiful face."

I asked him about attitudes towards school.

"People's attitude to school is slack," he said. "They don't take it seriously. Nowadays, the mentality of people, including me, is that I don't want a job, I want money. People will use any means necessary – drugs, robberies, whatever – to get money. I'll get a job in my mid twenties but, at the moment, I don't have time."

I asked why money was so important.

"It's a necessity," he said. "Everyone needs it. Like, if you go to a club in this day and age you couldn't just buy a bottle of water; you'd have to spend hundreds so that, when people look at you, they'll think well of you. That's what I mean about being a boss. If you don't have money or that kind of attitude, then you don't have respect and without respect you don't get girls."

"I've got girls around," he went on, "but I wouldn't call them girlfriends. Some are 'just any'; some are 'wifey' material. 'Just any' means a slut, just any old bit you'd send on the night bus home. They're the kind of girl who always likes intercourse, talks shit, has no expectations in life – is on a Level 1 beauty course or something; and 'wifey' means a female you'd have a long-term relationship with – girls who have got As in exams, maybe doing a Level 3 course – respectable girls."

His friends arrived, and we got talking about the police.

"They racially discriminate," one told me. "They search the black kids and leave the whites. I know they're only doing their job but they talk to us like we're a piece of shit. They smashed my brother's head against a windscreen, pushed me up against a wall, all for no reason. If they're going to be like that to me, I'm not going to be polite to them, am I?"

"That's why people rioted," he added. "They enjoyed having power over the police. They were saying, 'If we wanted to take over, we could.'"

As I left, I shook hands with them and noticed that one had a tattoo on the inside of his arm that read 'RIP Mum'.

I had spoken to everyone I could on London Fields, so I headed on to a nearby housing estate where I found five young men playing football in a caged concrete pitch in the middle of the estate.

"Even though we're not involved in gangs," one told me, "the way people look at you just puts you down. You don't feel welcome."

"We're stereotyped," he went on, "even us good people. No matter what you do, you'll always have that bad name of a black kid from Hackney, so some people think, 'I might as well be bad.' Some kids, their parents can't feed themselves, let alone the kids, so what do you do? Now the EMA has gone they have to steal to survive."

"There's a lot of talent in Hackney," another said, "but there are no opportunities to uplift yourself. We're left stranded; we have to fend for ourselves so, if you see people with a nice car, you say, 'I want some of that,' and dealing is the way to get it. Our generation, we like fancy stuff but we can't afford it – the riots were an opportunity to get things you know you couldn't otherwise get."

I asked if that was worth the risk of a criminal record.

"If there are no opportunities anyway," one said, "you might as well risk it."

"It's about leaders," another said. "If we had leaders, most of these things wouldn't happen. Like our MP – as soon as she got in that position she sent her kids to a private boarding school. She's meant to be representing us but she's just a hypocrite. They shouldn't say a thing about me until they've walked a day in my shoes. The same with Nick Cameron."

The others laughed at his mistake and corrected him.

"See?" he said. "I don't even know the name of the Prime Minister. How can we look up to someone if we don't know who they are? We need guidance; we need people to help us make the right decisions."

"Na mate," another said, "no one's going to do it for us. We've got to take responsibility for ourselves."

"But how can we do that without guidance?"

They began a long and animated debate about whether they should take responsibility for themselves, or whether others, politicians, in particular, had a responsibility to help them.

I had to leave. They wished me well and I thought how warm and friendly everyone I had talked to over the day had been, the young men I had just met most of all. As I walked back to the street, I could hear their discussion about responsibility continuing. In one form or another, that discussion would continue throughout my journey.

On the street outside the estate, I met a counsellor to young people from South London who was in Hackney visiting friends. We got talking about the riots.

"The brain of a child who is cared for grows larger than that of a child who is not," she told me, "so it's hardly surprising that children who are not loved behave this way."

"If these children see bad behaviour around them every day, then what else do you expect?" she went on. "That is why they have no empathy."

I asked her whether children could be taught to be more empathetic. She smiled at me.

"You don't teach empathy," she said, "you imbibe it from those around you."

3

Social Media and Social Class in London

A major topic of debate in the news after the riots that I wanted to understand more about was the role of social media, so the next day I got in touch with two young men with a good understanding of the issues.

First, over breakfast in a cafe in North London, I met Josh Feldberg, a thirty-year-old public relations consultant. I asked him about the role social media had played in the riots.

"The first thing to focus on would be BlackBerry Messenger," he said. "That's what a lot of kids used. They would change their username or put a status update saying, 'Let's go and smash up Tottenham,' and were encouraging everyone else to do the same. It creates a viral effect, but what's interesting about it is that it's closed – no one else can see it, so there's less fear of getting caught."

"It's not like that on Twitter," he went on. "Twitter's more open so you can see all the conversations and choose who to interact with. It's also a different type of person – they call it the 'Twitterati', and there's a sort of social type, to put it rather candidly, that uses it – what they'd call the ABC1 category in PR. That is changing now but it's still disproportionate."

I asked him why that was the case.

"Lots of reasons," he said, "whether it's access to smartphones, which make it easier to use, to being in jobs where you sit at a desk all day and can go online. To put it rather bluntly, you can't do that if you're stacking shelves. And the thing is that it creates a disproportionate influence, so places like Sky News look a lot at what's happening on Twitter for trends but obviously there are only certain people on there."

I asked him what people who were not on Twitter missed out on.

"I guess you miss out on instant news," he said. "It's just a constant flow of information, very up to date, very on the pulse. I don't think it particularly opens you up to new views, though, because you become more selective about what you see and you tend to lean towards people like yourself more. There are a few different voices around, but the reality is: people who really annoy me, I don't follow. Even the people with a different political view from me are all still in the political class – it's all just political gossip, which most people won't care about."

I moved on to Facebook, and asked what people who weren't on it missed out on.

"Time wasting," he said with a smile.

"I don't know," he continued. "It's got a lot of benefits, but, if it died tomorrow, would my life be worse? Not really. It's fun sharing your photos and having conversations and it does fuel your interests and give you more information."

"For me," he went on, "the bigger divide is not about Twitter or Facebook but the fact that some parts of the UK are still not on broadband. If you look historically, there was a proportion of the population who couldn't read, and that created a social divide immediately. Now the technology for the Internet has been created, it's about ensuring everyone has access because there are lots of benefits which can enhance life and make things easier."

"Take something like jobs," he said. "Something like LinkedIn – it's becoming *the* platform through which executives get jobs... TES Connect, for teachers, there's one for social workers, there's MyHammer, which is for people to bid to do building jobs..."

"But, then again," he added, "if it didn't exist, things would be a lot simpler."

I asked what he meant by 'simpler'.

"It drives attention deficit," he replied. "There's just too much going on at once… I remember when I was young, I used to watch Teletext for the football scores. Now I can go on my iPhone to get the latest goals on my ESPN app, go to Sky Sports News Centre on TV or on my phone, or I can watch a Twitter stream for #Arsenal, or I can probably see Facebook and get updates. It's just amazing amounts of information, and I've sat there with them all open at the same time, and I just thought, 'This is bonkers.'"

"Where it has been useful for me," he went on, "is I've been networking with people in San Francisco and New York and I've then met up with them. On a political level, I'm a big fan of Akala. I heard about his albums through groups I'm a member of online, so it does enhance my life in that sense, bringing me new culture. The other thing is that there's more variety but, again, I don't know if that's a good thing."

I asked why more variety would not be a good thing.

"Well," he said, "it's great to go on TripAdvisor and look at all these holidays and work out the best hotel and the best restaurant, but I go away for a weekend and I spend more time researching it than I do just being there and enjoying. Last week, I booked a random B & B and it was nice just to have turned up and not thought about it too much."

"It can make you less present, as well," he went on, "so you're in a restaurant, and you 'check in' on Facebook or Foursquare so people know where you are, you read a review online while you're sitting there, you take a photo and you tweet it – even in real life, you're always sticking towards your cohort of people."

I asked him why people did that.

"It's probably slightly egotistical," he said. "Like, if you've got a thousand followers on Twitter and you put a message out, people might read it. Everyone wants to feel heard, don't they? I've had times where you write something on your blog and suddenly thousands of people might be writing about it – and it's a good feeling."

"That's a real benefit of the Internet," he went on. "It can give you a voice; you can reach thousands of people really quickly. You can't get something published in *The Times* but you could write a blogpost that could get more views than any newspaper. There's a musician called LowKey who has no commercial backing whatsoever and he was on the front page of YouTube as the most viewed video of the day – it goes across all the arts and politics and I think that's the powerful thing, the ability to reach millions without having any money. Even if you don't reach millions, the technology really can fuel a passion, for music or whatever else."

He took a phone call, so I was able to pause for a moment and think back over my travels so far: the young people in Hackney, the anger in Suffolk and Essex. When he came off the phone, I told him about what I had found, and asked him where he felt social media fitted into the issues I had been considering.

"The important thing to consider is that it's more than just the digital divide," he said. "There's also a divide on who produces information, so there's no voice for disenfranchised people in Essex or the kids in the Tottenham riots – who's speaking up for them? Where's their platform?"

"I think one of the reasons for the rioting was about taking something back for themselves," he went on, echoing some of the young people I had met in Hackney, "because if you look at me, I know MPs, I have access to people via LinkedIn and Twitter who inform the news agenda which means I'm quite close to what happens. That call I just took was from a journalist who's going to meet the Vice President of a Global Fortune 500 company and write an article about him, just because I put in a few calls and wrote a few emails. That's writing the newspapers which you'll read on Sunday. But people in Tottenham, they're not connected to it at all. Some people are so far away from it, they don't feel like they have any influence on anything. They can write to their MP or go to a surgery, but really, what good is that going to do?"

"The other thing is about wanting to have 'stuff'," he added. "It's like that iPhone advert with the tagline, 'If you don't have an iPhone, then you don't have an iPhone' – like, if you don't have one, you're no one. But an iPhone is a bloody expensive thing, it's a minimum of £40 a month on a contract or if you buy it direct it's three hundred or four hundred quid – that's most people's wages for two weeks. The iPhone is a luxury good promoted as being a 'must have' even though most people could never afford it, so you get people like that kid in China who sold a kidney to get an iPad."

I suggested that it was unlikely that anyone in the UK would do that. He looked at me.

"No," he said, "we just smash shops up instead. Whether it's selling a kidney or smashing up a shop, it's still an extreme way of getting what you want."

* * * * *

Later that day, I met Alex Smith, who until recently had worked in the communications team for the Labour party leader, Ed Miliband. We met in a pub in Westminster for lunch, and I asked him about his interaction with social media.

"When I worked for Ed," he said, "I'd wake up and the first thing I'd do would be roll down on Twitter, just to access my news from people involved in Westminster journalism and public policy to see what they were saying. That way, I'd be informed about what was going on even before getting out of bed. And then on the walk to the Tube station, I'd continue to do that, so I was abreast of all the news stories before I arrived at my desk. The first thing I'd do when I got to work was open up twenty or thirty different websites and see which were talking about issues that we thought were important. And then throughout the day, I would periodically look at Twitter so I'd be constantly informed and connected."

I asked whether that level of interaction with social media was necessary.

"It's the done thing," he said, "but that's in a very PR/third sector campaigns/political world. I think it's only the 'Westminster Village' and the media set that thinks that Twitter is especially important – it doesn't exist like that in the City, for example."

He took a phone call, and I looked around the pub. I saw a group of men wearing T-shirts that read 'Save British Jobs' so I went over to see what was going on.

"We work at the Bombardier factory in Derby," one told me, "and we just lost a big train order to Germany. The knock-on effect on the supply chain, you're talking thousands of jobs, so we've come down to Parliament to make our point."

"It's the last train factory in Britain," he went on, "and if it closes, that will finish trains in this country. We're going to lose our heritage if we're not careful."

He wished me well and went back to his colleagues. I went back to Alex and said it didn't seem like social media was doing much for people like the man I had just met.

"The thing is," he said, "that social media is held up as this empowering, equalising tool that gives a voice to the voiceless and redistributes power. And around the world there are some examples of that happening – the Arab spring, for example. But here, the biggest campaign I can think of that really had an impact was for Rage against the Machine to be the Christmas Number One ahead of Simon Cowell's X-Factor winner. Social media hasn't led to a change in social policy in a way that most advantages those people who need most help. Those people are the most remote from this social media world, and it doesn't seem like this technology is empowering them to make changes in areas that really make a difference in their lives."

I asked him why not.

"Because the whole scene is self-selecting," he said. "There's still the same group-think that there was when people were meeting in smoky pubs in Westminster. I follow Westminster journalists and they all follow each other – they don't follow John who lives in Stockport. Until Twitter leads to a revolution in housing or social care, it's not going be the great democratising tool it's held up to be. But I'm a cynic…"

I suggested that the world that he was being cynical about was also the world he inhabited on a daily basis.

"Yeah," he said, "but I don't like it. Whether it's knowing or unknowing, I don't feel comfortable with people holding up social media to be a democratising thing beyond what it is. They say, 'Social media is great because it gives people a voice,' but until that translates into people feeling like they've got more power in their life then they'll continue to be angry."

As he left, I realised I had started the day thinking about technology, but ended it thinking about connection and class, and, in particular, the ability of some to succeed in modern Britain while others were left behind – an issue I planned to explore further as I travelled.

4

Identity and Nostalgia in London and Sussex

Later that afternoon, I went for a walk around Hackney, where I had been staying. I walked past a parade of shops that still had broken windows from the riots a few weeks earlier, and saw a pub with two large Union Flags in the window. I was interested in this statement of British identity so I went inside and met the landlord, Steve. He told me he had put the flags out for the anniversary of Armistice Day but had kept them up.

"I'm proud of it," he said. "We've got three saints on our flag – even the Pope doesn't have that. We put even more flags up for the Royal Wedding. No one puts flags up any more but we're proud of it."

It turned out it was not just a statement of identity for Steve but also of tradition.

"We call it 'The Last Bastion'," he told me, "because there are no other traditional pubs round here. We play the East End music on a Saturday night, we still serve warm beer from the barrel, the men stand and the women sit, and we have the keyboard and the drum like we did when I was a kid. I suppose it's a bit of a time warp but just because things move forward in time, it doesn't mean it's necessarily progress. Everything's changing but I like to keep things traditional, protecting things the way they were."

He wished me luck with the book and I walked out into the sunshine. On the street outside the pub, I got talking to Laura, a charity manager who lived nearby, about what Steve had said about tradition and the past.

"Harking back doesn't help though, does it?" she said.

I asked her what she meant.

"I just think that saying there was once a golden time when nothing was wrong is deeply flawed," she said, "suggesting that the way to help people who are struggling today is to recreate the family dynamics, the way in which we interacted and the way authority was structured in a bygone era… It wouldn't work, and it completely disregards the fact that there have been huge strides forward in British society."

I asked if that meant she was less concerned about tradition than most people.

"I think that there are things that are traditional which are amazing," she said, "but I just think it's really unhelpful to look to undo all this progress. I'm not saying things are perfect but you have to start from where you are."

* * * * *

Laura's argument had been persuasive, so I decided not to focus on the questions the landlord had raised about tradition and instead determined to focus on the issues he had raised around identity and patriotism. When I heard that the English Defence League was holding a rally in London the next day, I headed down, keen to find out more about them.

It was a sunny Saturday and the streets around King's Cross station were quiet when, suddenly, a large group of men appeared, singing and bearing English and British flags. They headed for a pub just along the road and congregated outside. I watched as more and more groups arrived – each cheered as they walked towards the pub – until the number outside the pub had grown to around a hundred. Many wore T-shirts and jumpers with the EDL logo and the name of their local branch – Berkshire, Wakefield, Manchester. The Scottish Defence League was there, too, its members holding a Scottish flag bearing the name of Kris Donald, the Glasgow teenager murdered by British-Pakistani men in 2004.

"No surrender, no surrender, no surrender to the Taliban," they chanted and the occasional car driving past gave them a hoot of approval.

Television crews appeared, prompting more boisterous and aggressive singing into the cameras, and the police numbers grew as well. Across the road, an EDL member was talking to a group of young white builders who had come over to see what was going on.

"We're not racist," he told them. "We've got black members and Sikh members; we just want to keep things British."

"Why should they cover their faces?" he went on. "If you come to England you should play by our rules."

It was a very similar argument to the one I had heard in Essex and Suffolk, and the builders seemed to be listening with interest.

Across the road, someone threw something at the crowd, and scores of the men rushed off in pursuit of whoever had thrown it. The police followed them around a corner, and there were the sounds of shouting and screaming and smashing glass before order was finally restored, and the men returned to the pub. Nearby, I saw one man pinned to the floor by six police officers, his face pressed into the pavement until finally he stopped trying to wriggle free. They picked him up and took him away.

Next to the pub was a bus lane that was set off from the main road with pavement on either side of it. As the buses came through the lane every few minutes, they were surrounded by the men, who stood in front of each one and unfurled the Union Flag before letting it through, banging on its windows as it passed. They stood in front of one bus waving the flag for a particularly long time, perhaps a minute, and banged hard on its windows. Surrounded on all sides, the driver had no option but to wait until finally they let him move. As the bus pulled past me, I looked in and saw a young boy, no more than three or four, clearly frightened by the men waving the British flag.

* * * * *

23

My next stop was Hastings in Sussex, and, on the train down, I heard the guard on his radio complaining to his head office about a broken toilet. I asked him what was going on.

"I told them to fix it four hours ago," he said. "It's pathetic."

We got talking and I told him I was writing a book about British society.

"That'll be depressing," he said.

"My son's in the army," he went on. "He hates it but what's the alternative? There are no jobs for young people here. OK, some English kids don't seem to want jobs, but there are also just too many people. Every time they propose a new law I think, 'Great, but how are you going to enforce it?' It's so overcrowded that it's ungovernable."

"I do this line a lot," he continued, "and you can go along an entire train and not hear anyone speaking English, and they're not tourists, not on this line. This isn't the country I grew up in. Every six months I go to see my family in Scarborough, and that's still England, but when I step off the train back at London I just get depressed."

As he went back to work, I couldn't get the sadness in his voice out of my head.

* * * * *

When I arrived in Hastings, I walked into the town centre and saw a tattoo parlour. With questions of identity and patriotism still in my mind, I went in, interested to find out whether demand for Union Flag and St George's Cross tattoos had changed in recent years. The four men and three women inside were interested by my question and, while they said demand hadn't changed much, it did get them talking.

"We used to have an empire, you know," one man told me. "I used to be in the army. That's what really annoys me when other countries go on about colonialism and say we ruined this and we ruined that – if the Empire hadn't moved in there, they wouldn't have anything – like the

Indian railway system."

"It is ironic, though," one of the women said, "that their railway system is now so much better than ours. We seem to export our nationality, not keep it for ourselves – like we're ashamed of it."

"We just keep apologising for things," the man said, "like apologising for slavery. It was a terrible thing but *I* didn't do it, so why do we have to keep apologising? Nowadays everything is done with an apology."

"As an outsider, I can say the country is letting its own people down," another man, originally from Trinidad and Tobago, said. "I've no problem with immigration – the Polish, the Gurkhas – they fought with us in the war. But it's got to the stage when they can fly the Polish flag but not the British flag…"

"… because that makes you a racist," one of the women said. "We're so scared of upsetting people – it's a very British thing."

"It's not about harking back to a golden age," she went on. "I'm not saying we should go back to the fifties when everything was wonderful – an idyllic time when kids were just scamps who played on the street. I just think there are elements of that era that were better – manners, for example. We just don't have those ethics any more."

"That's what the bike club we've set up is all about," said the first woman. "It's multicultural but we all stand up for principles and stand up for Britain. We have so many nationalities but we all follow the British way. We all believe in bikes and we all believe in our Britain."

I asked what they thought of people who used the British flag to say people should stay out of the country.

"Absolute scumbags," said one of the men. "The biggest mistake this country made was not pledging allegiance to the flag, so it becomes a unifying thing. You very rarely see the Stars and Stripes used as a right-wing symbol and that's the problem here – the flag has been captured by the right wing and that has to be corrected."

"We get people in here wanting a Cross of St George," he continued, "and people think it's National Front but I never see it that way. The flag is what you believe in, and, if you lose that, which I think a good part of this country has done, then everyone loses out. They should have said, if the BNP is going to fly the flag then everyone else should fly it too, so the BNP becomes diluted. But, instead, everyone else was told not to fly the flag, so it gave the BNP even more power. In France you can't move for the flag but if I put a Union Jack outside here I guarantee someone would call me racist."

"We're almost hiding who we are," he went on. "I remember, a few years ago, England won a match and Ian Wright – a black player – ran across the pitch in an England flag. That's what it should be about – it should be for everyone, regardless of their colour, and you should be able to wear it without anyone saying you're a horrible right-wing thug."

* * * * *

With questions of identity and patriotism still on my mind, I decided to go up to Wembley Stadium a few days later, hoping to find some England fans on their way to watch a match against Wales.

It was an hour before the game and a steady stream of people were walking towards the stadium. I met a father in his sixties and a son in his thirties, both sporting England shirts, and asked if they felt more English or British.

"English," the father said firmly. "I'm always told I'm British but you never hear a Scotsman saying he's British, do you?"

I asked his son what being English meant to him.

"Being downtrodden," he said, echoing the tattoo artists. "Never allowed to say who you are. We should be celebrating St George's Day. In the US, sometimes it's a bit much but they are proud to wear the flag, they're proud of their country and they support their forces. When I was staying in the States, as soon as they found out I was in the RAF they thanked me and gave me 50 per cent off the room."

"The Human Rights Act is greatly abused," said the father. "It's aimed in one direction – some people get more rights than the rest of us. I'm not being racist but that's the reality…"

"The main point," his son interrupted, "is that, whether you're from India, Pakistan, China, whatever, if you're here, you should say you're English."

They went on their way, and two women wearing England shirts appeared.

"Being English is important," one told me. "We're not as passionate about our identity as the Scottish. Maybe we're a bit lethargic about it, but I also think we're scared. England is a multicultural society and that's fine but anywhere you go it's rammed down your throat too much – we should be allowed to celebrate when England win, and people who've been born in Poland or wherever should celebrate, too."

"Nights like tonight are a chance to express our pride without feeling guilty about it," her friend said. "We should have our own English anthem, too, for events like this, but, again, it's something we're too frightened to say or the right people aren't saying it."

More and more people passed, predominantly white and all stating that they were proud to be English. I began to ask them why they felt such pride, starting with a man in his forties.

"Patriotism," he said.

I asked what made him patriotic.

"The Irish celebrate St Patrick's Day but we don't celebrate St George's Day," he said. "I know we're multicultural now and I'm not a racist but the Scots and Welsh don't worry about offending people so why do we?"

I wanted to press him on the things that made him proud, but he was keen to move on. Behind him, I met a group of young men from Northampton.

"I'm definitely English, never British," one told me, "but even coming through London you feel like you're a foreigner in your own country."

"Everyone should be proud to be English," he went on. "You live here so you should be proud."

I asked what made him proud.

"It's just great to see the St George's Cross all over the world," he said, walking off, and again I felt that he had not really answered my question.

More and more of the people I spoke to struggled in a similar way to answer the question, and kick-off was approaching. Just before the match started, I found a man who had come up to Wembley from Devon with a friend.

"This is great, isn't it?" he beamed, pointing to the crowds making their way towards the stadium. "The atmosphere, the feeling amongst people – we need to come together in hard times like this."

I asked him whether there was anything in particular about the country that he was proud of.

"My homeland, my country, our exceptional history," he said. "Just look at the exceptional train stations we've got and the magnificent gothic buildings."

His friend standing next to him, who was more cynical about the question of identity, was not impressed.

"Train stations," he said as they went on, "is that it?"

* * * * *

I left Wembley that evening concerned that so many people I had met felt inhibited about expressing their identity; but I was also troubled by people feeling proud without being able to explain why. I thought back to the pub and the train guard. Laura, the charity manager I had met outside the pub, must have been right about the country having moved a long way forward, but somehow it didn't feel that had translated into people feeling better about life in the UK. As I travelled around the country I wanted to understand why that seemed to be the case, but before I left London I wanted to get perspectives from migrants to the UK on the issues I had been examining.

5

Migration in London

The next day I arranged to meet Shoqo Warsame, a Somali woman who had come to the UK twenty years earlier. In her flat in Kilburn, North-West London, her baby son asleep in her arms, I asked her about her view of British society.

"The politicians were good before," she said, "like Tony Blair – he was a good man. When I came to UK, it was John Major. I applied for asylum seeker, and didn't receive anything for six years. Then Tony Blair came; it only took two weeks. Politicians are not good now; they cut too much. Both of them – Nick Clegg and David Cameron – they even cut soldiers and the police. The police are very important to keep us safe. Now London is not safe. This is a royal country, but even Prince Charles was attacked in his car. When I saw that I was so worried – they're trying to cut the money but they're cutting the country."

I asked her what she thought of British people.

"Very nice people," she said, "very kind, very respectful, very helpful when I come here."

"The language is very difficult," she went on, "so everyone must learn English – otherwise you can't understand everything. You need to learn the rules."

I asked her if she ever felt she was not welcome in the UK.

"I never had any problem," she said. "On the inside, people might have discrimination but I never see it since I came here. Other countries are different – I been to Italy and I was sitting on the bus. An Italian man said I must stand up. He said 'I am Italian – you can't sit when Italians are standing.' It's the same in France – when you are on the train, the ticket inspector only checks people who are not French. In the UK, it's more equal, and no discrimination. They don't stop you wearing the hijab or the scarf. That's the reason peoples come here – because it's freedom, more respect for our religion."

I wanted to look at religion in greater detail later in my travels but, given my conversations in Suffolk and Essex a few days earlier, and the fact that Shoqo wore a headscarf but did not cover her face, I decided to ask her view on the burqa.

"It is no good," she said. "It's not nice to wear in a public place. In the UK they don't stop you but I think Muslim people must respect the British society. British people respect people, but you have to show the face."

"I was at Heathrow," she continued, "coming back from Somalia, and there was a woman in the queue – she refused to take off the niqab for security. I told her, 'If you refuse, no one will trust you.' After September 11th, trust went, and we have to listen to what they say. I respect for British society – I don't want it damaged. If you leave your country, you have to compromise, you have to listen how they like security and society, you have to change. We're very lucky here – you get a solicitor, you get medical care, you get everything. It's a big opportunity, but they have to respect this country and listen to the people."

* * * * *

My next stop was Croydon, South London, to meet Crescencia Nga Che, a woman in her twenties who had moved to London from Cameroon six years earlier. While I waited for her at a bus stop, I got talking to a Polish builder. I asked him what he thought of people who said migrants were taking British jobs.

"We don't '*take*'." he said. "We work harder and we work better."
He pointed to a wall.

"Look at the brickwork," he said, "it's bullshit. I would never do a
job as bad as this. We're not tossers, we're not wankers – we come for
opportunity, so what's the problem?"

He wished me well and jumped on his bus.

When Crescencia arrived, she showed me around the area where she
and her brother had lived when they had first come to London. She
pointed out hairdressers that, she said, were centres of gang activity and
said she often could not sleep for the police sirens on the street below.

"I lived in that attic room for two years with my brother," she told
me, pointing at the top floor of a house. "The ceiling was so low he
couldn't even stand up straight inside."

I asked how she came to the UK and she told me her mother had
put her life savings towards them studying in London.

"My mother nurtured my love of the UK from an early age," she
said. "She told us the history, took us on visits here. We saw London as
a land of opportunity where people of all cultures came together to
achieve their potential – the centre of the world."

"We had high expectations in my country," she went on. "We went
to private school and grew up surrounded by entrepreneurs or people
holding senior positions in big companies. They expected us to emulate
them, so I've never suffered from the lack of aspiration which plagues
some of my peers in black British communities. I feel a bit like an outcast
because of it, but for me where I am is where I was meant to be."

With most of their mother's savings going towards tuition fees, the
attic in Croydon was the only place Crescencia and her brother could
afford. She told me she lived in constant fear of the gangs, trying to live
as a "ghost" in the area, hoping to pass through unseen on her journey
to and from the station each day.

As she progressed with her course and her career, she described how
she faced a fight with the Home Office to stay in the country. She said
she spent numerous days "being herded like an animal" at different

Asylum and Immigration Tribunals across London, and had to fight her case single-handedly because she couldn't afford a lawyer.

"I studied the British legal system late at night after work," she said. "Immigration law, employment law, the Human Rights Act – sometimes until four in the morning."

"I wrote to my MP," she went on. "I wrote to every Secretary of State, the Mayor of London, the Equality and Human Rights Commission, even to the Prime Minister. Eventually I got an apology back from Gordon Brown. And then there was another administrative error with my work visa in 2010, so I had to write to all the Secretaries of State again. That time I got a letter from David Cameron and three letters of apology from the UK Border Agency who decided to grant me my work visa."

In spite of all the challenges, she told me she still loved the UK. I asked her why.

"Love sometimes is irrational," she said, "but the battles I have fought have made me who I am today. They have helped me to grow up and become stronger. The British immigration system is difficult but it is far better than many other immigration systems in Europe and, when it was hard, my British friends helped me to fight against it. I am still fighting, I still have years to go until I become a British citizen, but one day I will be, and when I have my own children here I will be able to instil in them the British values which mean so much to me."

I said I couldn't imagine that most migrants to the country would be as successful as she had been in going up against the legal system or in advancing their career in the UK.

"That's why we have problems now," she said. "Some people give up and go home but some end up staying but feel very angry. The system treats you like a criminal; it makes you feel that you don't belong here. Some parents pass these feelings on to their kids."

"Also," she added, "you have many migrant mothers who have to work night shifts as nurses or carers just to support their families. This is why their children start roaming the streets as they are left with no father figure to look after them, because fathers sometimes do not take their responsibilities. As a result, we end up having children without parental figures, hating the country and getting into gangs and riots."

As we said goodbye she told me that, in spite of all the challenges she faced, she still loved the UK and that her mother's dream was still alive.

* * * * *

The next day, my last in London before heading to the South-West, I travelled to South-East London to visit a community education centre in Abbey Wood, Greenwich. There I met Ameen Hussain, the centre manager, and Jatinder Dhillon, who worked with similar centres across Greenwich, and we talked about perceptions of citizenship and identity in Britain and India.

"When our first Prime Minister Nehru came to power," Ameen told me, "there were problems with the caste system and between religions, but he said, 'You are Indian first.' You don't have that sense here, that people are British first."

"When I fly back to India," he continued, "everyone on the plane is on their way to work in the IT industry – that's where the growth is now in the world economy. British children need to be schooled in the ways of these countries – particularly India and China. They need to understand their culture and their language. But the council has cut funding to teach these languages and for projects to bring communities together, which means they are not exposed to one another."

"Comprehensive schools are failing miserably," he went on. "There is no preparation for the language and culture of emerging economies. We're not making use of our connections through the migrants from those countries who live here now. London is the capital of the world but we're not making use of that infrastructure and our global position. Speaking English gives British pupils such an advantage – anyone who can speak English can rise up very fast in India. But, even with that, multinational companies can't recruit here – young people don't have the skills or the ambition – they aren't saying, 'I want to be a scientist, I want to be an astronaut.'"

What he said really hit me. I knew that the Indian economy was growing rapidly each year, while Britain's was stagnating, and it felt that, while many of the people I had met were concerned about migrants coming to the UK, they could equally fear people leaving for better economic prospects elsewhere. I found it difficult, however, to reconcile Mr Hussein's model of British people immersing themselves in and learning from migrant cultures with the views of many of those I had spoken to on my travels.

I asked Jatinder what he thought.

"My father and my grandfather served in the British army," he told me. "My grandfather died in France in World War I and my father was stationed in Lahore and then went to Burma. He told me great things about the honesty of the English soldiers he served with. He spoke proudly of England, the Englishman's honesty and his word."

"As a young man," he went on, "I studied English literature and British history and was extremely impressed. It is my understanding that the English values and character made Britain great. I came here in the seventies for higher studies, and worked part-time in West Yorkshire textile mills to support myself. I appreciated the honesty, generosity and good manners of many English people, although, like any other new migrant, I also encountered my fair share of hostility from some quarters of the society."

"The problem is that our education system does not incorporate teaching English values," he went on, "and I'm concerned that those great values are being eroded. There is the pressure of immigration and of the far right, and many people don't know where they fit in. It is important to sustain what made Britain great to keep its central place in the world."

"Englishness has greatness in it," he added. "It has given so much to the world. At a discussion with the leader of a local authority, I was enlightened when he stated that other countries are learning from us and beating us in our own game. I would say that it is good that the world has learnt our values and the political system but there is no clarity on the direction that we are now heading."

We shook hands and they wished me well.

* * * * *

That afternoon, I headed for Waterloo, bound for Exeter for the next stage of my journey. I had only been travelling for ten days, but already I had many issues that I wanted to explore further. I thought a lot about myths and legends: the landlord trying to keep memories of the past alive in his pub, the lives the young people I met in Hackney aspired to, the Britain Crescencia's mother had dreamt of and the reality of the country I had seen so far. I also wanted to look in more detail at class, politics, the economy and why so many people did not seem happy in a country where so many advances had been made. But as I began to think about how I would spend my time in the South-West, it was what Ameen and Jatinder had said about the country's place in the world that concerned me most. As the train pulled out of Waterloo, I looked north across the Thames and saw the British flag flying above the Houses of Parliament.

6

The British Drinking Culture in Exeter and Bideford

When I arrived in Exeter, I was met by Jake Robey, a nineteen-year-old who had offered to take me out to a club in the centre of the city where he sometimes worked.

The atmosphere at the bar was happy and pleasant; it was the end of the summer, and the talk amongst the young people there – many just post A-Levels – was of universities, jobs and plans for the future. I asked them about life in Exeter and found them all very positive about it, especially compared with London.

"I feel like if I died in London no one would even care," one young woman told me. "It's like in TopShop in Oxford Street – you go in and you just feel like a fly. Same on the Tube – everyone's just in their own little bubble."

"Exeter's a neat town," another girl said. "Everything you need is here. It's not like London; you can go anywhere you want in ten minutes."

While everyone was very positive, Jake did mention violence at the other end of town: a friend who had had his jaw broken; 'chavs' who had attacked his brother on the bus; a lucky escape from attackers on a bridge.

"Things aren't perfect here," he said. "There's even one club – we call it the 'paedophile club' – because old men go there to watch young girls dance. Exeter definitely has a dark side."

As if to prove his point, things deteriorated as the evening went on. On the packed dance floor, people pushed one another to make space to dance, causing a girl to drop her mobile phone; she scrambled on the floor but was unable to find it. In the toilets, a man fell asleep leaning on the wall at the urinal; and, at the entrance, a teenager with a ripped T-shirt who had been thrown out for fighting remonstrated with the bouncers.

There was vomit on the pavement outside the club and down the road, by a cash point, a drunken teenager sat next to a woman who was begging and lectured her about the causes of homelessness. A girl walking home barefoot argued with her friend. A man grabbed at a girl who prised herself away. Around them, most people seemed to be having a good time, the air warm on a late summer night.

The police appeared and went into the club before emerging without making any arrests. The young man who had been ejected earlier paced up and down the street outside, apparently waiting for someone to come out. Two girls kissed passionately on a bench while two men in their forties chased a drunken friend down the road and brought him back to a taxi in a headlock. A girl in another cab leant over the driver's shoulder and pressed hard on the car's horn, causing the crowd to turn their heads. When they turned back to their conversations, she pressed it again. Other cab drivers standing nearby waiting for their own fares looked on without surprise.

Behind them, a man shouted at a taxi that had refused to take him. "Fuck you," he shouted, "I'll get you."

I agreed to meet Jake back at his house so I jumped in a taxi. The driver was originally from Afghanistan and told me how good the people of Exeter had been to him and how, in seven years of driving his taxi, he had never had any trouble.

"It's the friendliest place I have ever been," he said.

* * * * *

The next morning, Jake offered me a lift to Cornwall, where I planned to visit Cadgwith, the small coastal village where my father's parents had once lived. As we drove through a town on the Devon-Cornwall border, I saw a pub with a blackboard outside that read: 'Beer is proof that God loves us and wants us to be happy'.

When we reached Cadgwith, I headed down to the bay and met a local fisherman.

"They talk about Broken Britain," he said, "but it's not broken down here: business is alright, you can still leave your door unlocked and kids can still play on the roads."

I walked up from the bay to the house where my grandparents had lived. It was the same as it had been then, the garden full of little nooks and crannies where I had played as a boy. In fact, the whole village didn't seem to have changed at all, except for the flat-screen television with Sky box now in the local pub. As I walked back down to the bay, seagulls flew above and the mist blew in from the sea; two men emerged from the pub with a dog that looked just like one my family had once owned, and it felt like a dream of another time.

As we drove back into Devon that evening, Jake and I talked more about Exeter. He talked positively about it but he did also mention 'dark people' on the estates at the other end of town, girls who got pregnant in their mid teens and still continued to smoke and go out drinking.

"Everyone's so unhealthy," he said. "People eat so badly and that puts more pressure on girls about losing weight. There are lots of girls who are anorexic or bulimic and there's lots of depression and self-harm too – one in four people, I think."

He dropped me at the station in Exeter and as if to prove his point, when the teenager sitting next to me on the train put his phone to his ear, I could see a deep, straight scar on the underside of his wrist that I thought could only have been self-inflicted.

* * * * *

From Exeter, I headed for the north Devon coast, to stay with my aunt and uncle who lived in the small village of Appledore. The next day, in a cafe in the nearby town of Bideford, I met Elaine, a local street pastor. Street pastors, she told me, offered non-judgemental advice and support to vulnerable people in town and city centres across the country. They also handed out flip-flops to women who had given up on painful or broken high-heeled shoes and 'spikies' – plastic devices women could place over their bottles to ensure that their drinks were not spiked. She invited me to join their Saturday night 'patrol offering' around Bideford, which seemed an ideal way to continue to look at drinking in the UK.

We met at the church at ten that night and after prayers the pastors, most in their sixties and seventies, headed out on to the streets, led by Duncan, the coordinator. Three volunteers stayed back at the church as the 'prayer team', providing logistical support and offering prayers when incidents were called in.

As we walked out, Duncan told me that there were over eight thousand street pastors nationwide, all volunteers affiliated to churches.

"Non-religious groups are perfectly entitled to do something similar," he said, "but they don't."

The Bideford Carnival had been taking place during the day, and, at half past ten, there were hundreds of children and young people still out at the fair. Most were no longer using the rides but were instead drinking and dancing.

We came across a security guard who told Duncan that a young woman had been assaulted. The assailant, another young woman, was apparently nearby, but the police had not yet arrived. While we waited, Duncan talked to the security guard.

"I used to like the fair," he said sadly, looking towards the teenagers drunkenly falling over one another, "but normal life as you know it doesn't exist any more."

His sad tone reminded me of the train guard on the way to Hastings, but, before I could ask him any questions, the girl's father appeared. He demanded that action be taken, but, after forty-five minutes of waiting for the police to arrive, he lost patience, got in his car and drove off.

"He's decided to go looking for his own justice," Duncan said.

I asked whether it was unusual for him to see women involved in violence.

"No," he said, "and I tell you what else: when men fight, I'll get quite close, but when women fight I stand right back. Men just punch each other – ladies gouge and tear."

While Duncan had been speaking to the security guard, Elaine had been counselling a young woman who had clearly had too much to drink. They had been sitting on a bench by the quayside and as the young woman walked off she lost her balance and lurched to her left, almost falling into the water, before centring herself and walking on. Nearby a group of young people climbed over iron fences into a local park. Five minutes later, an ambulance appeared at the park's gates.

"Emergency services on scene," said Duncan. "Let's move on."

We walked up into the centre of town. The atmosphere was fairly peaceful as young people approached Duncan and his team asking for lollipops. Many spoke in baby voices as they made their requests, and I asked Duncan why they gave them out.

"We use the lollipops to build up relationships," he explained, "so they will talk to us if something happens later in the evening. You'd be surprised how many fights we've stopped with lollipops."

"It also gives them a sugar boost, which sometimes they need," Elaine added as we headed back to the church for a cup of tea and a rest, "plus it's more difficult to shout when you've got a lollipop in your mouth."

When we went back out half an hour later, at about quarter to one, the atmosphere had noticeably deteriorated. A girl was lying in a doorway, and Elaine gave her a bottle of water from Duncan's backpack. Along the street, a young man sitting on a bench vomited, and Elaine gave him a tissue to wipe his face.

Outside a bar, we found the police taking a young man away. We spoke to the bar manager, whose face was bruised.

"There wasn't a hint of trouble all night," he said, "and then suddenly one attacked another, and I tried to break them up and someone hit me."

"I can't be bothered with this any more," he added wearily. "Why can't people just enjoy having a drink?"

As we walked on, we heard two men shouting at one another. Duncan started to move towards the noise, but three police cars appeared, and he decided to move on down the street. There we met a teenager who was upset about her mother being arrested for being drunk and disorderly.

"She just falls into the wrong crowd," she said. "She's very impressionable."

Back at the church over more tea and biscuits, the conversation moved on to the fight that the police had broken up. Duncan suggested the police had been heavy-handed in sending three units to deal with it.

"Well, you never know," someone said. "It could have been another Tottenham."

The break lasted about forty-five minutes, and, after another prayer, we went back on to the streets. It was now two-thirty, and things were starting to quieten down. Caesar's Palace, the town's biggest club, was about to close. While the police kept watch over the drinkers milling around outside, Duncan and his team received more and more requests in baby voices for flip-flops and lollipops.

At half past three, a group of men and women staggered out of the club, and the women both took pairs of flip-flops, and the men both took lollipops.

"Thanks so much," one of the men said, unable to focus his glazed eyes on us. "I'll give that to my little boy in the morning."

It started to rain and Duncan called it a night. One of the pastors gave me a lift to Appledore, and Bideford was quiet as we drove out. I reflected that, while most people had clearly enjoyed their evening, some of the drinking I had seen seemed very self-destructive. I thought back to what Jake had said about depression, self-harm and eating disorders amongst young people in Exeter; in spite of all the economic and social progress in the UK, something didn't feel quite right.

7

Euroscepticism in Appledore

The next day, my aunt and uncle had organised for a group of eight members of the local community in Appledore, all in their fifties and sixties, to come to their house to offer their views for the book. The conversation started with them telling me about the village and, having thought I would have to facilitate the discussion, I was in fact able to sit back and just listen to their conversation.

"Having lived in Sussex," one of the women said, "the sense of community in a commuter town was almost non-existent because people were just so tired from going into London every day. There's so much more of a community feeling here."

"I've lived in my main home in Surrey for over thirty years," another woman said, "but I talk to many more people when I'm down here. There's a much more disconnected feeling in Surrey."

"That's why we moved here," a man said, "because it was a proper community. Everything was here – the post office, the pub... We're very lucky."

"It reminds me very much of the past, going back to the 1950s almost," another man said, "because people still care about each other, talk to each other. It's old-fashioned I suppose and some people think it's nosiness but it's not really."

"It's a bit like Narnia," a woman said.

"You go to buy the paper," a man said, "and it takes a good half an

2

hour because everyone stops to talk to you. They chatter away and you find out what's been going on in the village. It's a real community."

"And we have our festivals, which are all home-grown," a woman said, "like the book festival – so, all in all, it's delightful."

"And there's a good cross-section here, too – not just the pensioners like us."

"But an awful lot of the youngsters are single mothers – you see them around with their pushchairs…"

"I was in a supermarket the other day and a girl had a pod of peas and didn't know what it was – she didn't believe peas came from inside, she'd only ever seen them outside the pod. There's no common knowledge any more."

"And, of course, with the open borders we've got now, people coming in from other countries, it's all getting even more diluted. They all migrate to London because it's such a mix and you can lose yourself there, if you know what I mean."

"I heard that in one school in London, thirty-two languages are spoken – that's a big problem."

"The face of society has changed almost 100 per cent I would say. This is why we're getting more people moving down here to get away from it."

"You've got a situation now as well with modern technology where people can live down here and then commute into work once or twice a week."

"I do that – but I find it very isolating. I miss the banter, the cups of tea… People need that everyday human contact."

"That's why going to the post office or the newsagent is so important – a place where everybody knows your name."

"Plus, if you don't appear, people will look out for you – they'll knock on the door."

"There are people in big cities don't know their neighbours, you're completely isolated. There was a pensioner who died in London – he was there for months and, when they found him, the television was still on, the heating was still on. But here you get that sense of security – I know if there was a fire, someone would put it out."

"That's how England used to be, but there are too many people here now; they're letting too many people in. There's a real dilution of the ordinary people."

"I think they should be stopped coming altogether – our tiny little island is full up."

"But if they do come here they should try to integrate, and I'm sorry but they should be made to learn English."

"In Bradford they've turned a church into a Chinese restaurant. That would never happen in Iran; they'd never do that to a mosque."

"But it's our society that has let that happen – we're too easy-going."

"This country has always lived on people coming in and out, though, hasn't it?"

"But there are just so many of them – too many."

"And a lot of those who did come in the past were artisans making a contribution. Now they come here from Romania and they want a better life for themselves and want to take out, not pay in."

"We're a very fair and tolerant people but they take advantage of that."

"And it puts our own resources under pressure – like people coming over from abroad to have babies. They leave it to the ninth month to visit the UK, and then have thousands of pounds of obstetrics and then get a British passport for their baby. It's using all our resources while we're struggling to pay for the NHS."

"They should wait five years before they can use it… Someone from Poland – I've got great admiration for their skills; they do a good, honest day's work. But even if their wife and children are back in Poland, we still have to pay child maintenance for them. We've sold ourselves out to the Europeans and there's no way back."

I could feel the frustration rising as the conversation moved to Europe.

"It was supposed just to be about trade but now it's about human rights, telling us what we can and can't do…"

"We are paying for two governments, one in London and one in Brussels. And that European government is power-hungry – every year they want to tell us more and more about how we should live in our own country."

"Mr Blair sold us down the river – he signed our sovereignty away, with no referendum like we'd been promised."

"Because he knew we would say no…"

"Politicians have got a vested interest in keeping Europe because if you want to shunt someone aside, you can just send them off to a nice job in Brussels. It's absolutely appalling but that's just politicians, I'm afraid."

I didn't want to focus too much on politics in the discussion so I asked what in their view had been the social impact of the changes in society they had described.

"It becomes a social problem when people don't learn the language – people become scared because you don't know who they are, how they behave. Sometimes people get aggressive towards them because they feel attack is the best form of defence."

"But some of the resentment isn't so much that but the fact that if you burn your passport and arrive with five children you get a house. It's unbelievable."

"But it's hard to see what the answer to that is – what do you do?"

"Send them back where they came from."

"But you can't do that if they've burned their passport…"

"At the very least, you shouldn't give them any money – you should give them vouchers or food."

"Most of the people coming to the country *do* want to work…"

"I agree about some of them – like the Chinese. You won't find many of them on welfare. They do the jobs we won't do – because we've got an idle, lazy underclass – sometimes out of work for three generations…"

"We need to sort that out, too. We always blame the foreigners but we don't look at ourselves."

"What Britain really needs is a benign dictatorship like in Singapore – woe betide you if you drop chewing gum on the pavement there. But liberal thinking has advanced so much that there's no way we would accept tough rules like that here."

I was interested in the exchange, since the point about not simply blaming migrants was one of the first times on my travels that someone had suggested that we should take collective responsibility for our problems. But the remark about Singapore brought the discussion back to what the state should make people do, and the point about citizens taking responsibility for themselves passed without further comment.

"Bring back conscription, I say – at least two years. If they want to live in our country, they should be willing to defend it. But you watch how they'll run away."

"It doesn't need to be in the army – it could be a general service in the community or the public sector, teaching discipline, respect, a trade or skills, good manners… They would get the discipline they wouldn't get in school."

"But why is there no discipline in schools?"

"Because of these liberal educationalists, these liberal thinkers."

"They should bring back corporal punishment."

"You don't need to bring that back, but you do need to have good discipline."

"From what I hear, in some inner-city schools, the pupils run the classroom. It's impossible to discipline them."

"It's about parenting. The parents are lazy – *they* don't have the discipline."

"There are some children going to school in nappies – they can't speak, they can't communicate…"

"And then the slightest thing happens, and the parent talks about suing the school, 'We know our rights,' they say."

"It's all human rights, which brings us back to the EU… Like the rioters in Bristol and London, they were taunting the police but the police did nothing."

"I don't see why they didn't get the water cannon out."

"They would have said it was against their human rights…"

Everyone laughed and I asked for their views on potential solutions to the issues they had identified.

"Young people need a sense of direction. Kids that have a sense of direction don't go out and riot. They need boundaries – that's where good schools come in."

"But they stopped competitive sport – they sold off all the playing fields. There is no sport any more."

"And there's this nonsense about having no competition – it's liberal teaching in schools yet again. You've got to learn how to lose."

"But governments take education to the lowest common denominator so it's 'fair' for everybody. They've gone against grammar schools, gone against private schools, introducing the lowest common denominator rather than risking everyone not being exactly equal."

"We need grammar schools and secondary schools. And polytechnics. They were the base of the country – we were shopkeepers and engineers."

"But we can't keep harking back to the past, can we? We've got to move forward. The reality is that Europe and North America are dying and Asia is taking over – that's an inevitable fact. The Far East is the future of the world."

It was a similar point to the one Ameen Hussain had made in Greenwich and I was keen to hear how the Appledore residents would respond.

"If we are being overtaken by these economies, something radical needs to be done to correct the situation and you start off with the basics of education, money for schools and universities. And we need to move more quickly. In Britain, we talk about things for ten years and by the time we actually do anything it's already obsolete."

"Or we invent things and then other people take them. We invented the electric induction motor, which allowed trains to hover. The Labour government allowed the money for a mile of track, and then it was cancelled. And now China has got it…"

"But I think we need to have the attitude where we'll learn from other people, and how they live. We need to be more willing to accept other people – the Far East is the future of the world, and if we're not prepared to reach out, we'll never be successful. We've also got to remember they provide so many doctors and nurses in our hospitals – even down here in Barnstaple we have Asian doctors."

"But those doctors can't even be understood by local people – I read it in the paper."

"You have to have a common language, and you have to have rules as a society – so, in the case of the burqa, if your husband is forcing you to wear it, that isn't compatible with our freedoms."

"Someone I know was being interviewed for a job in the Olympic village – *a job in England* – by someone in a full burqa, and she said, 'That's not acceptable. I'm being interviewed by someone and only allowed to see their eyes.' And she walked out."

"Humans rely on face-to-face contact; it's a natural instinct. I'm with the French on that one – facial expressions mean everything. If they want to wear it in their home, that's fine, but in public it shouldn't be allowed."

"You must accept that there are rules which you must obey if you go to another country. It's just good manners."

The conversation drew to a close and they began to filter out. As he left, one of them thanked me.

"That was cathartic," he said.

The remark stayed with me, seeming to suggest that the feeling of people's voices going unheard extended to communities like Appledore. I felt the discussion had given them the chance to share their views on domestic issues and on Europe, but I couldn't help thinking I should have tried to hear more of their thoughts on Britain's future place in the wider world, an issue I wanted to explore further.

8

Religion in North Devon and South Wales

The following evening, my last in Devon before heading to south Wales, I went to meet John, a local vicar, to discuss the role of religion and values in modern Britain. John's wife Sarah joined us for the interview, and in their front room I told them about my experience with the street pastors in Bideford a couple of days earlier and asked for their view on the state of British society.

"I'd like to think that we were better in years past at looking after each other," he said, "but there's a lot of selfishness today and also a bit of fear about interfering in someone else's life, even if they're in a predicament – people think 'Is this a trick? Should I be interfering? Is this politically correct?' That seems to overtake the reaction of seeing someone in trouble and wanting to help them. From that point of view I think our society has a lot to answer for."

I asked him why he felt this change had happened.

"There are lots of factors, I'd imagine," he said. "I suppose one is that we are now a much more widely-spread society in terms of religion and ethnicity, and, although there are good aspects to that, it is harder to identify now what it is to be British and I think it's been a downward factor in creating a coherent British nation."

"The two world wars had a bashing on church attendance," he went on. "There were so many atrocities that people were brought into contact with, and people started to ask, 'Is there a God? What's the point of religion? Has it helped us?' I also think people question a lot more nowadays – people don't simply accept faith as handed down by the Church and very few children have the opportunity to learn about the Christian faith – it's almost an apology these days."

"Fifty or sixty years ago," Sarah said, "many people had a very limited intellectual education but everybody had some kind of spiritual education and it was deemed quite an important part of life, whereas now, if you don't send your child to school it is a criminal offence, but it is not a criminal offence if you fail to teach your child morals or values and a spiritual sense of life. That change is massive."

I asked how strong ethics and values could be maintained in a more secular age. There was a long silence.

"There's no easy answer," said John.

"I think people are still searching," said Sarah. "I think that hole, that not knowing, is still there. The sixties generation lost that link with traditional Christianity and its values. If there's any responsibility for what's happening on Bideford quay on a Saturday night, it's not just the fault of young people – we, as adults, must share some responsibility. Our generation wanted the freedom to say, do and behave just as we pleased. We passed laws and produced an education system that says 'Everything is relative' – whatever you feel is right is OK. But actually it isn't – values and principles of lifestyle and behaviour are important and do have consequences."

"I think it is the kids' responsibility, most definitely," said John. "They need to know the difference between right and wrong. You can't just say it's not the kids' responsibility – they know perfectly well what they're doing. It's like those riots in London – all those kids knew what they were doing, so I don't think you can absolve any responsibility from the kids who were rioting and stealing…"

"It's the speed of change," he added, "that is undermining a sense that society is stable. Technology is pushing massive changes – you hear people on the bus telling everyone about their business, talking about their private life as if everyone else is going to be interested. It's brash and it's arrogant – I sound like a grumpy old man but it really annoys me and I don't think that kind of thing would have happened years ago. It's all got blurred – what's acceptable and what's not, what's private and what's public – to the point where anything goes."

I asked how he felt we should respond to these changes in society.

"I would get back to basics," he said. "I don't think you can go far wrong with the teachings of Christ, the ethics, his challenging of the ills of society – aggression, greed, selfishness, injustice, cruelty, all the rest of it. Those teachings are open to everyone whether they've got religious convictions or not – they help people to understand how to get on with their neighbour, how to act responsibly and so on. We need to get back to God's way, rather than man's selfish way."

"My faith gives me a peace and a confidence that we are in safe hands," added Sarah, "but, if I didn't have it, I think I would be quite depressed about what's happening in the world. Before the fifties, British law was made in line with Christian values and biblical teaching – I'm not saying everyone was living up to the laws but, because there was a plumb line, we knew what we were aiming for. I think many people in Britain today are in rebellion against God and spiritually the control of the country has gone. Fifty years ago, health, education, the law, business and family life all looked to traditional Christian values. When I was at school, we used to start the day with prayer, we worshipped God in assembly, we said thank you to God for our food. There was a sense in which God was pervading all of society. Now, John gets hauled over the coals for praying with someone in the local hospital..."

"I understood I had the authority to pray by asking the woman if she wanted to pray," John explained, "but some nurse tried to stop me. We seem to be dominated by PC considerations, over and above what is humane or kind or considerate. All the other values go out of the window – if it's not politically correct, it's wrong. People are so scared of doing something that's not politically correct that they don't do anything, which leads to apathy – and the whole society suffers."

"We've gone too diverse," Sarah added, "and in some respects we have become too inclusive. We're bending over backwards to teach children about Hinduism and Islam at the expense of Christianity. Many Christians are having problems trying to uphold their beliefs and values but we seem to be very tolerant in society of all the other expressions of faith and belief."

"Over the years, many British Muslims have become more tolerant and inclusive by living and working in this community," she continued, "but, when you look at the Islamic countries, they still have a very controlling and dominant regime. In Bristol, schoolchildren who were becoming more tolerant now have a different imam at the mosque. Teachers have noticed that attitudes of the young people have begun to become more radical in recent years. We really are in danger of sharia law being adopted in some of our cities. I think we are quite ignorant of the power of other faiths and of the determination of Muslim people to control their environments and laws."

"In Muslim countries," she went on, "you don't find the level of tolerance we have here. People of other faiths are denied jobs, punished or imprisoned. Many Christians in Arab countries are living in fear when trying to worship or live out a Christian faith. You don't get the reciprocity of tolerance you have here."

They warmly wished me luck as I went on my way.

* * * * *

The next day, I headed to south Wales. My first stop was Swansea and, in the city centre, the sun was shining. As I talked to people on the street, I heard echoes of what Sarah had said about Islam in light of an incident a couple of days earlier when a small group of protestors had set fire to the American flag outside the American Embassy on the tenth anniversary of 9/11.

I felt it was time I got a Muslim perspective so, when I saw an Islamic centre, I knocked on the door and was greeted by the volunteer who looked after it, a man in his sixties of Iraqi heritage. He told me he had come to Swansea from Baghdad thirty years earlier to study, and had stayed ever since. He was now retired, and spent much of his spare time at the centre.

"Swansea city," he told me, "the Muslim people here about twenty thousand. Most are Indian and Pakistani, Egyptian and Iraqi. Most of them are student. There is three mosque. All of the student go to university mosque inside the campus of the university. There is an Islamic cemetery, too – in Saint Thomas. The imam comes from London every week to give speech, either in Arabic or English. We also have an Arabic school here – for both girls and boys. Most of the staff are women".

I asked about attitudes towards the mosque in Swansea.

"Thanks God we are lucky," he said. "Whole Swansea is peace city, no racism or anti-Islam – thanks God, touch wood."

"I am establish here now," he went on. "I have sons and granddaughter. My sons both mathematic teacher."

I asked if he felt British.

"For my generation," he said, "we still feel half-half but, for my sons, they feel British – they are relaxed, they are happy. For me, it is difficult – I live in my country thirty-five years, so it is not easy to forget but thanks God I am here. It is free country, everybody likes the freedom – I am lucky to finish my life here in such country."

I asked about negative perceptions of Islam in the UK.

"There is Islam and there are Muslims," he said, "and there are different levels in how they follow the religion. Not all Muslim people are completely Muslim, like in Christian faith or Jewish faith. Lots of Muslim people reflect bad things about Islam – they do many things that are forbidden – like they steal or they kill or do terrorist thing. It is forbidden in Islam."

"The name of Islam," he continued, "if you translate it, it means peace. We should live in peace every time. Every Muslim should be looking for peace, not to hate or to kill. Every Muslim must be in peace. But what to do about Al Qaeda or the Taliban? People think this is

Muslim; this is not Muslim, this is Al Qaeda, this is Taliban, they are not reflect, represent Islam. Islam is not responsible, *they* are responsible."

"It make me ashame," he went on. "They kidnap, they kill, and they say they are Muslim. No, no, no, they are not Muslim. They kill everybody, even the Muslim – you see in Iraq now. I feel sorry about that. The British people think that is Islam, but it is not."

"There are some who say if you are not Muslim, we will not talk to you, you are not human," he added. "But all human are equal – to deal with them, to talk with them, we are equal."

He had to get back to work.

"God help you with your travelling," he said, shaking my hand warmly as I left.

I was pleased to have heard his perspective, but I was concerned that the discussion of Islam had distracted me from John's points about values and ethics in a more secular society, which I felt might be part of the reason for the sense of unease I had encountered on my travels. I resolved to look further into this as I travelled. First, however, I wanted to focus on south Wales.

9

Changing Communities in Milford Haven and Llanelli

From Swansea, I headed west to Milford Haven. The Welsh coastline was beautiful, with wet sand marches and the sea on one side of the train, and hills and trees on the other, all bathed in glorious sunshine. On the train I met Gareth, a man in his thirties, who was reading a book about Welsh identity. I asked him how people felt about Welsh independence and nationalism.

"There are still Facebook groups about independence and rallies in places like Carmarthen," he said, "but mainly people are more focused on their communities now – like people not being able to afford houses in their towns because of holiday homes, or supermarkets tearing communities apart."

"Some parts of Wales are just depressed," he went on. "Lots of the places in the Valleys haven't recovered since the mines closed – on a scale of poverty, they're like parts of Eastern Europe. So lots of people are moving away, and ending up homeless in Bristol and Cardiff, or you've got the spate of suicides in Bridgend where kids just feel there's no hope. We've got more to worry about than the English."

* * * * *

As the train pulled into Milford Haven, the first thing I saw was a large out-of-town shopping centre right next to the station. I walked up the hill towards the centre of town and, in the local Conservative club, I met two men, Ron and Harry, who told me a bit about the place.

"It's been very quiet for a long time," Ron told me.

"Haverfordwest gets everything," Harry added, "and we're the forgotten neighbour. They've got a Wickes, a Marks and Sparks, a Laura Ashley, all the perks. We have cruise liners come in, but they ship them all straight out to Tenby or St Davids."

"It's a ghost town," Ron agreed. "People just pass through."

I left them to their drinks, and walked up towards the heart of town where I began to see what they had been talking about. It was very quiet, but I did meet Ali, the manager of the local Indian restaurant.

"I like it here," he told me. "Everyone is very friendly and, until recently, business was good. But now it's too expensive; people don't go out since the last three or four years. Since they built the supermarket out of the town, the high street has gone dead. It's killing the small business – it's just a place to live here now, not a working place."

I walked down to the main street, Charles Street, which was as run-down as he had suggested, with many of the units lying empty. I got talking to Robert, a local man, and asked him what Milford Haven was like.

"Crap," he said, "rubbish, dead. All the trade has gone to the docks. We used to have four shoe shops up here; now we don't have any. And look at the mess they leave."

He pointed into the window of a former cafe, where plug sockets had been smashed, cabinets ripped off the wall and a sink lay in the middle of the room. He took me up the street, pointing out the mess that had been left in virtually every abandoned shop, including a unit that had once housed a kitchen shop, where raw sewage was now leaking in.

"What kind of message does this send about our town?" he asked.

By the time we'd walked the whole street, I had counted twenty abandoned units.

Robert took me into the local newsagent's, and showed me the postcards on sale. Each depicted idyllic scenes – the countryside, the sea, boats on the quayside in front of beautiful sunsets.

"It's not how we live," he said.

I walked down the hill to the marina, which, while only five minutes away, felt like another world. Hundreds of boats stretched out along the quay, the water shimmering in glorious sunshine and seagulls flying above. At the quayside, there were boutique shops selling designer fashions, arts and crafts, jewellery and sunglasses.

Outside a cafe, I met a man, Chris, who was on holiday with his wife. He told me he owned an electrical store in the West Midlands, which he had decided to close.

"The market has just changed dramatically," he said. "Twenty-five years ago we had to have a big store to put our whole range out. Now people can go on the Internet and the range is right there in your face. Now people come to my shop, touch and feel the washing machine and then go on the Internet and buy it. All the manufacturers sell direct on their sites at the same price they sell to me, so why would anyone buy from me?"

"It's a family business," he continued. "My parents started it and it's caused real heartache, but it's happening to everyone. I belong to a national group of family electrical stores that used to have over a thousand members; now there's less than six hundred."

I wished him well and walked back towards the railway station and the out-of-town development that seemed to be so controversial, hoping to get a sense of why people preferred it to the high street. I saw a woman in her fifties walking towards her car with five or six shopping bags in her hand. I asked her why she shopped here rather than on the high street.

"Convenience," she said, and then added, "It's terrible what's happened to Charles Street; it's so sad."

I asked if, by shopping out of town, she was contributing to what was happening in Charles Street.

"But there's no alternative now," she said.

"I know things have to change as things progress," another woman told me, "and I know there's an economic situation, but this is killing our town. You used to have a chat on the high street, but not any more. We had a nice town and we'd like it back."

I asked her if there was anything she could do to change things back.

"It's not going to happen," she said, shaking her head.

As I talked to people, while many expressed reservations about the impact of out-of-town shopping, they all felt the changes to the town were beyond their control and they just had to accept them. I was thinking about leaving when I met a young woman with her foot in a cast and asked what had brought her down to the shopping centre while she was on crutches.

"I'm a student," she said, "plus I've got to pay for an operation on my foot, so anything where there's a deal, I'm in. I know we're killing the town centre and I feel sorry about it, but times are hard and food is cheap here."

"You've made me feel bad now," she added, hobbling off.

* * * * *

I travelled from Milford Haven to Llanelli and arrived late in the afternoon as the sun was starting to go down. I walked away from the station and found myself in a residential area made up of street after street of terraced houses, and little else. A couple of children played around an abandoned shopping trolley but otherwise the streets were empty and I was about to move on when a group of volunteers from the Salvation Army on a door-to-door collection appeared. They agreed to let me join them and, as they knocked on the doors, they told me about their fundraising.

"It's not good this year," one of the volunteers told me, although as we went round they seemed to be getting a decent response given the economic circumstances of the time.

"Collecting is a thankless job," another volunteer told me. "It's a poor town and it's getting harder every year. Some people can be very rude, or just silly – last year when I knocked on one door, someone shouted out, 'There's nobody in.'"

"Some people can be rather aggressive and belligerent," she added, "and I don't know why."

At one door, a mother gave her daughter a few coins to put into the collection tin, and there were smiles all round. A few doors along, there was no answer, even though, when I looked in the window, I could see a man watching television. On the next street, an elderly man said he couldn't give anything.

"I'm sorry," he said with deep sadness in his voice, "I just don't have enough."

Glyn, who was leading the group, said I could follow him for a while, and, as we walked, he talked about the challenges of door-to-door fundraising. Sometimes, he said, members of the team would end up knocking on the same door twice, or knock on both the front door and the back door of some houses.

"Our volunteers are also getting older," he told me as we walked, "with more ailments."

I asked about the next generation.

"There is no next generation," he said. "They went off to college and didn't come back. There's no industry left so we lost young people altogether. We lost a complete generation – that's the group that should be here now to let us oldies off."

"Collecting is getting much more difficult," he continued. "People aren't answering their doors as much. Some are at work and others just won't open their doors after dark any more. People are more afraid of strangers at the door these days."

It seemed like this was quite a safe community so I asked him what people were afraid of.

"It's what they read in the papers," he said.

"The economy is also affecting people," he continued. "There are so many appeals these days that people can't give to all of them, so we're looking at other ways to raise money – coffee mornings, events and concerts in community halls. We're trying to get outside people to come because it's usually only our people who turn up."

"Church attendance is down," he added, "though people still appreciate our work and they still give even if they don't attend."

The sun was setting in a clear blue sky, and it was a beautiful evening as children played in a playground next to the houses Glyn and his team were visiting.

He knocked on one door and the man who answered said, "I don't speak English."

"We get a few of those," Glyn said as we walked on. "They should just say, 'No, thank you' – it's much more honest."

As the sun went down, Jen, Glyn's wife, rubbed her hands together to warm them against the cold.

"It's not the best job, this one," she said, "but, if you remember the people you're collecting for, it's well worth it."

She knocked on one door.

"I'm unemployed with seven children," said the woman who answered.

"You need the money more than us," Jen said. "Good night, God bless".

The sun had finally set, and, as the light faded, fewer and fewer doors were opened. There were hardly any cars on the street, and Glyn decided it was time to call it a night.

"We'll start again tomorrow," said Jen as they set off home.

As I made my way back to the station, I thought about the impact of changes in communities like different shopping habits, reduced church attendance or fear of strangers, and how these might be contributing to the sense of unease that I had encountered on my travels. I also reflected that the well-meaning efforts to do good in this changing context seemed to be deeply-rooted in the older generation, with fewer younger volunteers apparently coming through. Yet what stuck in my mind most of all were the conversations in Milford Haven, where so many people had expressed reservations about losing their high street but had felt powerless to do anything about it and, indeed, had arguably played a part in its decline.

10

Decline in Swansea, Cardiff and the Welsh Valleys

Back in Swansea the next day, I headed to the indoor market in the centre of town, and was immediately struck by how quiet it was – the market was packed with stalls, but there were very few customers around. At his stall, I met John, a grocer, and asked him for his view on British society.

"It's fucked," he said. "I don't recognise it any more – there is no Britain. It's a country where your average, heterosexual white male feels totally ostracised and that his view doesn't matter. Who decided without my permission that there's a whole pile of words I can't say any more? Who gets to decide what's racist? One man's racism is another man's joke, and tell me a race on earth which isn't racist anyway."

"Since Thatcher, things have changed," he went on. "Communities have been destroyed. You can't trust the old institutions, you can't trust a bank, you can't trust the police or the government. It's every man for himself."

"A couple of years ago, I saw a female police officer chasing after a man who had stolen a handbag. She caught him and tried to hold him down. There was a man there selling helium balloons – he gave a teenager the balloons and helped the policewoman hold the man down. Well, you know what happened? The balloons were stolen, and then the police superintendent said in the local paper that members of the public shouldn't get involved in police operations in any circumstances…"

"I like my photography," he went on, "but I can't even take pictures in the street with children nearby for fear of being called a paedo. It's totally intolerable – it's becoming 1984."

He said he had to get back to work, but first he wanted to tell me a joke.

"Who was the last man to enter Parliament with honest intentions?" he asked, paused for a moment and then said, "Guy Fawkes."

He smiled as he said it, but it seemed to capture very well the feelings of many of the people I had met on my travels about politicians of all political parties.

I moved on to the next stall, which sold Welsh cakes. There I talked to Jan, the owner, and asked her for her views on how things were going in British society.

"Family values aren't what they were," she said. "We need to teach parenting in schools – the values my parents taught me are not being taught by parents today. A lot of children don't have values or life skills."

"I don't know why it stopped," she went on. "We all had values, we all had respect, whatever class you were. It's not just here, it's countrywide. Society is breaking down a bit."

I asked her what could be done about it.

"I don't know," she said. "People who are far more savvy than me don't know the answers, so how am I supposed to? I'd hate to be David Cameron – there's not enough money in the world they could pay me to sort out this mess."

She stopped for a moment, and then said with a smile, "We just need to keep trying."

John walked over.

"What's the point in trying?" he said. "It's all fucked."

"We need to keep trying," Jan said again.

* * * * *

My next stop was the University of Glamorgan, in the picturesque town of Treforest, just north of Cardiff, where I was meeting Howard Williamson, a professor at the university, who had offered to take me on a tour of the Welsh Valleys.

"A lot of what you read on Wales is about the coastal belt," he said as we drove out of Treforest, heading for Merthyr, "and, in particular, Cardiff Bay, which is quite an elite and privileged place. But you get out into the Valleys and it's very different."

We drove past Aberfan, where a mining disaster had killed a hundred and forty-four people, most of them children in the school beneath the mine, in 1966. The National Coal Board – based in London – had been warned of the dangers but hadn't acted, Howard told me, and, in spite of the scale of the disaster, there had been a delay before anyone from the government had come to Aberfan. The story held particular resonance, as four Welsh miners had been killed in an accident in Neath the day before, and there had been anger in Wales that the London-based media hadn't given the news greater prominence.

The main road veered around the town, its route altered to steer clear of the graves of the children who had been killed, and we continued north. As we reached Merthyr, Howard told me about the town.

"It's grim," he said. "There's no employment, and big industry has vanished. Young men struggle, in particular, because their fathers worked in the mines, and they don't see working in call centres as man's work – but there's very little else. And that's when the problems with SAS start."

I asked him what he meant by SAS.

"Sunbeds and steroids," he said.

"When you don't have control over your job," he went on, "when you don't have anything else to give yourself self-esteem, you manipulate your own body, so they go to tanning centres, they get tattoos, steroids. And then there's ketamine, mephedrone…"

I asked him what he thought the future held for Merthyr. He told me about numerous education initiatives, but there still appeared to be the basic problem of a lack of employment opportunities.

"There's no real money circulating," he said. "I once went on a visit to the jobcentre near here, and the manager told me that his was the best-paid job in the whole town."

We headed across a mountain and then south into a series of long, thin mining villages squeezed into the Valleys, a single road with houses on either side stretching for miles on end, the communities rolling into one another. Many buildings were boarded up, including a number of former miners' institutes – social and educational institutions for miners – that were now run-down and dilapidated.

We pulled off the main road and headed up to a large housing estate set on a hill high above the main road. Howard told me unemployment there was around 90 per cent, and in the winter buses were often unable get up to the estate because of the snow, leaving the residents cut off. I told him I was surprised by the level of poverty we were seeing.

"No offence," he said, "but there's a naivety about London. When I used to advise politicians, they didn't think circumstances like these existed – they'd never been near it."

"For me, that's the biggest tragedy in British society," he continued, "the complete separation in understanding between rich and poor. It's built on prejudices on both sides – the poor stereotype the rich and the rich lock themselves away, never seeing how poor people live. There's a woman living near me, I've never seen her on foot – she drives everywhere and only gets out of her car once she's safely inside her gates."

I asked him what could be done not just for the area but for British society as a whole.

"We broke down the classes but we've lost a sense of respect," he said. "The question we need to ask is if it is possible to create respect in a non-hierarchical society."

"I've always supported a national citizen service," he continued. "We need to bridge the division between the least advantaged and the most advantaged young people. When they do things together, they find more that unites them than divides them."

"We also need to remember that this isn't such a bad place to be," he went on, "the fifth or sixth largest economy in the world. But I wish we could build a society with more manners, courtesy, consideration – a more watchful society. Outside my house is a dedicated space for blind people to cross the road – and people park across it. But then I've also seen teachers park on zigzag lines outside schools – it's predictable what will happen when educated and knowing people behave that way."

"In my heart," he went on, "I worry about the consequences of the austerity measures. I think they could leave a hole which is just too big for things to grow over it – I just don't think enough people are ready to take responsibility. Too many of us are passing by on the other side of the road, although it's also possible that harder times will produce greater mutuality. You never know, it could re-civilise society."

As we drove on, I thought about what he had said. I believed he was right that there was a chance that a difficult economic time could bring people together, but I was also struck by the sense of powerlessness and apathy I had encountered on my travels and felt that this would need to be overcome if we were to build the more watchful society he had spoken of.

We arrived in Pontypridd, left the car at his house and headed for the station. As we walked, we heard three impeccably groomed young men talking about their hair.

"I rest my case about young men and their bodies," Howard said.

We reached the station, which had once, during the boom years when huge trains were needed to carry all the mined coal from the area, had the longest platform in the country. It was a sense of the best days having passed that stuck with me as I said goodbye to Howard and headed for Cardiff.

* * * * *

I arrived in Cardiff that evening as the sun was setting and headed into the city centre. In the main pedestrianised shopping area, a crowd of Asian men, women and children had gathered outside a clothes shop. I went over to see what was happening.

A young man taking photos explained that it was the Indian cricket team in Cardiff for a match the following day. It turned out his name was Kesh, and, as his friends followed the cricketers around the shops, he and I chatted. He told me that he was studying for an MBA in Cardiff, but planned to return to India when he finished his course.

"I think I made a mistake coming to the UK," he said. "Lots of people in India think that it's the land of opportunity here, but it's changing – that's not the reality any more. I'll go back to Bangalore – that's a real metropolitan city, people from all over the world. People say it's just call centres, but there are so many opportunities there now."

As I walked back later that evening, the city centre was very quiet for a Friday night and, everywhere I looked, taxis were lined up waiting for customers who didn't seem to be coming.

I couldn't help but be worried by the feeling of decline I had found in south Wales, even in Cardiff, the economic centre. As I headed back to England, with plans to visit central and north Wales later in my journey, Kesh's words about opportunities lying in India rather than the UK echoed in my ears like Ameen Hussain's before them, and I realised I had no idea how the country should respond.

11

Role Models, Networks and Education in Malvern and Woodmancote

As I travelled back to England, there were a number of issues that I wanted to look at in greater detail. The experience in south Wales had made me think about the impact of economic decline, while John, the vicar in Appledore, had raised interesting questions about values and role models in a more secular society; I also wanted to make sure that I spoke to more young people and to migrants to the UK outside the London melting pot. I set these as my priorities as I headed north towards Scotland.

My first stop was Malvern, where I met Ann and Alan Courtney, social work managers. Over dinner at their home, we talked about British institutions and role models, what Alan called 'anchors' in society, which he felt were not as firm as they had been.

"There was a huge debunking of things and people you could look up to during the 1980s," said Alan, "and, whether it was Mrs Thatcher or secularisation or a lack of respect for institutions, it's certainly something that has become more pervasive."

Ann said she agreed but stressed that people still did a lot for one another.

"I come across people all the time who look after elderly relatives," she said, "or foster carers who also cook meals for the people next door."

Alan asked her where she felt the motivation for that kindness came from.

"It's probably the fact that they live in sufficiently small communities that they actually know people," said Ann, "that old-style community where everybody knows everybody and they'll still go and dig somebody's garden because it's what you do."

Thinking back to my conversations in London and the South-East, I asked whether they felt there had ever actually been a golden era of strong communities and social harmony in the UK. The conversation moved to the Queen's coronation and Ann said she felt that the idea of every street in the country celebrating was misleading.

"Those photos, they're so evocative," she said, "but they don't necessarily paint an accurate picture, do they?"

"No more than the jolly Cockney's blitz myth," said Alan, "which has been exposed so many times. And that's the point for me – we've got so much knowledge and cynicism about everything now, including the people who were perceived to be role models."

"Everybody questions things now," Ann agreed, "and people know so much more. Even without the media, people seem to feel the right to know everything about everybody, and nobody is going to stand up to the scrutiny of 24-hour news."

I asked whether these trends made it more difficult for role models to emerge.

"I don't think it's the case that there's no one to look up to," said Alan, "but the obvious people to look up to have been exposed, so perhaps you have to look harder."

"There are some really good role models that crop up," Ann said. "I just can't think of any at the moment…"

There was silence as they tried to think of strong role models in British society. They couldn't.

"I think there's just a huge amount of information around now," said Ann, "about everything and everyone and it all comes at you as if it has equal importance – there is no filter in terms of significance or even its truth. If you read newspapers, they're just making statements and then reproducing them – no one's evaluating the evidence."

"I don't know what you do about that," she went on, "because interpreting all that information requires advanced analytical thinking and many people just can't think in that way. That probably didn't matter in the days when people were just told what to do and think but now everybody can act for themselves and influence their own lives in a way that they couldn't before. Everybody's got more power but not necessarily the resources to use it."

I asked about solutions to the issues that we were discussing.

"I don't think there are obvious solutions," said Alan. "We're in a period of great uncertainty and great gloom at the moment, but there will be things that pull us out. My only reaction is to find the things that you feel are really important to you personally and try to do something around them. I suppose I have a faith that there are so many people who do tremendous things, so despite any feeling that nationally we're in free fall, I don't think that's the case at all."

"I suppose I feel a little less positive," said Ann, "because it's such a dilemma – all the changes are things that we would have advocated and wanted to see, but the outcome hasn't actually been very good, because it's been too difficult to cope with. All the advances have made people quite rightly more questioning and challenging, which of course means that there isn't that sort of cohesion or acceptance of any form of authority. And I think deferring to people in the right circumstances is important, but perhaps a lot of people are struggling to know who those people are."

"I don't think I'm particularly unusual in wanting somebody to emulate or know better than I do," she continued. "You want those people to be there because we all realise we don't know enough about most things, and have huge amounts of doubt about even the things we do know about. You want to think there are people who are wiser and know more."

"But then there are people," she went on, "who spend their lives trying to find 'the right answer' and keep thinking that if they just pay more and keep looking, they'll find it, whereas often there is no answer or no cure or no solution. Perhaps I'm just as guilty as anybody of looking for the 'right' answer – I certainly would if I had a medical problem – but deep down I'd probably realise that even our experts don't know all the answers. I suppose there's something in-built in us to try to find someone to tell us what to do, but you realise that most of the time they don't know any better than you."

Her words really struck me, and I felt took me further in understanding the sense that things weren't right in British society: if educated professionals like Alan and Ann sometimes found it difficult in a country where people felt there were few people to look up to, I could imagine that would be very challenging for other Britons too.

* * * * *

The next day, I went to stay with Sylvia and David, a retired couple who lived not far from Ann and Alan in a small hamlet in the Malvern Hills overlooking the Severn Plain. That evening, as the sun set, I watched lights come on one by one in houses in the valley below, and David pointed out the birds preparing to migrate south for the winter.

Over dinner, they told me about the various groups that they had joined over the years, helping them to make new friends in Malvern having moved from London: the cinema society, a Spanish class and a Roman history group.

"It's very pleasant," said Sylvia, "that there are so many ways to come in as a stranger and meet people. It's even possible to join a Sunday lunch club or go on excursions with a geologists' group."

We talked on, and David told me about the local country houses that opened their gardens to visitors during the summer.

"It was very important to us when we were creating our garden," he said. "Almost every Sunday we'd pootle out into the countryside."

They told me about the difference at such events between 'tea', which meant simply a cup of tea, and 'teas', which meant tea and cake.

"It was very feudal," David said. "I think the village ladies were put on a three line whip into doing the catering."

They also told me about the strength of culture, particularly theatre and opera, in Malvern and Sylvia told me about the satellite broadcasting at Malvern Theatre of live opera performances from the New York Met, and the 'very English problem' of whether to clap at the end.

"Some people do, some people don't," David said, before adding, "Sylvia claps."

"I think one should," Sylvia said.

David said that one of his disappointments about life in the area was that staff from the local private school had not contributed more to the cultural life of the area.

"It's like having a liner in port," he said, "but no one leaves the ship. The school doesn't have a jot of impact on the town; it's entirely self-contained."

"But we're all the same," he went on, describing a walking group he knew in France that just involved English second home owners. "We all create our own networks."

We talked on and the conversation turned to London.

"I enjoy going back," Sylvia said, "but, while it's obviously important in structural terms, in many ways London is now irrelevant to my day-to-day life."

"We observe London as a centre of power," David added, "but for Sylvia it could be the subject of a sociology essay, or for me rather like looking at ancient Rome."

As the evening drew to an end, I thought how happy they seemed in the new networks they had joined in Malvern, somehow separate from the issues I had heard other people raise during my travels, almost as if they were viewing those issues from afar.

* * * * *

My next stop was Woodmancote, a small village just outside Cheltenham, where Dave Aukett and Karen Hawkins, youth justice consultants, had offered me a room for the night.

Over a curry that evening, Dave, Karen and I were joined by their friends Ian and Tracey and Dave's daughter Molly and we talked about modern British society.

"I think we're very lucky to live in a society where we look after those who are weaker than others," said Karen, "but I am worried that that caring side is going."

"I think it's already gone," said Ian.

"I don't think people give a hoot about each other," Dave agreed. "We're too self-centred – everyone's out for themselves and their families."

"I just think a lot of people are frightened to help other people," said Karen. "You don't see people stopping in the street, do you, if someone's being attacked?"

"I would," said Tracey. "I would get myself probably killed…"

"But that's not true," said Karen. "The *Daily Mail* and the news makes us think that. Every day somebody stops something, but we only ever hear about the ones who get stabbed."

"As with everything," she went on, "we always expect somebody else to fix things. Every time there's a problem we expect the police or politicians to fix it. *We need to fix it*. They can't fix it for us; we need to fix it. We should be stepping in, saying, 'Don't do that…'"

"I agree about the media," Tracey said. "It does put you off and we drum it into our kids – don't get involved, so, as society rolls on, nobody helps anyone."

Karen agreed.

"I worry," she said, "because Molly always says, 'They'll kill me, I'll get stabbed.'"

"Yeah," said Molly, "because you don't know what people are thinking. They've all got their own agenda, haven't they? Even if they seem nice on the outside, it doesn't mean they're genuinely nice people."

Karen said it was sad that Molly's default view of people was mistrust.

"I have these conversations with the kids," she said, "where they'll say, 'If I don't do it, someone else will,' and I say, 'If everybody has that attitude, where does that lead?' You have to stand up for what you believe in; you have to say, 'That's wrong.'"

"I blame the class system," she added.

There was a sharp intake of breath around the table – this was clearly a regular topic of debate in their household.

"But is it still there?" Ian asked. "I think, with the increase of multiculturalism, with the different mix we've got, the class system has kind of broken down."

"If you look at the people who run this country," said Karen, "the vast majority are privately educated – the Etons, the Harrows – and, I'm sorry, but how can they know about everyday life? They are making decisions for people who they don't know, who they don't understand and who they don't care a lot about."

"Sweeping!" said Dave.

"Seventy-three per cent of our judges are privately educated," said Karen, "but 7 per cent of the country is privately educated. Is it because they're the smartest or is it because of who they know?"

"I think it's a simplistic view," said Dave, "because people, whoever they are, will do whatever's necessary to get the best school for their kids. Sometimes they will pay a fee, sometimes they will move to a higher mortgage in an area with a better school – what's the difference?"

"It's not like buying a car," said Karen. "Each child deserves the chance to make the best of their ability and, as a country, we deserve the best of the best, and if that means someone from a council house, then let's have that, not just someone who's daddy had more money."

"I think private schools have a place," said Ian. "I think we're going to be fighting a losing battle if we're trying for a level playing field, because at the end of the day money will always talk. We've got to try to find a better balance, a *better* chance rather than an *equal* chance, because you're always going to have people who are up here and people who are down there. Competitiveness lives throughout all walks of life."

* * * * *

In the car on the way to the station the next day, I talked to Karen about being a parent in modern Britain.

"It can be a nightmare," she said, "because, while your own morals may be less materialistic, if you push them on your children, they suffer. I lived with my kids on my own for ten years, and all their friends were from relatively well-off backgrounds so there was always a pressure to give them holidays and things they could talk about with their friends."

I asked if she felt she was swimming against the tide.

"Definitely," she said, "but I also feel a huge responsibility to bring up children who are going to make a positive difference and that's what I'm determined to do."

As I travelled north towards the Midlands, her words from the previous evening – "We need to fix it" – stuck with me, reminding me that the task I had set myself before setting off on my journey was not only to understand the problems the UK was facing, but also to consider what could be done to resolve them. Alan Courtney had advised me to find something important to me and focus on that, so I began to look for ideas.

12

Multicultural Communities in Wolverhampton and Burton

My next stop was Wolverhampton and, when I arrived, I headed for Penn Road, an arterial road leading to the town centre where my mother's parents had once lived. The road stretched for miles and seemed to have everything – a Sikh gurdwara, a Hindu temple and a Christian centre, as well as a McDonald's and a Waitrose. It seemed an ideal opportunity to look at how multicultural communities worked in the UK.

I started by visiting the Hindu temple. I knocked on the door and was welcomed warmly, told to take off my shoes, and taken upstairs to the main prayer room to meet the head priest. While worshippers came in and paid their respects, he told me about his attitude towards different faiths.

"Christian, Muslim, Sikh, Jewish," he said, "we don't want to convert. You're born where you are born, you do as you do. British people rarely come to this temple, but, if they do, we explain to them about the religion but we don't try to convert. We want to live and worship in our own way in Britain, but we respect British rules 100 per cent."

As I left the room, a volunteer gave me an apple from a large basket of fruit and, on the noticeboard outside, I saw letters from a local hospice and the Red Cross thanking the temple for sizeable donations.

I left and walked down the road, and saw people of different ethnicities walking together and talking to one another. It was the first time since London that I had seen people of different backgrounds really interacting, not just living side by side.

By a bus stop, I met an old man with a pipe.

"Wolverhampton's a shithole now," he said. "It's just gone down and down. There's too many Jamaicans, and they don't want to work. I don't mind the Asians, they work hard, but the Jamaicans have been brought up to believe that the state will provide."

I asked whether people of other backgrounds acted the same way.

"Oh yes," he said. "It's about how the parents bring them up – it's what happens when they're this high that matters."

He gestured to show a toddler's height.

"If you've got a plant in a pot," he continued, "you've got to help it grow, or it will grow wild. I mix a lot with Asian people – they look after the elderly, they look after their children. There's a lot we can learn from them."

The bus appeared, and he shuffled slowly towards it, wishing me luck with the book.

I walked up to the house where my grandparents had lived. I knocked on the door and was greeted by the Sikh man who lived there now. He invited me in.

"It's a good community," he told me with a huge smile. "We mix together; everyone is good neighbours."

I asked him about British society more generally.

"It's generally fine," he said. "In any society you'll find a few bad people – but mostly they're OK, honest people. It's hard to bring up children, though – there are so many things parents can't do. Even schools, the teachers haven't got much rights at all."

I told him about the man down the street who had suggested there was a lot to be learnt from Asian families.

"We can all learn from each other," he said. "When I came here from India in 1962, I was told, 'You have left your country – this is your country now.' There are good things and bad things in the English culture, just like in the Indian culture – you must collect all the good things from English culture and join them with all of the good things from Indian culture and become a good society."

He proudly showed me photos from his daughter's graduation and told me about his son, a chartered accountant. He showed me round the garden, and then offered me a cup of tea before wishing me well on my way.

Before I left Wolverhampton, I decided to stop in at McDonald's, where both the staff and the customers were from a diverse range of ethnic backgrounds. I bought a drink and sat down, and, as I reflected on the day so far, a toddler in a booster seat at the next table smiled over at me, waved and said hello. She was with her grandparents, who smiled too and then went back to their lunch, showing the child how to clean up after herself and making sure she didn't leave a mess. The girl kept waving at me, and, when they finished, the grandmother took her out of the booster seat and said, "Go and say goodbye to your friend." The girl walked a couple of paces towards me, stopped, smiled and waved. The grandmother said goodbye and they were gone. It had been a nice moment, and I reflected that it was the presumption of trust in a stranger, not just from the girl but from her grandparents, which had made it possible.

As I walked to the station, I got talking to an Asian man on a market stall selling soaps and beauty products. I told him about the book.

"If you're talking about British society," he said, "then it gets a bit racial."

I asked him what he meant.

"I don't like to be told what to do," he told me. "Asda has a halal section now – what about the other ethnic minorities? Why should we be force-fed something? I don't tell people how to live – I just do what I think is best for me and my family."

"I'm from India," he went on, "but I've lived here for over fifty years. My upbringing and education is here so I see myself as British and I get annoyed with people complaining about it. If you're not happy, you should just go. I'm happy here… apart from the weather and the cricket and football team."

I told him the England cricket team were currently at the top of the world rankings.

"Well, the football team then," he said. "I tell you, they should be paid per goal – that would get them going."

* * * * *

From Wolverhampton, I headed east towards Burton, still interested in how multicultural Britain worked. I walked into the town centre and found a cafe with a mix of ethnicities amongst staff and customers. Inside, I met a British-Pakistani man who worked there. I asked him what Burton was like.

"Compared to other places, Burton is a friendly place," he said. "There are a few parts – rough ends you could call it – but if you don't mess with them, they don't mess with you. Probably you hear someone got mugged once in a blue moon or something. Otherwise, it's a beautiful place."

"In this cafe, everyone comes in," he said, looking at the mix of customers eating, drinking and chatting. "Old age people, students, black, white, Asians coming in and getting mixed together. It's a multiculture place – before you would see Asians on their side, whites on their side, Polish on their side – we're trying to bring them together like to mix with each other."

Two children came in and asked to leave their bags behind the counter while they went to pick up a friend. He let them.

"Here we don't have to be strict," he said, "but we can tell who the troublemakers are and we tell them to 'Go from this place'. We want a safe place. Every Wednesday we have the church group come in and we have the inter-faith meetings as well; every Friday, the young people play cards here – the toy shop organises it. We used to have a night where we played films on the projector and then we'd have a discussion after that – what was the moral of the film, that kind of thing."

I asked about the staff.

"We've got Polish, Afghan, English, black, Latvian as well," he said. "We've got about three Pakistanis – the owner is Pakistani. He's doing a lot of work in the community, too. He's a member of the mosque community and he's on the council as well."

"He took over three years ago," he went on, "and the community was the main thing. We're not making that much money but, on the other side, we're doing the charity work, like charities if they want to have their evenings here, they're most welcome. We have the gallery upstairs where the students from Burton College can display their artefacts. We say, 'If you've got any talent or anything, come around.' This is the heart of Burton."

I asked about the economic situation in Burton.

"Ten years ago it was much better place," he said. "We used to have a lot more jobs – we used to have national distribution centres and everything. But now half of Burton's industry has been shipped out, gone to Poland, which is giving bad effects to people – they are frustrated, they don't know what to do. I mean, we're not saying don't give your jobs to these people, but at least saying don't take your industry out of your country. It's just like chopping your own fingers."

"The way I see Britain," he continued, "give another five, ten years, people needs to leave from here because there are no jobs. Many of my friends, they are gone already. A couple to Holland, Dubai, Pakistan. They haven't got job security; they don't know when some company is going to go busted."

It struck me that it was the third time on my travels, after Greenwich and Cardiff, that I had heard about migrants leaving the UK in search of opportunity elsewhere.

"Plus economy-wise," he continued, "they're saying, 'Recession, recession' – I think last year was no recession, it was just the hint, but this year, you can see it. You can even see it in the cafe – people spending less. Our boss, he is really good guy, he doesn't want anyone to lose jobs, but, if it was someone else, he would shut it down."

"Other than that," he added, offering me a cup of tea, "people-wise, I think no one can beat Britain. You know what they call the humanity, you've got it in this country – you've got animal rights, you've got all rights, nothing can beat that. Even your social security system, no one can beat it. Only problem now is politicians; they're the worst you can get – I compare them with our Pakistan politicians. They're just with their own things, their own power – forget about people."

I had to get to Sheffield, my next stop. I offered to pay for the cup of tea, but he told me it was on the house.

As I walked back towards the station, a member of staff from the McDonald's I was walking past chased after a young girl and handed her a packet of chips, which she had forgotten to take, and the girl thanked her warmly. I was reflecting on what a positive experience I had had in Burton when two teenage girls started arguing in the street.

"You better fucking stay away from my boy," one shouted. "You and your fucking mum better stay away from my boy."

"I don't want your fucking boy," the other girl said.

"Yes, you do – if I ever see you in the fucking city centre I'll fucking have you, so you better fucking turn and walk away right now."

The girl slapped her and she began to cry.

"I'm going to fucking kill you," she shouted through her tears. "You're going to be in fucking A & E tonight. Your friends are going to see you in fucking A & E tonight."

She walked off, still crying. The few people who had been watching turned back to their shopping, but most had just ignored it altogether. It was an unhappy note to end on but it didn't detract from the positive experience at the community cafe. Both there and in the McDonald's in Wolverhampton, there had been an assumption of trust between people of different backgrounds. Building that trust seemed important, and I wondered whether some statement of common British values, signed up to by both migrants and non-migrants alike, could be one way to do it.

13

Young People and Urban Life in Sheffield

From Burton, I travelled to Sheffield, where Paul, a teacher in a local secondary school, had invited me to spend a day talking to his pupils. The school had a mixed catchment including both inner-city and suburban families and it seemed an ideal opportunity to get a perspective from young people growing up in the UK.

I started with a class of fifteen- and sixteen-year-olds who reflected the ethnic and social mix of the school. Paul had briefed them in advance about the book and the questions I was likely to ask but I was still surprised by how keen they were to talk about sometimes difficult issues. We started by discussing where they lived.

"I live in the inner-city ghetto," one boy said. "It's like Peckham in London. Most people in that area are in prison – they're drug dealers, init."

Paul clarified that there had been a major drugs raid in the area, and a number of members of the local community had been imprisoned.

"Students have come to the area now it's safer," another boy said. "They come and have their parties. They never used to come – they used to shit it, they'd get a taxi to their front door."

A girl was amused at the idea of students coming to live in a neighbourhood like the one where all the arrests had taken place.

"I'm not saying this in a bad way," she said, "but that area is more black than white. It's not a racist area, that's just how it is – the white people don't come down there."

"Britain's meant to be a multicultural area," a boy said, "so why is it, when you go to certain places, it's full of blacks or full of whites? It's not right, is it?"

I asked the rest of the class if they agreed that Sheffield was racially divided.

"If you looked at Sheffield as a whole," a boy said, "you'd think it was quite a varied culture but I understand what people are saying because there are parts where some people are mostly of one culture. But I don't think I've been to a place where there's been no black people or no white people and, if you go into the town centre, you always see more than one culture."

"I live in a mostly Asian area," a boy said, "mainly Pakistanis and Bengalis and next to my house, there's a bridge that goes to another area. Every single time they have fights on the bridge, it's between the Pakistanis and the Bengalis, but then sometimes Pakistanis and Bengalis help each other to beat up whites."

I asked why they were fighting.

"Basically, it's coloured against whites," he said, "because they don't want to see any Pakistanis or Bengalis in their area; they're protective of it. I walked past there once and this old lady started shouting, 'What are you doing in our area?' at me."

"But sometimes it goes the other way," said a white boy. "Sometimes *we're* not included – only certain people are made to feel British and the rest are just left out."

I asked him who the people were who were left out.

"I think it's the ethnics," a Somali boy interrupted. "People judge you on your colour and your religion. Like yesterday, we were playing football and this police officer started searching everyone and then he was swearing at us and all of this, and one of us started swearing at him, and he arrested him and took him home. It's all focused on the coloured people – they think of us as criminals."

"I'm not being racist," the white boy said, "but that never really happens. Black people try and say everything's racist, and I'm not being racist, but if something happens to them, they'll just think the first thing is that it's racist."

"But most of the time they are being racist," a Somali boy said.

"But when you get stopped by the police," the white boy said, "you think he's just being a racist twat, but it's also about what you wear, what you're doing. If I was walking around with certain people acting a certain way, I know I'd get stopped, too."

"But it's embarrassing," said the Somali boy. "Your neighbours see you and think you're a bad family and don't want to associate with you."

"But that's how it's always going to be with the police," the white boy interrupted. "They're always going to think the bad people are the young ones, and then when we want to settle down and have a nice life, we're going to think, 'Oh yeah, it's the young 'uns making trouble.'"

I asked the others what they thought.

"A lot of my friends and family are black," a girl said, "and they've all been called different names around Sheffield, but, on the other hand, it's dealt with quite quickly and people stick up for them, so that's good."

"I don't think Sheffield is racist," another girl said, "but there are the odd people. Like I was in this shop and there was this older man picking on this mixed-race boy, saying, 'You're this, you're that' – but loads of people were sticking up for him, nobody was supporting the old man, so I think Sheffield is quite a good community."

"But after what happened in that drugs operation," a Somali boy said, "all the black youths got sentenced to prison, and then this one British lady got sentenced for doing heroine and crack, and they gave her community service, and there was a Somali guy, younger than her, and they gave him four years – I thought that was racism."

"It probably wasn't because of that," another boy said. "It was probably because she told on other people – the police probably made a deal with her."

"And nobody's taking into account her previous record or the fact that she's a woman, she might have a family... You can't just say it's racism without knowing the facts."

"It's definitely because she was white," the Somali boy said. "It's like if you're British, yeah, the police are nice to you, but, if you're coloured, they're more aggressive towards you, giving you cheek and backchat for no reason."

I asked whether this was still a good country even if it wasn't perfect.

"I think it's really good," a girl said, "because, in places like Saudi Arabia, women aren't allowed to go outside without a man and stuff like that. But in England and Britain, it's not like that."

"That's why people from all over the world come here," said a boy, "because you ain't got nothing to fear. Like, no offence, in Somalia, there's war happening, in Pakistan there's poverty, they come here for a better living standard. But then you get treated like crap by police officers, like it ain't your country, it's the British country."

The class came to an end. Many of the students wished me luck as they filed out, and I was left thinking how complicated the world they had to negotiate their way in was.

* * * * *

My next class was a smaller group of sixth-form students, aged seventeen and eighteen and with a similar ethnic and social mix to the first class. As they were a high-ability group, Paul suggested we stretch them with a discussion of identity and values, issues that had been raised throughout my journey. I started by asking them about British identity.

"People actually do have a strong sense of identity, they just don't know it," one young man said.

"Ours is just a very British way of doing it," a young woman added. "We're not a big country for ostentatiousness – except for the Royal Wedding. Everybody would feel a bit silly saying 'I pledge allegiance to the Queen' – it's too American…"

"But I think Americans are quite insecure," the young man said, "because they're still quite a young country. Britain's like the grandfather, just chilling in his armchair."

"People do have a strong sense of being British," a young woman added, "but it's less of a culture and more of an attitude; we have that British humour, it's slightly different from everywhere else and maybe an underlying cynicism, whereas the Americans are really out there. We just take the piss out of ourselves – we're secure in our identity."

I reflected that their security in their British identity reflected their own self-confidence and clearly, for others, British identity was more of an issue. I decided to move the conversation on to ethics and morality by asking where they got their sense of right and wrong.

"The BBC," one young man said, "from *Eastenders*."

Everyone laughed.

"But actually," a young woman said, "we've got that idea of an ideal family, two kids, two parents, middle-class dog. When you watch the TV, that's what you want to aim for even if there aren't actually many families like that."

"Children are more influenced by celebrities and their friends," another young woman said, "because they think their parents are boring."

"And I think the newspapers, they're always trying to say like, 'Single parents are on the rise' – almost subconsciously, they're trying to make you think something."

My conversation with John, the vicar in Devon, in mind, I asked whether any of them took their ethics and values from religion.

"It depends," a young woman said. "As a non-religious person, it has no bearing whatsoever. For some young people, it does, but, even then, you see some who follow certain religions breaking aspects of that religion because of peer pressure, like Muslim kids drinking on school trips or whatever."

"Some people," added another young woman, "they don't think they're even breaking the religion, they just say they're interpreting it in their own way."

"But I think that, even if you're not religious," another young woman said, "a lot of British culture has a sort of moral grounding which comes from religion, so you might not think it's consciously from religion but it probably does come from it."

"I'm religious," a young man added, "but I don't feel religion made my morals what they are. It's down to parents and friends as well, but you're never going to get away from the fact that, in the past, we did have a strong religious society. It's still going to have a bearing on what we do today, but I also think we have moved on and changed. People who are not religious are not going to start going against everything in the Bible. Everyone's morals are still pretty much the same in the most important areas."

"But it has to change," a young woman said, "because otherwise people, like gay people, would still be being discriminated against, so it's probably better that it's a bit more loose, a bit more interpretive…"

"But then if you've got a 'loose cannon' in society, without any of the same morals as anyone else, that's quite scary, isn't it? That's where you see criminals, people who are making decisions which the rest of society wouldn't see as morally correct."

"But it's like the riots," said a young man. "They knew they were doing something wrong, but they did it anyway because they were angry. You know when you're doing something wrong so it's not about the moral code, the moral code's fine. It's just getting people to care about it."

His comment struck me as really important, and suggested that the country's problems stemmed not from a lack of a clear moral code, but rather from a lack of commitment or attachment on the part of some people to the British society itself.

"If you were to say to all these young people," the young man went on, "'We'll give you better schools, we'll give you better education, you can be like the rest of society,' then they probably wouldn't take it out on the rest of society. I mean look at MPs and bankers taking massive bonuses, and then kids get in trouble for thieving…"

I asked what the link was with politicians and bankers.

"If the people who are ruling you are not following that code, then you lose a bit of respect for it," one young woman said, echoing comments I had heard in Hackney. "If MPs are going to do that, then it's really hypocritical for them to say, 'We're going to enforce a moral code.'"

"The media says it's an underclass," another young woman added, "but the politicians went to the best schools, went to like Oxford and Cambridge and stuff, but they are still greedy and they still steal."

I asked whether what MPs had done was not different from the rioting.

"It's all part of the same moral code," said one young woman. "The MPs knew what they were doing was wrong, and the rioters knew what they were doing was wrong."

"I think what the MPs did was worse," a young man said. "They're supposed to be the people who are meant to lead this country. How can you have trust in anyone who doesn't follow the moral code they're telling you to follow?"

"It doesn't justify what they did," said one young man. "There are ways of putting your point across and that doesn't include going out and ruining other people's lives."

"And it's got to stop somewhere," a girl agreed, "because you can't have it that the rioters did something because the MPs did something, and then it'll be the shopkeepers – it can't keep going like that."

Our time was up, and Paul brought the class to an end with many questions still unanswered, although it was clear that, as in Hackney, there was a great deal of anger towards politicians amongst young people.

As they left, I was pleased: the discussion had helped advance my thinking a great deal in a number of different areas, particularly the point about not focusing on the rules of British society but rather on why some people didn't feel committed to them. It felt, from what they were saying, that resentment about the way MPs and other leaders had behaved had led to a reduced commitment amongst people to society as a whole, an idea I wanted to explore further as I travelled.

14

National Identity and Values in Sheffield

That evening, Paul had organised for his friend Steve and a couple of his colleagues, Jeremy and Peter, to come over to his house and continue the debate about values and identity. Steve, who was studying in Sheffield but held dual American and French nationality, began by comparing British culture with that of his home countries.

"This is the most divided society I know," he said, "more divided than France, more divided than America. There are all these unwritten rules that if you don't know, you can't get by. There are people who know how to get around and people who don't know how to get around."

"There I do agree," said Paul. "It can be very difficult – you do need to have a certain amount of cultural capital."

I asked what he meant by cultural capital.

"It's about being able to turn up at an interview," he said, "or go out for dinner with a potential employer and feel easy and able to talk about a diverse range of subjects – to feel comfortable in the established order as it is today. There are a lot of kids who feel really alien to that and unable to negotiate their way through it. If you've got those really subtle skills, it's a very easy place to live, but if you don't, it's not."

His point about division not on the basis of money but on the basis of the ability to negotiate the modern world made me think about what Alex and Josh in London had told me about Twitter, which was open to all but nevertheless divided between those who knew how to work it and those who didn't.

I asked Jeremy what he thought.

"I just think there's a feeling of despair in the country," he said, "and the media like to put it out there – 'Broken Britain'. But then maybe that's just part of being British, the middle-class debate, endlessly talking about what's wrong with us."

"I think every society has something similar," said Paul, "but maybe that's important, and maybe if you have an idea that your society is really good and is moving towards a set goal, it feels a bit authoritarian."

"So maybe it's good to have a more pessimistic society," said Jeremy.

"It's a delicate balance," said Paul, "because I quite admire countries with a good constitution which you can have a dialogue with – it gives you some kind of fixed point. It's important for it not to become too fixed a point, otherwise it becomes dogmatic, but without that fixed point the discussion can become loose and nebulous and you end up with nihilistic despair."

"I think the problem is the word 'citizenship'," said Jeremy. "We're not citizens, we're subjects – if we were citizens, we would take this more seriously."

"But if we were citizens, we'd need to know what we were citizens of," said Paul. "You need to have a charter to sign up to. And then there's a problem whenever a politician tries to establish a set of values – it always ends up with embarrassing platitudes."

"And with the economy potentially heading into a recession," Peter added, "you need that sense of community and togetherness otherwise it could quickly become a 'them and us' kind of mentality."

Paul asked him how he felt that could be countered.

"There's definitely something about schools," said Peter, "children getting buses together, having lessons together. A few years ago I went out to China with a group of schools, both private and state schools, and it was a great advert for modern Britain, and there wasn't very much 'them and us'. There were a few funny comments like, 'I thought you'd be dead posh, but you're alright!'"

It turned out the trip had been funded by the Chinese government, and Paul noted the irony that it had taken the Chinese government to bring British children together. We discussed China further and Peter told me had lived there for two years.

"It's good to go to there", he said, "and it gives you a good perspective on Britain. Like, I taught at Beijing University and we had a debate with the students about the monarchy, and at the end, they voted seventeen to three in favour of the Royal Family, which, for communist China, is quite surprising. They said that it's good for the morale of the country, it represents the country abroad, and, in a changing society, it's something to hold on to. After that, I was a bit more pro than I had been."

The idea of 'something to hold on to' struck a chord: a number of people I had met had seemed very lost and confused in modern Britain and fixed points – 'anchors' as Alan Courtney in Malvern had called them – seemed more important in that context. I knew that the Royal Family's popularity had been increasing even before Prince William's wedding earlier in the year, and I wondered whether the stability of the institution in a changing world was part of the reason why. Around me, the conversation about China continued.

"Obviously there's that concern about China and human rights," Paul said, "but I think it's important just to engage in as open a way as possible, and acknowledge that if China is going to become more and more important globally, we need to engage with it, not mythologise it. If there are things we disagree with, we should say so, but in a spirit of conviviality, of being part of the same global concern."

"I also think," Peter said, "there's a massive temptation to moan about China and have negative views, and that makes us feel a bit better about ourselves – like there was a big story recently that China had banned a TV talent show because it was getting four hundred million viewers and people texting in to vote for the winner was a bit too much like democracy. Everyone here was feeling a bit smug when it was banned but what have we got – *X Factor*? Lucky us…"

"The Chinese are fed up about getting lectured about the economy or human rights," he went on. "Like the economy at the moment – it's in a mess and the Chinese are quite keen to report that, because it makes them feel like this model that the world has been trying to ram down their throats isn't quite as good as we all thought."

I asked about the UK's place in a world where China's influence was growing.

"It's easy to knock Britain," he said, "and say it's just a small island and it hasn't got a role but I think it is important to acknowledge that we do punch above our weight with films, and royal weddings…"

Paul asked why the Royal Wedding was so important.

"I guess it's that realisation that we're a little island and we've lost our Empire," Peter said, "but we still do A-plus celebrities."

"We've got a good education system," he went on, "not world class possibly, but, still, you only have to walk around Sheffield to see five thousand Chinese students coming here to learn. So it's got a lot going for it. It might not be quite as important as it was – we've certainly lost a lot of power and prestige – but it's taken it quite calmly and reinvented itself as a modern, liberal country. In places like China, it's seen as America's little poodle, so with America's decline in the next ten or twenty years, people will see Britain as declining too. That causes a bit of a loss of confidence, but people just get on with it."

"Everything that's happened with the Murdoch empire and MPs and banks, too – it's shaken people's confidence a bit," he continued. "But, then again, the Brits are quite phlegmatic; we ultimately 'keep calm and carry on'. It's just a shame that funding for the World Service is being slashed – it's a genuinely world-class institution, one hundred years of experience and we're just losing it. And I think that changes people's perspectives of Britain and lowers our self-esteem a bit."

"There's a sense that Britain has been great," Jeremy agreed, "and that's why people still expect the England football team to win the World Cup. There's a sense that Britain has been great – we have the distorted view of the British Empire. But let's not forget there was also Wilberforce. We know that we freed the slaves – so there are things to feel good about, too."

We moved on to discussing solutions to the problems the country faced.

"The thing for me is don't wait for government," Peter said. "I'm a great believer in people-to-people exchange and education. Just get on with it, almost give up on the negative people with their negative views, and the politicians will see that they're increasingly marginalised – and boring and bitter."

"Hopefully the politicians will catch the mood," said Paul, "because they've probably got noble intentions in the main and at the moment it's a nasty little trade-off, because they pander to the electorate, and the electorate aren't really sure what they want so nobody's really stepping up."

"Everyone is happy to abdicate responsibility," Peter said, "and they're lazy – it's easy to blame someone else but they should look in the mirror. Just do your little thing on a small scale, and slowly but surely that will affect a change. Look at racism – it's so much better than it was ten or twenty years ago – environmentalism, feminism, ageism – there's been an awful lot of improvement."

"Most of it has been driven through education and we should take that very seriously and be more confident about it," Paul said, "and I think the key thing about education is to teach people how to be good people. But you can't say that."

"Why not?" Peter asked.

"Because people are scared to say the word 'good'," Paul said, "because it comes loaded down with value judgements about what you're saying is good and what's not. We just concentrate on making kids the best they can be academically, not morally, but if you're not going to pick it up in school, where are you going to pick it up?"

We left it there, but Peter's challenge to look in the mirror got me thinking again about what I should do once my journey was over. The point the young man in the class earlier in the day had made about attachment to society rather than focusing on values seemed helpful, and I also wanted to think about how young people could be helped to build the skills to navigate an increasingly complicated world; but the discussion of China also made me worry again that by focusing on domestic questions I was missing the bigger picture of the UK's place in a rapidly changing world.

* * * * *

The next day, my last in Sheffield, Paul and I met up with Guuleed, a former student of Paul's, in a cafe that was run by members of the Somali community. We chatted about what being British meant, and, as the conversation continued, two brothers in their twenties entered the cafe and joined in.

"Britain is my country," said one of the brothers, who wore an Arsenal football shirt. "British people are the most friendly."

"Go to Toronto," said his brother, who was clearly more cynical about the UK, "then you'll see what welcoming means. But as long as Britain doesn't try to stop me practising my faith I'm not bothered."

"You don't know what you've got," said his brother, and this began a fractious debate between the two of them about whether any aspect of Britishness could ever be consistent with, or as important as, the key tenets of Islam.

"Name me one thing, *one thing*, which matches the faith," said his brother, increasingly angry.

"Human rights, human rights," said his brother, equally angry.

As they continued the debate, they raised their voices and the cafe owner had to quieten them down, abruptly bringing to an end a debate that they both clearly felt strongly about.

They left soon afterwards and I returned to the conversation with Guuleed.

"I think this question of Britishness is one for the eighteenth or nineteenth century," he said, "when the nation state really mattered. Now when people ask it, I'm always a bit suspicious. It seems to be asked as if some people are not British enough. Every so often, it seems like a journalist doesn't have anything to write about, so will try to investigate this question, and it ends up being divisive."

"I don't mind when it's asked out of genuine curiosity," he continued, "but it's still a question for another era. Now that we have the Internet, I can connect with the people who have the closest values to my own, wherever they are in the world. These value systems are more important than the nation state – so let's go back to values, rather than trying to force the same culture and identity on people who haven't even met."

"The Internet changes the conception of the state," he went on. "It used to be all of us behind the leader, and leaders still live that way, British institutions are still constructed for the Empire – but we're free now, we don't have to be stuck. That's not to say I'm not British – and, if anyone asks, I'll tell them that – but I would prefer a world in which that wasn't necessary."

He had a confidence about him that I had not come across since meeting Alex and Josh, the young men I had talked to back in London about social media. His argument about identity was also really persuasive, although it challenged the idea that the concept of 'Britishness' might provide a 'fixed point' that could bring people together. I knew the idea of Britishness was one I would have to look into further when I got to Scotland but, first, I was heading to Rotherham.

15

Obesity, Depression and Decline in Rotherham

I arrived in Rotherham on a beautiful Tuesday morning. As I walked into town from the railway station, I saw a man fishing in the river below. It was an idyllic scene, the water shimmering in the sunshine, so I climbed down the embankment to reach him. He was bald and perhaps in his fifties, and spoke softly and quietly, so I could hardly hear him over the gushing river. He told me that it was a good spot for fishing, and that he came occasionally when he wasn't working. I asked him what he did.

"I work in the factory up there," he said, pointing along the river. "We take the labels off candles from China and then send them to supermarkets to sell them on. Basically we just get the Chinese writing off – best before dates, that kind of thing."

Before I could ask my next question, he caught a fish and reeled it in. As he held it in his hand, the fish thrashed desperately, the hook still caught in the side of its mouth. He gripped it harder and it was unable to thrash any more; motionless, it looked out in apparent terror. For perhaps a minute, he tried to prise the hook out of the side of its mouth, reaching further and further in as he did so. Eventually he freed it, and threw it back in. For a moment, it didn't move in the water, and I thought it had died, but then it began thrashing again and swam off. He looked back at me.

"Up there," he said, pointing to a bridge down the river, "a few darkies got caught eating the fish they caught. They just got warnings. If it had been me I would have been fined."

I left him to it and walked into town, where I got talking to three women. They agreed to be interviewed if I referred to them as 'three old biddies from Rotherham' and called them by false names they gave themselves – Emilia, Gertrude and Nora.

"Make sure you note down that we're all cheeky," said Emilia, "and that I'm the cheekiest."

I asked her about the town.

"I'm not a racist," she said, "but there are too many of them – on market days, you can't move for them."

"They come out of the woodwork," said Gertrude. "I said to Nora the other day, 'Did a plane just cover over? Because it's like they've been parachuted in.'"

"Enough's enough," said Emilia. "Feed them but no more. We don't have enough for ourselves. We've got nothing of our own here."

"What I don't understand," said Nora, "is how they can afford to smoke and go to the betting hut."

I asked if white British people did the same thing.

"Of course, love," said Emilia, "but no more of them."

They needed to go and walked off smiling.

"Bye-bye, love," said Emilia.

I walked into the heart of the town, which was full of people enjoying the sunshine. I was struck almost immediately by the number of people who were clearly obese. There seemed to be a large number of fast food restaurants, cafes and bakeries, and many of the people I saw were eating pasties and sandwiches out of brown paper bags.

I saw a man on a bench, and walked over. It was only when I reached him that I saw his legs were shaking. His face was drawn, and he looked exhausted. I tried to talk to him, but he just said 'No, no, no' in an accent I didn't recognise. Across the road, a young woman spat in the street, walked into a shop and emerged a moment later with a bottle of Coke.

I walked past Jamie's Kitchen, the cafe set up by the chef Jamie Oliver to encourage healthy eating in the town, and on the other side of the road found two women smoking.

"There's not much here," one told me. "All the shops are shutting down – they're all gone to Meadowhall. There's nowt for the kids to do."

I asked her about Jamie's Kitchen.

"Never been," she said. "It's all very well and good to want to eat healthy but it's cheaper to buy chips."

"It's just quicker as well," said her friend.

I asked whether she had considered buying cheap ingredients and cooking them up.

"People can't be bothered to cook themselves," she said. "Everybody is too busy to sit down for dinner together. I'm a single mum; I work part-time, too – so it's lots of convenience food."

In the heart of town, a man sat alone on a bench staring straight ahead intensely. He was muscular, tattooed, with a shaved head. I sat down next to him and asked him about the town.

"It's all changed," he said. "I've been away the last four years and it's all new buildings now."

I asked where he had been.

"Let's just say I've been away," he said.

"I was born here, I grew up here," he continued after a moment, "but I've been sat here for half an hour and not seen one person I know. I worked in pit when I left school and it was all sons and fathers and grandfathers. Not any more."

"I don't even recognise it round here," he added, motioning towards the pedestrianised area. "Last time I was here, you could drive down there."

"And that," he added, motioning at an empty building, "that used to be Woolworths."

Market stalls lined the streets in front of the building, one of them with a sound system playing music, and the street was full of people. With the sun shining it was a happy scene, but he didn't seem part of it at all.

I asked what he wanted to do now that he was back in Rotherham.

"There aren't many jobs," he said, "and it's not for the lack of trying. I'm a qualified gym instructor, baker and brickie, as well. A lot of people I used to work with in the pit, they're just sat about drinking all day and they're looking really old. People just live day by day."

I asked about the sense of community that came from working in a mine.

"Everybody knew everybody," he said, "but that died with strike."

"There used to be paths in the woods where I played when I was a boy," he went on. "Now they're overgrown and all the kids are sat in front of their PlayStations."

He sat quiet for a moment, and then decided he had said enough.

"Has that helped you out?" he asked, and I said that it had.

He got up, shook my hand and wished me all the best. As he walked off, I wasn't convinced he had anywhere to go.

I walked on and saw a woman sitting on a bench. I went over to her and asked about Rotherham.

"It's a shithole," she told me.

I asked why.

"It just is," she said. "Everything's bad. People are scruffy… It used to be nice, but now it's all just drunks and druggies. Nobody's got any money – it's just full of bookies and pawnbrokers. I'd leave tomorrow if I could."

I asked if there was anything else I should write about Rotherham.

"Don't come here," she said and walked on.

"It's a poor town," another woman told me. "Nobody's got anything. Everything's so dear."

I asked her how people in the town were feeling.

"A lot of people have probably given up," she said. "It's sad really."

What she said struck me. I had seen some difficult things on my travels but nowhere where people had given up. She was quiet for a moment, and then added:

"You should go and talk to them youngsters – they might say something different."

She pointed over to two young women on the next bench along. I went over and asked them about the town.

"You don't want to know about Rotherham," one said.

"It's a shithole," the other said. "There are too many foreigners, no jobs, and a shit load of pigeons, druggies, convicts and alcoholics."

I asked if there was a problem about unhealthy eating in the town.

"It's just cheap Greggs," she said.

"They're all lazy cunts," the other said. "They've got no jobs, they eat loads of takeaways, cheap bread… They've probably got six kids, too."

I asked whether the people she was talking about cared about their health.

"They don't care about anything," she said.

It was lunchtime by now, and the town centre was even busier than it had been. At the town's McDonald's, I found all the staff waiting around outside – the power had gone down, and the restaurant was closed. One by one, people came to the door, saw the sign telling them that food wasn't being served, and made alternative arrangements.

"Thank God," said one young man, who had been clearly forced to come by his friends.

"KFC?" said another man to his friend, and they headed on.

"Looks like a chippie job," said someone else.

I talked to one of the employees about weight problems in the town.

"Don't say in your book it's because of fast food," she said, "because it's not. I've been working in cafes and chippies for fifteen years and I haven't put on any weight."

"It's not our fault," she continued, "because it costs a fortune to buy fruit and veg. People can't afford it, especially with the bus fare into town. If you've only got so much, you've got to live within your means. Kids aren't shown how to cook – they grow up and, rather than cook a meal, they buy it cheap. But that's the whole country. Rotherham might be rough and down to earth, but it's got some lovely people – they tend to be warm and open to friendship so once you've met them, you're friends for life."

I had a train to catch, but wanted to try to understand more about the eating habits in the town before I left. I sat down next to a grandmother, perhaps in her late forties, who was watching her daughter and young granddaughter play around the town's fountain.

"It's unemployment and fast food," she told me. "People tend to eat microwave food now – cooking's an art of the past."

I asked if people worried about their health.

"I don't think they do," she said. "People just live from day to day – they don't think about the future. You just get used to lounging around in casual clothes. I used to get dressed up for shopping but it's a tracksuit and trainers these days."

"But this is a good place," she continued. "People are very sociable – a few are nasty but you get that anywhere. Most people are lovely."

Her daughter called her over, and she left, wishing me luck with the book. I believed what she said about the people of Rotherham but I was still deeply concerned by my visit. Despite their friendliness, the sense that some people in the town had almost given up on life was disturbing. The circumstances were different from those of the communities I had visited in south Wales but the sense of depression and decline was equally affecting. As I headed for Scotland, I thought back to the conversations in Sheffield about the rise of emerging economies like China, and worried that, if the UK's economic position worsened, the pain and loss I had encountered in Rotherham and south Wales might become more widespread.

16

Scottish Independence and Identity in Edinburgh, Dumfries and Aberdeen

I started the Scottish leg of my journey in Dumfries, a town known for having a strong sense of Scottish identity. It seemed like a good opportunity to explore the issue and its links to the question of Scottish independence, so, on a sunny morning in the town centre, I began approaching shoppers to get their views.

"There's a preconception that we're all subsidy junkies eating deep-fried Mars bars," one man sitting on a bench told me, "but you've got pockets of deprivation everywhere, not just in Scotland. And while we've got 8.5 per cent of the UK population, we contribute 9.6 per cent to the economy."

"We've been in a budget surplus for years," he went on. "We send more down than we get back up. And that's before you even mention the three-letter word – oil. If you include that, then we're the fifth richest country in the world."

He was clearly passionate about Scottish independence and I asked why he felt so strongly about it.

"It's a feeling that you can do it better yourself," he said. "Remote control government from four hundred miles away doesn't work."

"There's also a unifying bond," he went on. "We're historically, culturally and socially bonded. Our history is more than the last three hundred years of forced union, and we realise we can do things better for ourselves. There's ambition about the place now, it's linguistic, it's cultural, it's our literature, our songs..."

"You look at art," he continued. "All the Turner Prize nominees seem to come from the Glasgow School of Art... Literature – since devolution, writers are not afraid to identify themselves as Scottish. The cringe factor has gone, and people feel there's nothing wrong with writing about your people, your place."

I asked him what he would say to people who felt that England and Scotland were stronger together.

"It's a perfectly valid view," he said, "but I disagree with it. You come here and you know you're in a different country. The humour is different, the accents are different, the people are different."

"I'm ambitious for England," he went on. "I think England can be a prosperous country again, but, when we find people down south complaining about subsidies for Scotland, they should be looking at their own government, asking whether it's really better to fund Trident than get their pensioners free prescriptions."

"Speaking of Trident," he continued, "can you name me any country in the world where they have a nuclear weapon within twenty minutes of a population centre? You can't, because there isn't one, except us. Twenty minutes from Glasgow, that's where the nuclear sub is. It's a constant worry for us, but I saw an article the other day making the case for the Union by saying that England has nowhere to put a nuclear sub. So we're just a parking space for nuclear subs now? You can see why we feel like second-class citizens."

He had to go and wished me well. It was clear he was very engaged with the independence debate and I wanted to find out whether other people in Dumfries shared his strong sense of Scottish identity.

Outside a shop, I found two young women.

"I'm Scottish definitely," said one. "Only English people say they're British. Even though we're with England and they give us all this support, I still always tick 'white Scottish' on a form – I even write it in if it's not an option."

"I sound like such a racist," she went on, "but I don't want to be English. It's just the arrogance – when I was in Carlisle, someone shouted 'Oi, Haggis' at me..."

"No, they didn't," her friend said.

"They did," she said. "I swear on my granny's grave. That was just one person, and I don't want to be ignorant but they all come across like that, especially politicians."

"We're like hamsters for England," she went on.

"You mean guinea pigs," said her friend.

"Yeah, guinea pigs," she said. "They try everything on us first – like the smoking ban."

"And Andy Murray is Scottish," she went on. "They try to say he's British – he's not, he's Scottish."

I asked if she would support Scottish independence.

"Well," she said, "we've not got much money. We kind of need them a wee bit but, if you ask most people, unless they're old or they like the Queen, they're Scottish. My pal drew a moustache on the Queen on a banknote..."

"Don't say that," said her friend.

"I'm just being honest," she said. "We're not in the William Wallace times, against the English, but I cannae think of anyone here who would be proud to be British."

I walked on, and found two young men smoking outside a pub. I asked their view. They were both wholeheartedly Scottish. I asked why.

"Because, if you think about it," one said, "when Andy Murray wins, he's British, but when he loses, he's Scottish. And they weren't *British* riots, they were *English* riots."

I asked his friend what he thought.

"Aye," he said, "especially within the likes of the BBC, we always get bad publicity. We're always portrayed as fat, ginger and Scottish."

"It's the border," his friend said. "We go down to Carlisle, and we're hated. No offence to English folks, but they're always dicks."

"Snooty," he added, "that's what they are."

Outside a carpenter's shop, I found the owner, and asked him whether he felt more Scottish or British.

"Scottish, I'm afraid," he said. "They never do anything for us – like the Poll Tax and Maggie Thatcher. If there's owt to be tested, they'll test it on Scots."

I asked him what was good about being Scottish.

"We've got an identity," he said, "that's where we belong. No matter where you are in the world, you know you're part of it and, wherever you go, people will welcome you."

I asked if he supported independence.

"I didn't," he said, "but I do now."

I asked why he had changed his mind.

"The way we got treated with the Poll Tax," he said.

* * * * *

The next day I went to a pub in Edinburgh to watch a crucial rugby World Cup match between England and Scotland, which seemed like a good place to continue to explore Scottish identity. The pub was packed full of fans, including a few England supporters who were being completely out-sung by their Scottish counterparts. Scotland took the lead early in the match and, as the minutes passed, a fan next to me clasped her hands together, almost in prayer. When Johnny Wilkinson, the England fly half, missed a series of crucial kicks, the Scotland fans grew in belief.

"Come on, Johnny," one shouted sarcastically.

"You couldn't make this shit up," said another, grinning.

Their confidence was growing and the noise was rising, but, in the penultimate minute, almost out of nowhere, England scored a try, and the pub fell silent. The final whistle blew shortly afterwards: England had won and the pub emptied quickly.

Drowning his sorrows by the bar, I found Kevin, a Scotland fan in his forties, and asked him about Scottish independence.

"It'll never work," he said. "We're thirty-five years too late. North Sea oil, the gas, all the electricity, none of it belongs to us any more. Besides, I'm ex-forces so I'm not Scottish, I'm British. The nationalists hide behind the safety of knowing it's never going to happen, so they can say what they like."

"None of the people I know vote for the SNP," he continued. "They only do well because the nationalists are the only ones who vote. We're the UK, we're Britain, and having another set of Parliaments and governments just costs people money. There's seventy million people in the UK, and only one tenth of them are in Scotland – do they really think that we're going to be better off on our own? It's nonsense."

"You've got so many kids coming out of schools with no qualifications," he added, "and all these ex-mining towns where nothing is produced. That's what they should be worried about, not having another layer of politics."

I headed outside and on the street I got talking to George, a Glasgow man visiting Edinburgh for the weekend. He was also against the idea of independence.

"Scotland benefits enormously from its ties with England," he told me. "We get more from them than they do from us. It defies logic as far as I'm concerned: right now, I've got a local councillor, a Euro MP, a Scottish MP, and a Westminster MP – someone needs to explain to me what I need another Parliament for."

"And people think we'd be accepted to the EU," he continued, "but why would they? We've got no money. RBS would have gone bust if wasn't for the British government. And say Scotland did become independent – do we block the BBC? Why should England allow us to benefit from their broadcasting system if we're not going to contribute to it?"

"We're a small country," he concluded. "We need to stay as we are."

* * * * *

The next day, I headed to Aberdeen to catch a ferry to the Shetland Isles.

On board, with a fourteen-hour journey ahead – including a short stop in the Orkney Isles – I took the opportunity to speak to the other passengers. Having heard the case for independence in Dumfries and the case against in Edinburgh, I wanted to see what the people on the ferry thought.

The sea was choppy, and, as the ferry was being tossed around, I got talking to an electrician sitting in the indoor seating area about the potential for Scottish independence.

"It would be too hard," he said. "They all talk about Scotland having the oil, but things could backfire. It's been this way for so long, it's probably best to stick with it."

"Everyone talks about being separate from the English," he continued, "but that's just a natural hatred thing. A lot of people just say it off the top of their tongue, but whether it's feasible or not, nobody knows."

I asked what he meant about hatred.

"I've not got it," he said, "but you hear people, with sports in particular, who have this stigma where they are just for Scotland. It wouldn't just be England, it would be Northern Ireland, Wales, everybody. It's just stupid, really."

I asked where that feeling came from.

"Stupid people," he said. "Anyone with any intelligence would happily bypass that and support a successful team. It's just idiots who jump on a bandwagon."

I wanted to continue the conversation but the movement of the ship on top of the beer became too much for him and he staggered off towards the bathroom, just managing to wish me luck as he went.

I headed out to the smoking bay at the back of the ferry and found a collection of people – lorry drivers, tradesmen travelling to work on Shetland and Orkney and locals returning from shopping trips to the mainland – and asked them about Scottish independence.

"It's a no-win situation," one man, Mervyn, told me. "We'd like to be independent – at the moment, we're being taxed to the hilt and it's subsidising England, you catch my drift? No offence meant – that's just my opinion. But independence? No, not yet – never in my lifetime. We'll never get enough folk to vote for it because they're frightened. People aren't going to take that chance; you don't know how it's going to work out, especially with all the turmoil in the world right now. What if it went wrong – then what would we have? Sometimes it's better the devil you know."

His friend came out and joined him, and I asked him how he felt about independence.

"I'd love it," he said, "I really would. Then we couldn't blame anyone else; we'd have to take responsibility for ourselves."

I asked whether he would still support independence if it was economically damaging for Scotland.

"That's the question," he said, "but I'd still support it – it's about more than money."

They headed back inside, and I talked to another man, Ivan.

"I'd vote for independence," he said. "I know there are a lot of things against it, like, if you did get independence, you couldn't just stop the British army – the whole country needs to stick together as far as that's concerned – but if we got the oil grounds and the fishing grounds, then we'd be pretty well off."

I asked whether his support for independence reflected badly on the rest of the UK.

"Not at all," he said. "We just want to be our own country so why not go the full hog? I've no problem with the English – my girlfriend is English – but there is bigotry and you'll never stop that. Some people are just very small-minded. It stems back to the 1300s and 1400s and it's time to let go. Films like *Braveheart* didn't help – it was extremely well-dramatised, shall we say, but that's how lots of people learn about history."

A young man came out and asked him for a cigarette. Ivan obliged.

"Magic," the young man said.

"It's not magic," he said, "it's the same shit as the rest."

I headed inside, and on a table sitting alone I found Rachel, a young woman who told me she had moved from the mainland to Orkney.

"I studied history at university," she explained with a warm smile, "and I want to be a curator, so I'm volunteering at the main museum on Orkney. I felt really ready for an adventure, and for me that came true in Orkney."

"It's a really nice culture," she went on. "I fell in love with the landscape; there's lots of independent shops, and there's a real community spirit. I always dreamed of living on an island – it's like a little microcosm, with its own identity."

I asked her about that identity.

"It definitely has its own Orcadian culture," she said. "I'm Scottish, and even I feel foreign. It's very different from mainland Scotland; it's more correlated with Viking culture. I'll never be considered an Orcadian because I wasn't born there. Even if I lived there fifty years, with my accent I'd still stick out like a sore thumb."

I asked where British identity fitted in.

"Probably way down the list, to be honest," she said. "It would be Orcadian first, and then Scottish, and then reluctantly British. Shetland's even more complicated – there's always been a good friendship between Shetland and Norway through the ages. It feels as Norse up there as it does Scottish."

"Identity is funny, isn't it?" she added, still smiling. "We start dividing ourselves the moment we're born."

* * * * *

As I went back to my cabin, I reflected that I didn't know who would win the Scottish independence election but I did know that many Scots clearly felt their own identity, separate from the UK, even if their fears about the political and economic implications of independence meant they might vote against it. This sense of a separate identity so soon after my conversation with Guuleed in Sheffield once again challenged the idea of Britishness as a uniting force and I decided that if I wanted to take positive lessons from my journey, I should focus on trying to identify more practical steps that could help to bring people together.

17

Money, Industry and Tradition in Shetland

The ferry arrived in Lerwick at dawn, and I headed straight into town to meet Victor, a local landlord who had a room to rent in a shared house on King Olaf Street, just off the high street. I asked him about Shetland.

"People have been spoilt by the oil," he told me, "and young people are being brought up very differently to the way they were twenty years ago. Some don't have a clue about practical day-to-day things – they expect money but they don't want to work."

"There's a great culture here of claiming benefits," he went on. "One of my Latvian tenants was talking about that today – he's a great worker and believes in grafting for whatever he's doing. It's born out of poverty. But here it's a different attitude – the affluence of the oil makes them lethargic – they've had it too good for too long."

He told me about a new gas refinery at Sullum Voe, just outside the town of Brae, to the north on the main island. He said it wasn't going to do much for Lerwick.

"They're unscrupulous businessmen," he said. "They're buggering a lot of people around and most of the money is going to be held up there – they're going to run it like an oil rig on shore. I don't think it's going to do much for our economy at all, apart from Brae. Just look at how quiet Lerwick is, and this is only October. It used to be full of people but now there are units sitting empty."

It was clear that oil was a big issue on Shetland so when he left, I headed into Lerwick to find out what other people thought.

"The biggest economy was the fishing," one man walking down the main street told me. "Then the oil came and that just changed everything; it's been the saviour. Go to the Hebrides where there's no oil – there's no work there. Shetland would have been finished, too – especially after the EEC finished the fishing."

He walked on, and I found a woman who agreed that oil had been a good thing.

"There was some resentment as first," she said, "but the island was being depopulated and we got a good deal with the oil companies so everybody benefits. There's still a lot being found, too, which keeps the whole infrastructure going. And there's more on the west coast, I know there is."

Down the road I found an electrician over from the mainland and asked him what he thought.

"Shetland is just a place of work for me," he said. "It's just work, a couple of pints, something to eat and then bed. The oil basically rules the place. They used to have a mad accent, but they've totally lost it. If you go to the villages or the islands, you hear it, but here in Lerwick it's gone."

I asked him about what would happen to Shetland if the oil went.

"It'd die," he said.

* * * * *

That afternoon, I drove out of Lerwick to explore the main island. The hills outside the town were stark and bare, the landscape barren and exposed, covered by a brown-green moss punctuated only by sheep and the occasional house. I was particularly struck by the complete lack of trees but, while the environment was desolate, the infrastructure was excellent, with high-quality roads funded by oil revenues and wireless Internet in every population centre.

I drove to the far west coast of the Shetland mainland and found a lighthouse with the sea beating into the cliffs below. As I walked over to the house, the wind and rain battered in and it was hard even to stand up straight. I knocked on the door and the caretaker let me inside. We got talking about the lack of trees on the island.

"The legend is that they cut them down for firewood," he said, "and then the sheep grazed over them, so now they don't grow back."

I moved on, heading north towards the new refinery in Sullum Voe, which Victor had mentioned. The sun came out and I ate lunch in Brae, just next to the refinery, at the most northerly fish and chip shop in the country. I spoke with the owner about oil.

"It's changed a lot," she said. "We had been so rich in our traditions and it's a bit of a fight to keep them alive now with outsiders coming in. Things have been watered down a bit but they've built new schools, new roads, new leisure centres."

"Though it has endangered everything else," she went on, "like the knitwear which was passed down between generations – everyone started making money from oil and that tradition stopped being important. Some pockets around the islands still live the same way, surviving on fishing and knitwear, but here there used to be half a dozen houses. Now there are hundreds and the local people have done very well out of the oil."

"That's changing a bit now," she continued, "like, they promised to employ locals but that hasn't happened so we haven't seen the benefits so much. And the new refinery – they're bringing their own people in – but, even if that's the case, they'll still need to live somewhere, they'll need to eat somewhere…"

I asked if the oil was ultimately a positive thing.

"There's always been a divide," she said. "Some people want to keep things the way they are – but there are fewer and fewer people now who remember what it used to be like. Ultimately, it's bringing the young people back because there are jobs here."

"Nobody really knows how long it will last," she went on. "I can't see an end to it, in my life at least. I would imagine the wind turbines will eventually replace the oil industry but it's the same thing again – some people want to maintain the land, some people see financial benefits, some people won't get anything – there'll always be winners and losers."

She smiled, and I left. As I drove south, the wind battered in again, rocking the car. I found a village and asked a local man if there was a cafe nearby where I could escape the weather.

"Lerwick," he replied, pointing along the road. "It's about twenty-five miles that way."

The wind was getting wilder so I followed his advice.

* * * * *

Back at the house, Victor was moving in the man who would be staying in the spare room. His name was Craig, and he had come over from the mainland to work at the new refinery. He had worked in oil, gas and coal his whole life, and it seemed to show in the lines on his face and his heavy cough.

"It's booming up there," he said of Sullum Voe. "It's worth trillions. The farmer who owned the land, they're giving him loads of money for it – so he's hardly going to keep running around with his sheep, is he? I know I wouldn't."

We talked on, and he told me about his home town of Mauchline, in Ayrshire.

"Everyone used to know everyone," he said, "but it's all PlayStations now. When I was young, we used to go out and kick a ball, and during Wimbledon we'd paint a court on the street and play tennis – but not any more. People come into the town because they work in Glasgow but they want to live in the countryside. We had three roads, but now it's a town and you have no idea who people are. It's shocking man, shocking."

"Everybody's too busy," he went on. "Gaffers are putting too much pressure on; people don't have time. You get in from work, it's time to go to bed and the week just goes. I'm forty-seven now; it feels like years are flying, the years are like weeks."

In his voice I sensed the sadness and sense of loss I had encountered before on my travels, but I felt he was glad to have said his piece.

* * * * *

I decided to go out for a drink, but the town centre was virtually deserted. Many pubs were empty, although I did find one where five men had crowded around a small bar. One of the men was giving the barmaid a difficult time but he eventually became so drunk that he went over to a sofa, took off his shoes, put his feet up and fell asleep.

I left and was going to give up for the evening when I walked past a bar that seemed to be full of people. Inside, I realised to my surprise that it was full of young, middle-class English people, the atmosphere like a postgraduate bar at an Oxbridge college. I was even more surprised at how much everyone was drinking on a Monday night, downing shots and pints like there was no tomorrow.

At the bar, I got talking to a woman who explained that she and her colleagues were surveying for oil around Shetland, but the bad weather had forced their ship into port and they had nothing to do now but kill time. I asked if she liked her job, and she answered slightly awkwardly that she was comfortable in what she was doing.

I asked her about the environmental implications of oil and her face contorted slightly.

"There are no environmental implications of North Sea oil drilling," she said, "because they're so careful and precise."

I said that I had meant the environmental implications of climate change.

"The oil that we drill for doesn't cause climate change," she said. "When they turn it into oil to be burnt, that's a different story – but climate change is a big catch-all term and the science is more complicated than you think."

"Obviously the climate is changing," she went on, "but when you get into the causes it takes you into a big political debate which I don't want to get into now."

She went back to her friends.

Along the bar was an older man, perhaps in his late thirties, with a big beard, drinking tankards of beer. I approached him and asked for his view.

"We all know it's bad," he said, "but how did you get here from the mainland – boat or plane? Yeah, we'd all rather be doing something else, but at the end of the day people want to travel and oil lets them do that. It's about money, isn't it?"

"People think that other forms of energy are friendlier," he went on, "but do you know how much energy is required to go into a wind turbine? It's huge. So these energies which seem environmentally friendly, they're not really."

He had mentioned money, so I asked if that was also a factor.

"Yeah, of course," he said. "I'm sounding really cut-throat and I'm not like this myself but I'm just trying to be realistic – at the end of the day, money makes the world go round."

They were all still drinking heavily when I left at midnight. That night, I was kept awake by the sound of Craig coughing violently in the next room. Unable to sleep, my mind went back to the conversations of the day: the sometimes uncomfortable trade-offs and compromises that came with money and industry; and Craig's description of a home town changed beyond recognition.

18

Isolation and Community in Northern Scotland

The next day, I headed back to the mainland. Aboard the ferry in the late afternoon, the sun shone brightly as we headed south. As I looked out to sea, I could see patterns of weather – sunshine in places, intense rain in others, and a hint of a rainbow.

I went inside, and met a couple of men from the RNLI who had been visiting the lifeboat stations on Orkney and Shetland. I was interested in finding out more about an institution that was very well regarded in British society, so I went over.

"If you listen to Mr Cameron's big society," one told me, "the RNLI have been doing it for two hundred years. These are people who take boats to sea to save people they don't know, generations of the same family going out, all for the good of us. In every other country, it would be a paid service."

"It's a very British institution," he continued. "The Netherlands have something similar, but it's tiny in comparison. The US coastguard is essentially just the navy."

I asked whether the lifeboats were viable without government funding.

"Oh, God, yes," he said. "There are a few sparsely populated areas where we struggle with volunteers but, all around the coast, people still answer the call of the bleeper."

"There's certainly an element of danger involved," he went on, "but, in the islands, lifeboats are quite well respected and people are keen to do their bit. Unless some big rescue happens, there's no recognition – but they're not looking for that. They're just looking to do the job they're there for."

"It would also be a very different organisation with state funding," his colleague said. "Everybody sees the men in the yellow jackets, but the old ladies who raise the money are just as important – and they turn out come rain or shine."

"Fundraising happens all over the country," he went on, "not just on the coast. I was talking to one mechanic who had got a huge donation from the Salford RNLI Committee – they don't have any lifeboats in Salford."

"I went to a station last week," the first man said, "and they tell you how much they've raised – tens of thousands – and it's humbling. That's the best part of this job: you meet the best of people. There isn't one person on any station I've visited who I wouldn't want to go for a pint with."

"And it's not only them," his colleague said, as the ferry pulled into port, "it's the families left behind, it's the employers. One guy I know, he had three shouts in six hours. When you're on call you're tied to the pager, you can't go out and get drunk, you can't go to the next town, you're on your guard 24/7 – but that's just what people do."

* * * * *

By the time I drove off the ferry at Scrabster, the sun had almost set, and there were dark clouds on the horizon. As I drove past the Doonray nuclear power plant, I could see the moon to one side and the sun setting behind pink and grey clouds to the other.

The sun disappeared and it became dark very quickly. As I rounded one corner, I almost ran into a flock of sheep in the middle of the road, and had to wait for them to scuttle off. The men from the RNLI had recommended a hotel in a small village on the north coast, so I headed for it.

At the hotel bar that evening, in front of a roaring fire, I talked to Chloe and Gillian, two young women in their early twenties who both worked there.

"I like it here," said Chloe, who was looking to build her hairdressing business in the village. "There's not much to do but it's a really good community."

Gillian agreed.

"I'm studying from home," she said, "an online degree course from UHI, the University of the Highlands and the Islands."

She explained that UHI provided distance-learning courses to students in remote areas who wanted to study for a degree but didn't want to leave home.

"I get to study from the comfort of my own bed," she said. "People don't think we have the Internet here but we do – it's not as remote as it seems. You do need to wait until ten or eleven for a paper, but I can just check online anyway."

"I've always wondered if I should have gone away to uni," she went on, "if I was missing out, but I'm just so much happier with my family around."

Chloe was working behind the bar, and as people walked in, she greeted each of them by name and knew which drinks they would be having.

"The main thing I love about round here," she said, "is that you can only be here for a couple of weeks and immediately know everyone. Everyone is really friendly; it's such a great community."

"I grew up here," said Gillian, "and I had about seven or eight people the same age as me and it was great. We just made use of our imaginations, came up with things to occupy ourselves. Before we came to pubs, you had to think of ways to amuse yourselves – my childhood was the best time of my life."

I asked whether she felt childhood had changed as a result of the Internet.

"My younger brothers spend all their time on the computer," Gillian said, "the laptop and the X-Box. They just don't have the opportunity to go out and play with others."

"It's the same with my brother," said Chloe. "After-school activities only go to half five and football is just once a week so he just comes home and sits on his computer."

Everyone who came in was greeted by those already at the bar, and when one young man entered they all sang him 'Happy Birthday'. Lorna, one of the hotel owners, came in ten minutes later and bought everyone drinks.

It was perhaps the most relaxed and friendly atmosphere I had found on my travels, so I asked her about it.

"We try to give this place a family feel," she said, "but, to be honest, it's like that anyway round here. People look after their own; it's old-fashioned like that – if there's someone who's older and getting ill, they'll do most of the support within the family."

"They'll tell you it is less community oriented now," she went on, "but compared to London... It's just too fast there and in all the rushing around we forget about the human contact that really sustains us. I was a nurse for nineteen years and I know that's what ultimately matters."

Around us, people drank and chatted happily in front of the fire and, when the bar had to close, there were smiles and hugs as people said goodnight.

* * * * *

The next morning, I headed west along the north coast, with beautiful countryside on one side of the car and the sea on the other. On a road with no other houses nearby, I saw a number of odd pieces of pottery along a wall and stopped to investigate. Set off the road, I found a small workshop, surrounded by more odd and beautiful pieces of pottery. I went inside, and met Lotte Glob, a ceramic artist who lived there alone.

She told me she was originally from Denmark, but had lived in Scotland for forty-five years.

"I was a student of pottery in southern Ireland," she told me, "and I came to Scotland and fell in love with it. I came with my two children – my son is now an artist in Harris; my daughter got to eighteen and went straight to London."

I said it felt very quiet, particularly for her, there on her own.

"It's not quiet enough," she said. "I've always got friends and family and people like yourself popping in. When I came, in 1968, we lived in an old army camp where my children grew up – now that was remote."

"I just love the landscape," she went on. "I don't like cities. I'll go to see exhibitions and so on but I enjoy coming back. People say this is the end of the world, but for me it is the beginning."

I asked whether she ever got lonely.

"It's not lonely here, not to me," she said, "and you can be lonely wherever you are. You might be able to distract yourself in the city, but you can still be lonely."

"Besides," she continued, "places are becoming a lot less remote with computers and transport and exchange of people. In fact, the only bad thing is when you get a toothache – the nearest dentist is a hundred miles away…"

I asked if she got scared on her own in such an isolated place.

"What is there to be scared of?" she asked. "Just a few stags. I have a friend who grew up in Glasgow – he says this place is spooky. But I get claustrophobia in London – so maybe you've got agoraphobia here."

"This is my home," she went on. "I planted four thousand trees here. I stayed in a caravan for five years while I built this place. I wanted to create my own culture croft, where I could be messy and wild."

She showed me some of her work, and I asked about photos up on the wall, which appeared to show her pottery placed around the Scottish hills.

"I've put seventy-five pots in hills between here and Skye," she told me. "It's like putting them back where they came from. One day, I'd had a bad response to my work, and I was depressed so I went for a walk to make myself feel better. I just saw a place and thought, 'This pot, it would really belong there.' So I left it and then I saw another place where one would go well. Some will have gone by now but some will be found by archaeologists in two thousand years' time, and they'll be so confused…"

She smiled and I asked what had prompted her to start doing this.

"Everything just happens," she said. "It's just something to do."

I let her get back to work and she wished me well. As I drove off, I thought about her story, the friendliness of the people in the hotel and the commitment of the men from the RNLI. There seemed to be a discrepancy between the many negative views I had heard about the UK and the kindness and decency that I had found throughout my journey, and I wondered whether the country needed to find better ways to enable people to see that kindness and decency in each other.

19

Physical and Online Communities in Skye

My next destination was the Isle of Skye and, at the bed and breakfast where I was staying, I met Matthew Anderson, a civil servant from Sussex who was on holiday there. Over dinner, we got talking about the book and he said I should put something in about the impact of technology on modern Britain and offered to share his experience of Internet dating. My discussions at the hotel in northern Scotland had identified how the Internet could keep communities together and this seemed like a good way to explore the impact of technology on people's lives further.

"The Internet is an excellent way of meeting people," he told me. "Facebook creates a lot of superficial relationships and I've seen some young people use it in a very mixed-up way but I think dating sites are helping to create real, lasting relationships."

I asked him what his love life would be like without the Internet.

"I'd probably have stayed at home and rotted," he said, "because, for someone like me, who doesn't get out there that much naturally, it would have been much more difficult. At parties, you've got to summon up the courage to introduce yourself whereas on the Internet it's a more passive rejection. There are still lots of people who get messed around but I've had quite a good experience."

I asked if there were any downsides to Internet dating.

"I do wonder if they raise expectations," he said. "If half the people on these sites exaggerate, do women's ideas of what's average rise? But then they probably see through it… I guess the problem is that, in an average social situation, you're much more likely to talk to a wide range of people so it's more one-dimensional in some ways, and you end up going for the really beautiful women who you wouldn't have a chance with anyway."

"What it does do," he went on, "is enable you to meet more people, although, again, I don't know whether it's good to meet large volumes of women: I guess the more you meet, the more chance you have but it doesn't feel like it should work like that."

I asked him what he was hoping to find through Internet dating.

"Companionship," he said. "The women in my life, the serious relationships, have been really good for me, they've made me better. I know the pressures of not being in a relationship – I can't share my anxieties… I'm looking for someone to care about me, to ring me on the train and check I'm on my way back, so you can show your fellow passengers there's someone on the end of the phone. Hearing those conversations on the train really annoys me, but, if I was in a relationship, I'd love it."

"Tim Berners-Lee invented the Internet," he added, "and, in my view, it's the greatest invention ever because it's got such potential. It's a junkyard in many ways, but there are little corners of it where something beautiful is being built."

* * * * *

The next day, over breakfast, I got chatting to Oli Mansell, a man in his late twenties from Leeds who was staying at the same B & B. He told me that he was originally from London and that the Internet had helped him establish himself when he had moved to Leeds.

"I'm involved in a really social running group that meets once a week," he said. "It got set up two years ago on Facebook and something like that really helps when you move to a new area and you don't know your neighbours. At university, your social world is handed to you on a plate and that doesn't necessarily happen when you buy a house, you have to create it for yourself, but that's been a lot easier because of social networking."

While it was clear that Oli had benefited from social media, he told me he had concerns as well.

"The idea on paper of the Internet was that it would bring people together," he said, "but there's a definite argument that it reinforces tribes in a way. I've experienced the good but I think it can also have quite a corrosive effect – you only have to look at groups that have been set up on issues in relation to the Baby P killers being freed or Ian Huntley allegedly being given Internet access in prison – there's a herd mentality and these groups just become full of mass outrage."

"Those are extreme examples," he went on, "but there are plenty of others – like recently there was a son of an *Observer* journalist who'd gone to South America on his gap year and they were serialising his experiences. They had to shut the page down because it was attracting comments from readers that were so full of bile – they were throwing abuse at him, saying that he was upper class and wasn't doing anything meaningful. It wasn't just people rolling their eyes and being cynical, it was really personal."

I asked him what he thought prompted this behaviour online.

"There's a school of thought that there would always have been that impulse anyway amongst a certain part of the population," he said, "but I think it is also linked to the anonymity of the Internet so people aren't held accountable for what they say. It could also be linked to another question I really struggle with, which is the idea of the British as being reserved."

"I've wondered for ages," he went on, "does this stereotype and expectation of the British being reserved result in there being more aggression when it comes to anonymity of online forums? I think we're guided by these rules that we are meant to carry ourselves with extra decorum and the Internet or drinking on a Friday night is just an outlet for what we keep pent up."

He left soon afterwards and I found myself thinking back to the drinking I had seen in Bideford and Exeter.

That evening, I logged on to some of the forums he had mentioned and could see what he meant. A number of the messages, not just on campaign-based sites but on mainstream social networks like Twitter, seemed full of anger and hate, the bitterness running in stark contrast to the kindness and decency I had found throughout my journey.

* * * * *

I wanted to explore physical communities as well as online networks while in Scotland, so the next day I headed for Plockton, a beautiful waterside village just over the Skye Bridge. I walked up the hill above the main street, Harbour Street, and met an elderly woman walking her dog outside a house being built. She told me she lived on Harbour Street, in the house she had lived in as a child.

I said it was nice that she had been able to stay in the village her whole life.

"Yes," she said, "but local people can't afford to now. A lot of the youngsters have to leave."

"I own this croft," she continued, pointing at the fields behind us, "so my daughter is building her house here and she'll rent out one room to help with the mortgage. Her brother is helping to build it – she can't afford big firms. We have nothing against the outsiders who come here, but they do kind of take over."

She took me up to the house and introduced me to Dan, her son, who was busily working on the kitchen. His accent was strong but he was very softly spoken.

"Even a wee house in this village is half a million," he said, "because of the tourist industry. Most of the houses are being rented as holiday homes at six hundred a week so local people can't afford them. People are retiring up here, not people who have made their living here. My grandfather worked on the railway and there's no way he could have afforded to have lived here with prices the way they are now, and then a lot of the houses are empty in winter."

I asked how long he'd been working on the house.

"Two years," he said. "A lot of time was taken digging out the rock. If you saw the site, you'd never think you could'a built on it. We had the outside frame done by a firm from Glasgow – I've never seen a worse job. After that we decided to make the staircase ourselves – at least when it's finished, we'll know it was done properly."

"In the end, they gave us two hundred pound or something," he said of the Glasgow firm. "It was just nonsense, but we just decided to get on with it – in ten years, it'll all be forgotten about."

I asked about new people moving into the area.

"It's economics," he said. "You can't stop the tide. Once an area gets popular with tourism, it affects everything, especially the house prices. But what can you do? There was a local guy who sold his house to a local couple for a knock-down price – two years later they got divorced and sold it for the going rate to outsiders…"

"My sister would have been happy with a small house in the village," he went on, "but the way the market is, no one can afford it. Friends of mine are having to pay childminders to look after the kids because they both have to work to afford the house. It changes everything."

He had to get back to work, and I felt myself again leaving a conversation with a sense of unhappiness and powerlessness in the person I had met.

I thanked him for his time.

"I enjoyed the wee break," he said, "but next time you come bring a hammer."

Beyond the house was a bench that looked out over the water. It was dedicated to a local resident who had died in 2009. 'The principal business of life is to enjoy it', the inscription read. The sea wind blew in but, apart from that, everything was quiet.

* * * * *

That evening Bob and Carolyn, the owners of the bed and breakfast where I was staying, agreed to be interviewed. They told me they were friends from southern Scotland, and had set up the B & B together a few years earlier. In their front room, with their dog, Max, on the sofa next to me, I asked them about their experience on Skye.

"We were smitten with the place," said Bob, "but we never even thought of the people. I came here thinking, 'I'm a sociable guy, I can mix' but someone told us they're not nice to incomers and it is slightly true. My theory is that history of the clans has not gone too far away from Skye. There are so many forts around – I thought they were to keep the Romans out, but they were to keep each other apart."

"They're very reserved," he went on, "and not as warm as one would think – it's an untrusting, wait and see approach. My first year, I made a point of saying hello to most folk and eventually people do return that, but one of the curious things I've found is that they will never ask you about your stories. I don't know why."

"I've got a theory that it's about the Clearances," Carolyn said, "where the people were thrown out and replaced with sheep. The culture of Skye was obliterated and they don't have anything to call on now. People drifted back eventually and the more entrepreneurial people came back and became landowners but they haven't put any culture back – there's no music, nothing."

"The other thing," said Bob, "is that your neighbour is often an empty house. It's like you flick a switch each winter and everyone is gone to the big cities. When we came, it felt a bit like that film, *The Wicker Man*… There are days when no one passes the door, and that makes you change as a person – I've become a lot quieter. I freaked out at a party the other day – all the people, I found it quite scary."

"In a certain way," he went on, "it's disappointing for me, working as I did as a sparkie – an electrician – there was always lots of banter, but here there are fewer people to talk to, and you have to be careful what you say because of the gossip."

"We've had to keep each other going," said Carolyn, "because there's no out. You can't just go to a gallery or something."

126

"I like to think, though," said Bob, "that if something happened, people would rally round."

"I don't believe that," said Carolyn. "If the roof came off here I don't think they'd be round in the morning."

"I haven't made friends with anyone from Skye," she added. "The only two friends I've made here are not from Skye."

"Friendship is a dying art," said Bob.

"When I grew up it wasn't easy but you knew people," he went on, "and I don't know if you'll ever get that back."

They were quiet for a moment.

"We've got Facebook, though," said Carolyn with a smile. "It's alive and well here. And the funny thing is they're doing more talking on Facebook than they are face to face and they're more open on it than face to face. It's a kind of mixed-up world."

* * * * *

I left the next day, headed for Glasgow. The conversations with Matthew and with Gillian and Chloe in northern Scotland made me think about ways in which technology could be used not in the divisive way Alex and Josh in London had described, but rather to bring people together. There was a sense that communities had been changed – with some people, like Dan's sister, having to make a huge effort just to stay in their home town and others, like Bob and Carolyn, struggling without a strong social network around them. I wondered whether technology could fill that gap, but was still worried by the anger on the Internet that Oli had pointed me towards, and what that said about the way people were feeling in modern Britain.

20

Free Speech and Football in Glasgow

My first day in Glasgow was a Saturday, so I decided to go to Ibrox, where Rangers were playing against St Mirren. On the underground, spirits were high because Celtic, who had already kicked off in their match against Kilmarnock, were three-nil down. On the Metro, two fans told an older supporter with his young daughter the score in the Celtic match, and when he turned to them I saw he had a deep scar running from his lip to his ear.

At Ibrox, there was a quiet atmosphere around the stadium. There were thousands of fans, but very little singing. I saw two Rangers fans, a man and a woman who looked like father and daughter, wearing T-shirts that read 'Supporting your club is not a crime'. I went over and asked what was going on.

"It's against the SNP and their stupid legislation," the man told me. "They're trying to outlaw sectarian chants at football matches, but it shouldn't be against the law to support your team."

"It's all a one-way street," added the woman. "They sing about supporting the IRA, but it's us who get arrested."

"You remember the IRA bombing London?" the man asked me. "Well, the Celtic fans celebrate it in their songs. Our songs are just against what they're doing."

It seemed like an interesting opportunity to explore questions around free speech in the UK so I asked if they had their own songs that they sang about Celtic fans.

"Yeah," the man said, "but 'The Billy Boys' is just a song about a Glasgow gang, and it's got a word in it, 'Fenian', which is supposedly a word for a Catholic woman. It's not, but under the legislation they're pushing through, if you mentioned that word in front of a police officer, you'd be charged with sectarian aggression and could get five years."

"They're just trying to get votes from the Catholics," the woman said. "The Rangers fans call us 'huns' – as in Germans – so what's the difference?"

I asked why Celtic fans used that term.

"It's to do with the Royal Family," the woman explained. "It's a hatred of all things British. We're proud to be British. We bring troops on to the pitch at half time but we get condemned for it, or our players get poppies sewn into their shirts and then Celtic fans put out a banner saying 'No bloodstained poppies on our shirts'. Any human with any decency will support our troops – but they don't. They're living here, they're taking everything from British society, but they're slagging us off."

"They can't say we're sectarian," he added, "because both my sisters-in-law are Catholic and I love them dearly. And I work beside Catholics – they're good people."

"There's no hatred on our side," said the man. "We've no problem, none whatsoever."

"There's an old story," he went on, "that Rangers fans prefer to watch England than Scotland."

I asked him if that was true.

"Aye," he said, "the Tartan army are a disgrace – they've watched *Braveheart* too many times. William Wallace wasn't even Scottish; his father was born in Wales."

"And now they want Roman Catholics to be able to marry into the Royal Family," the woman said, "so in twenty years' time, we could have a Catholic as head of the Church of England – it makes no sense."

"We ask them, 'Could the Pope be Protestant?'" said the man, "And, of course, they say 'No way' – the whole thing is madness."

I asked whether the violence around Scottish football worried them.

"What violence?" the man asked. "There are fights and scuffles but the media just plays it up. After a Rangers-Celtic game, domestic abuse goes up but that's not just down to football."

"And besides," the woman said, "the story I saw was about a woman beating up a man, not the other way around."

"Mainly it's just the police and media," the man continued. "Not every killing is sectarian-related but, every time someone is killed, the police and BBC Scotland ask what team they supported. Football – it's just a ninety-minute thing. We sing in the ground but, once you go away from the stadium, that's it."

He gestured towards the crowds approaching the stadium.

"Most of these will go home after the game to a Catholic wife or girlfriend."

The woman agreed.

"It's a load of rubbish that we hate each other. We've got Catholic relatives. Do we hate them? No. Do we have good banter with them? Yes."

I still wasn't clear on their position on freedom of expression, so I asked about it.

"It has to be equal," the man said. "It's just a one-way street at the moment. I couldn't care less if they sing their songs if they want to."

"But supporting the IRA with their banners, that's a different story," the woman said.

"But either way," said the man "why are they wasting their time with this? Why aren't they sorting out drugs and knife crime?"

They wished me well with the book, and I went into the ground.

Before the game, an announcement was played over the tannoy stating that unacceptable chanting would not be tolerated. Supporters were encouraged to inform the authorities of sectarian chanting through an anonymous hotline.

The ground wasn't full, and the atmosphere was underwhelming. Two or three hundred fans in a small section of one stand sang throughout the game, but otherwise the ground was fairly quiet. It was an uneventful first half, with no goals, and the crowd grew restless, especially when they heard that Celtic had come back to draw three-all with Kilmarnock. There were even a couple of boos at the half-time whistle.

Rangers scored early in the second half but the crowd's excitement quickly turned to booing as a Rangers fan was escorted out of the ground.

I asked the man next to me what had happened.

"Probably shouted something they didn't like," he said.

The atmosphere became tense again as Rangers pressed for the second goal, but without success. After one particularly poor attempt on goal, the man next to me buried his head in his hands.

"He's one of our best players," he said. "The standard is shocking. All the half decent players go to England – that's where the money is."

As the match approached its conclusion, people began to stream out, and the ground was only two-thirds full when the man of the match was announced over the tannoy.

"Best of the bad bunch," said the man behind me, "like winning a tallest midget competition…"

A few moments later, in the last minute of injury time, St Mirren scored an equaliser, and the few hundred of their fans in the stadium went wild with delight, while the boos rang out from the Rangers fans. It turned out to be the last kick of the game, and the Rangers fans who had remained left the ground shaking their heads.

Outside a pub by the ground, I got talking to a Rangers fan.

"It's poor," he said of his team. "We used to be one of the richest clubs in Europe, we were signing boys like Gascoigne – *England internationals* – but those days are long gone. Anyone who is any good goes to the Premiership now."

I asked about the law on sectarian chanting.

"Football's not a place for politics or religion," he said. "It's just football. I just like to watch my team. There's a lot of deep-rooted religious problems in Glasgow and it all gets associated with Rangers and Celtic. There's not the nicest atmosphere in Scottish football at the moment; there's a wee bit of ill-feeling."

"The majority of fans don't want to see the chanting," he went on, "it's just a small element. It's like the rioting in Manchester a few years ago. A hundred and seventy-five thousand fans from Rangers went down for that game, and a couple of hundred rioted. The entire club got dragged through the gutter by a hooligan element – how does that work?"

He wished me luck with the book, and headed inside. As he went in, a woman was thrown out of the pub and berated the landlord, while inside the pub I could hear 'God Save the Queen' being played at full blast. The woman continued her argument with the manager while separately a bouncer ushered a man away from the doorway.

"Move away from the door," he said. "You're chancing it, boy, you're chancing it."

An Asian man in a Union Flag shirt walked past. I guessed he was a Rangers fan, so I asked him about Scottish football.

"We're getting a terrible time from the police," he said. "Fans like to have a sing-song, it's just a bit of harmless fun, but now the police are arresting people. It's a load of nonsense; they should be going after rapists."

"It's going to kill the atmosphere," he continued. "First they made you sit, now they don't let you sing. It's just banter – Celtic fans don't actually support the IRA. There's a small minority take it seriously but then everyone's tarred with the same brush. It sickens me when people get arrested for chanting – even Celtic fans – it's just a bit of fun and games. If you want to blame someone, blame whoever made up religion. Everyone's just the same to me – I just like to have a bit of a sing-song."

A man he knew came over.

"They're all tottie-picking bastards," he said. "If they want to be Irish, they should be living there. It's not racist to say the tottie famine was two hundred years ago, so it's time for them to fuck off. They don't respect the Queen, don't respect the country."

As I took notes, he noticed me writing with my left hand.

"My boy's a left-hander," he said. "We call him a Fenian… The thing about that word is that they call themselves the 'Fenian Army', but we just change the word 'army' to 'bastards' and we get put in jail for it."

He turned to the Asian man.

"If I called you a bastard, nothing would happen," he said, "but if I called you a Fenian bastard, or a Paki bastard, I'd end up in prison. It's just the same, I'm still calling you a bastard. Along this road in the eighties you'd see cunts getting slashed the whole time. You can't even tell a cunt to shut the fuck up now…"

"Most people round here would think he's a Paki first," he went on, gesturing at the Asian man, "but he explained that he was born here, he's a Scotsman, he supports the country, he's one of us."

"The Muslims say I'm a traitor," the Asian man said, "but they're just using this country – I say they're the traitors. I say if you don't like it here, go somewhere else."

"I say the same to Catholics," his friend said. "We don't sing the famine song to say fuck the cunts who died, we're saying if you want to be Irish, go live in Ireland. But I can't sing it now – our free speech is right out the fucking window."

I asked if Celtic fans should also be entitled to the right of free speech.

"But there's a difference," the Asian man said. "They're chanting for the IRA. This is Scotland, this is Britain. If they want to chant for the IRA, they can go to their own country. It's like the Pakistanis, they've got floods, they've got wars – they should be grateful for what they have here."

"I went down to the American Embassy to observe a minute's silence on the 9/11 anniversary," he went on, "and there were a hundred Muslims there singing anti-American songs. I asked the police why they could get away with it, and they said it was freedom of expression. So I thought, 'Why do I get arrested at Ibrox for having a sing-song when they're glorifying mass murder?'"

"I just don't understand the rules," he added. "They're all topsy-turvy."

21

Fatalism in Glasgow

The next day I headed for Glasgow's East End, near to Celtic's football ground. Having spent time with Rangers fans the day before, I wanted to hear a Celtic perspective, but there was another reason why I wanted to visit the East End: its reputation for ill health, a subject I had been interested in since visiting Rotherham.

On the edge of the East End, I met a man walking his dog who told me he lived in the Gorbals area where the average life expectancy was fifty-six. I asked why he thought that was the case.

"I suppose there's an apathy about it to a point," he said. "What do they want to stay healthy for?"

"I just found out yesterday," he went on, "a friend of mine died of cancer – fifty-four… I think people just ignore the health warnings; they think it won't happen to them. And there's nihilism – they just don't give a shit."

I asked why people felt that way.

"I think probably the stark contrasts in lifestyles between what they see on the telly – they don't have these lifestyles, and they're never likely to – so they just live their lives, which probably involve smoking and drinking, and that's that."

"I knew two brothers," he continued, "they died within ten days of each other – they couldn't even have been in their fifties. They had been drug addicts in their time – it's very sad, people don't see the point of keeping going. They're looking at the state of society and of the economy today and it's not going to get any better."

"If you go to the East End," he went on, "most people don't work, and that just adds to feelings of desperation and hopelessness. There used to be steel works and engine works, shipyards, all down the Clyde. It's more of a service city now and apparently it's got the second best shopping in the whole of the UK. And it's actually turning into a high education place, but not for East End people."

"The other day I saw a man who used to be an insurance salesman behind the till in Asda," he added. "People are taking jobs they never would have considered just so they have a wage coming in at the end of the month."

He told me he was taking photos all around the city and putting them on a website for Scots living all around the world to access.

"I'm trying to be a social historian in the last few years I've got left," he said.

I had to move on. He pointed me in the direction of Barras Market, which he suggested would be a good place to meet people, and wished me well.

* * * * *

I walked down to the market, and took a few photos outside. Behind the main market, men were making sales from their car boots and, when they saw me taking photos, one of them followed me for a while. I moved into the indoor market to get away.

Inside, I got talking to a man on his stall, which was packed with Celtic scarves and memorabilia. One scarf read 'Our Fallen Comrades' and named the members of the IRA who had gone on hunger strike in Northern Ireland's Maze Prison in 1981. I asked him about Glasgow.

"It's like this," he said, widening the gap between his hands. He wouldn't say any more.

I walked on and met a man on a stall selling kilts, tartan and Scottish memorabilia. We got talking about my visit to Shetland and how some people had said traditional ways of life were dying out.

"Traditional," he said, "what's that? Women at home not being able to go out? Things move on."

I asked him how things were in Glasgow.

"Terrible," he said, "it's all doom and gloom. I started my business in 1989 and I made more money at eighteen years of age doing that than I do now. The standard of living is so much less; the cost of living is so much more. You're working twice as hard, fighting for nothing. I'd always work but you almost think, 'What's the point?'"

I asked whether he got any help from the government.

"Don't get me started on the Scottish government," he said, "it's a PR stunt, it's not a government. It's a joke, it's nothing – a waste of time, waste of money, small men in charge and for what?"

"All the bank managers with experience have gone," he continued. "A bank is now just a shop – sale, sale, sale. My business, if I lose that money, I'm out of business, but not the banks. If I put in false accounts, I'm jailed. But the politicians, are any of them in jail? It makes me sick. Normal people who are working, trying to get ahead, are getting shafted. And I'm quite generally cheery, but I just see bleak."

I asked about health in the area.

"It's a sweeping generalisation to say we're all unhealthy," he said, "and, anyway, what working man can afford to smoke? And are people alcoholics if they go out at the weekend and have a drink, or have a wee bottle of wine with dinner? Healthy food costs more money so people buy shite. But it's education, you know, fitness, exercise… That's where the problem is – no work, no aspiration, no nothing."

"And then you've got these jokers in the Scottish Parliament," he continued. "They could have got somewhere free but they said no, let's have a new Parliament, let's pay all that money. It makes me sick. You get people who are leaders, even the British leader – Cameron… Clegg, who's the Labour leader? Miliband… They're all ineffectual, it's shocking."

"We're a society where, if you want to get ahead, working hard is not the answer," he went on. "Learning to play the system, that's where the money is. There's no encouragement to get people working. If you're working, you're earning, you're a valued member of society. But disaffected people, not working, property means nothing, life means nothing. People just say 'Fuck this, I've had enough.'"

"Food and energy bills going up, petrol's never been more expensive. And they talk about Scottish independence. To do what? Why worry about an idea when you're struggling to feed your family?"

I asked him if he had anything more positive to say.

"Here's one," he said. "Prozac sales are going through the roof!"

* * * * *

I walked on, and found a pub, the Emerald Isle, across the road from the market. I didn't feel I had answered the question of why people didn't take care of their health, so when I found some men smoking outside the pub I approached them.

I asked the first man I met, Graham, what the area was like.

"Dodgy," he said, "but the people are friendly. This is obviously a Celtic area – for the Catholics. We fight with the Rangers fans, but we're all great guys, we're sound as fuck."

I asked why, if people were so nice, they all fought one another.

"When it comes to the Old Firm," he said, "it's just a fucking riot. When Rangers play Celtic at Parkhead, it's like *Braveheart* on the streets, right here."

He pointed to the street in front of us, and I reflected that it was the third mention of that film that I had heard since I came to Scotland.

"They call it 'bigotry'," he continued, "we hate them, they hate us. It's just Scottish culture, it'll never change."

"They try to stop it," he went on. "Even the Prime Minister of Scotland tried to stop it, but it's Glasgow culture, that's it. My old man was Protestant, my mam's a Catholic. We used to have good banter, but when it comes to the Old Firm games, they just go for it. That's just how it is."

I asked about smoking and drinking in the area.

"Binge drinking, they call it," he said. "I started smoking when I was ten, drinking when I was twelve. I'm twenty-seven now."

I asked him why people drank and smoked.

"Because they've got nothing to do, that's the bottom line. You've got all these youth clubs but as soon as they finish the kids just go off and get pissed and have a fight – it's just Glasgow."

I asked if people didn't care about their health.

"No," he said. "Personally, my dad died of cancer, he died at fifty. He didn't smoke, he just drank. You only live once, people live life to the full and then, when your time's up, your time's up. That's the good thing about Scottish people, we don't give a fuck but we're the nicest people you could ever meet."

Graham's words reminded me of my conversations in Rotherham a few weeks earlier. His attitude of living life to the full and not worrying about the future felt a little more positive than the sense of hopelessness I had encountered in Rotherham, but the result – not seeming to care about one's health – appeared to be the same.

A friend of his joined us outside for a cigarette and I asked him why people drank and smoked so much.

"I wouldn't know," he said. "Some of the oldies, they think there's no point in giving up now… I don't know why I don't stop smoking – I suppose it's a mentality. It depends how you've been brought up."

A couple of others came out, and, while I tried to keep the conversation on health, they wanted to talk about Rangers.

"Rangers didn't sign a Catholic player for years," one said. "We had Protestants years ago – we signed Stephen Pressley, we signed Kenny Miller – we'll sign anybody – Protestants, Jews, Hindus… so who are the bigots?"

"Even if Celtic loses, you'll still get a party here," he added, "but Rangers fans can't take a defeat. They're all hun cunts."

He put his arm around me.

"You're the soundest English cunt I've ever met," he said. "You're brand new."

"I usually hate the English," his friend said. "You go to Turkey and it's full of English; they're all arrogant bastards."

They went back inside and I was left with Graham. He showed me a tattoo of his father's face engraved on his chest and it was clear how much he missed him. We talked about him for a while and then he suggested we went inside to talk to some of the other drinkers.

Inside, there were Irish flags flying and music playing and men drinking at the bar. I found one drinker and asked him about healthy lifestyles.

"From my point of view," he said, "most people don't care. They think it's just natural. It's the done thing – because your pal's doing it, you do it. They know it's wrong but they don't care; that's just how it is."

I asked him whether it would ever change. He thought about it for a moment. In the background, I could hear 'The Wild Rover' being played on the jukebox.

'Been a wild rover for many a year; spent all my money on whiskey and beer' went the song.

"It might change in the next generations," he said finally, "because there are that many warnings on fag packets – but it's no' guaranteed. Some people think they're no' going to live forever, so they just think, 'Fuck it, we'll enjoy ourselves while we're here.'"

"Some people just don't care until it's too late," he continued, "like my dad. Sixty-nine he died at. He told me not to smoke and by fuck he was right. A lot of people think the health warnings work, but they don't seem to realise people just ignore it."

It was getting late, but there was one more drinker at the bar I hadn't spoken to, so I approached him.

"I think people are just born into it," he said. "You follow in your parents' footsteps and your education is poor. People just refuse to adopt a healthy lifestyle. You see your mum and dad do it, and you think 'I'll do that,' and when they catch you and say 'Don't do that,' it's too late because you're already addicted."

"The National Health have been trying to stop it with nicotine and helplines and stuff. It's helped quite a lot of people but a lot of people are not listening. They think it's too late anyway, or they think, 'I enjoy it, so I'm not going to stop.' We've had plenty of warning, we really should stop…"

I asked why he didn't stop given all the warnings.

"I cannae answer that," he said.

We were quiet for a minute. Just as in Rotherham, it didn't seem like people's attitudes about their health were going to change. In Rotherham, this seemed to have been linked to depression and economic decline; here in Glasgow there also seemed to be a link to a fatalistic social attitude passed down through generations. I was thinking that both seemed equally impenetrable when he said something that made me think a little differently.

"You know what has changed a bit," he said, "people used to see their ma and da smoke, everyone would drink and smoke in front of their kids, but people know now that passive smoke kills. A lot of parents now are stopping smoking in front of their kids."

Graham came over and agreed that this was one thing that had changed.

"I don't smoke in front of my nephew now," he said. "People are starting to take heed of it. Not everyone but a lot of people…"

The pub was about to close so I shook hands with them and they all wished me well. Graham wouldn't let me leave until I promised him a mention in the book, but when I did he shook my hand warmly as he said goodbye.

* * * * *

That evening, I went to stay in Whitecraigs, an affluent suburb in the hills overlooking Glasgow. From there, I was able to look down over both the East End and Ibrox, the lights of the city flickering in the dusk.

As I prepared to head to Northern Ireland, I thought about my initial conversations in Scotland about independence and reflected that, for most of the people I had met, it was not at the top of their list of priorities. People in Scotland faced a range of others issues – violence, ill health, mistrust of politicians and the breakdown of a sense of community in a rapidly changing world – similar to those I had encountered in England and Wales. In spite of these often difficult issues, I looked back very fondly over my time in Scotland for one reason: the people I had met.

22

Sectarian Division in Belfast

I wanted to start my time in Northern Ireland by getting a feel for Belfast and was fortunate that Ken Robinson, a local charity manager, had offered to take me on a drive around the city, telling me about the neighbourhoods we were visiting and giving me a bit of their history.

As we drove around on a sunny autumn day, it was immediately clear that, in inner-city Belfast at least, there were still divisions between Catholic and Protestant communities with many of the inner-city areas split into what Ken referred to as 'ghettos': neighbourhoods, some as small as one or two streets, populated almost exclusively by Protestants or Catholics. The Protestant areas were often lined with British flags or other symbols associated with Unionism; many Catholic areas were dominated by Irish flags and symbols of the Nationalist movement. Both had huge murals on buildings and street walls, depicting paramilitary organisations and highlighting the history of Northern Ireland from what were obviously very different perspectives.

As we drove on, we saw a new mural being painted.

"There's a very Lady Diana, mawkish sentimentality to the murals on both sides," Ken said, "though there have been some successful efforts to de-politicise them. But you wouldn't want to try and stop them painting that one – a local hardman will have approved it."

While the symbols and the murals were different in the Protestant and Catholic areas, there seemed to be some common factors in both communities so I asked Ken whether there were any differences in the attitudes of the two communities.

"In the Catholic areas there is a very vibrant community spirit," he said. "It's not perfectly harmonious, but there is a 'pulling themselves up by their bootstraps' mentality, whereas the Protestants have more of a 'We've supported the state for years, now they should support us' attitude."

This difference in attitude between the two communities interested me a great deal, and I resolved to look into it in more detail as I travelled around Northern Ireland.

Ken and I drove past a police station in a Catholic neighbourhood that looked like a maximum security prison and then, as we entered a Protestant area, he pointed out a kerb painted in a faded red, white and blue.

"That stuff isn't so obvious now," he said, "but years ago, come July, you'd see people repainting it for the parade season. There's a parade here every two years but, because the populations have shifted, the Protestant Orange parade now goes through a Catholic area but they still don't change the route. That can cause quite significant tensions because the Catholics, as you might imagine, can't see why they have to put up with it."

I saw a tour bus come past, and tourists got out and took pictures of the murals and the flags that lined the street as local residents went about their business. I asked if there were mixed areas as well as the divided communities.

"There are," he said, "and in the middle-class areas it mightn't be an issue one way or the other. But you wouldn't find many Protestants in west Belfast, and you wouldn't find many Catholics on the Shankill Road. Outside the city, in the farming community, there are some unreconstructed bigots, who wouldn't do business with Catholics or sell land to a Catholic. Even amongst people I know, you still hear hints of it."

As we entered the Shankill Road, he told me that the two communities had lived side by side peacefully before the Troubles.

"Catholics would live towards one end and Protestants towards the other," he said, "and you'd shop in your own end but people got on OK. When the Troubles started, the ends of the street became more polarised until it came to a point where they had to put walls up at the interface of the two communities – peace walls they were called ironically – and there were a ridiculous number of them all over the city."

We drove past one peace wall, which stretched high into the air with additional fencing on top and murals on both sides, and Ken told me there were now more of these walls than at any time during the Troubles. We drove through the wall at some gates, and Ken explained that if there was tension in the area, the gates would be closed, separating the two communities until the tension eased.

We drove out of the inner city and into affluent south Belfast, the streets lined by trees with no sign of the murals, flags or peace walls of the inner city. As we drove, we talked about the inner-city neighbourhoods we'd seen.

"I wouldn't want to live there," he said, "but I can understand why people close in when they feel vulnerable and embattled. The consequences are awful – the rest of us talk about cultural diversity and embracing difference but they're stuck in ghettos. It's particularly sad for the young people, because they go to school in 'their' community, so they wouldn't see anything else. For some Protestant children, Catholics – who they might call 'Fenians' – might as well be a different species. For many of the kids, going to university will be the first time that they've spent time with children from a different culture, and for those who don't make it to university it's entirely possible that they'll never cross over with people from another community."

"You think you stop thinking about it," he added, "but, even at my age and relative maturity, it still registers that somebody is a Catholic, not a Protestant. You don't go looking for it, but it does register. My mother grew up on a farm and she always associated the smell of burning turf with Catholics and with poverty, because the men who worked in the farm were Catholic and could only afford to burn turf, they couldn't afford coal. So wee associations like that become built in and engrained, they lurk there in the background. It's not pretty, I'm not proud of it, but it's there."

* * * * *

From meeting Ken, I headed into the centre of Belfast and, in a cafe, I met two female students. We got talking about the sectarian divide at Queen's University, where they studied.

"You never ask what religion people are – it just sort of happens," one told me. "You would know who is who, from their first names or their surnames, and Catholics are more out there too – like, I wouldn't come into class wearing a Rangers shirt, which would make me stand out as a Protestant, whereas Catholics would have no problem wearing a Celtic top or a GAA – Gaelic Athletic Association – sweater."

"And if you wear a poppy," her friend added, "it's, like, spot the Protestant."

"You just feel like you're looked at," she went on. "We feel a bit like a minority at the university and there are places, Catholic areas, where I wouldn't want to live. Some Protestants do live with Catholics but, in my case, I'm living with two Protestants. It's not that I said to someone, 'You're a Catholic, I can't live with you,' it just happens."

"There's still a divide," said the first girl. "Like, at election time, it was hammered into us: you have to vote DUP because, if you don't, Sinn Fein will get in. If you're Protestant you vote DUP or UUP; if you're a Catholic, it's Sinn Fein or the SDLP. I'd say the DUP would be more right wing – more conservative/moral; Sinn Fein would be more socialist/progressive, but I'm a politics student and I had to look up the difference between left-wing politics and right-wing politics on Wikipedia because it's not relevant here."

I asked them how these divisions affected their lives.

"It would be things like marrying," her friend said. "Like I would only marry someone if they agreed to bring our children up Protestant. I'm involved in the church you see – a group for Protestant girls to make sure that traditions don't die out."

"I think that we as a community are definitely looked down on by more traditional Catholics," she added, "because I know a Catholic who would have taken a very judgemental view of me, and that affects how we make friends with people."

"But we wouldn't want to go back to fighting," she went on. "You wouldn't want to go back to everybody being stopped going into Belfast, having your handbag searched. We're strong in our views but we would never condone killing people just because they're Catholic. But, still, if I went home and told my family I'd met a boy called Sean from West Belfast, they'd be appalled. My uncle was with a Catholic girl for years and that was why they didn't get married, because of the religion thing."

They had to get to their next lecture, but before they left I asked if they were typical in feeling this way.

"I don't know," one said. "Some people are more like, 'Let's just get on with it,' but I'm standing in our student elections and so is this Catholic girl, and I bet that she'll get more support than me because she's a Catholic – it's like, you support your own."

"Well, we would anyway," said her friend.

* * * * *

Outside the cafe, the sun was shining and the atmosphere was pleasant. As a young man went out of his way to hold the door for a woman with a buggy, I found a mother with her teenage daughter. I asked her what Belfast was like.

"It's what you make of it," she said. "The Irish are very friendly, it's just the British rule that's the problem – it's like the Irish coming along and taking over England – they're invading our country."

"She was born before the ceasefire," she continued, gesturing to her daughter, "and it's a lot better now, but they still put out this propaganda – the IRA have done this, have done that, but nothing about what the UVF or UDA or the police or the army have done. But I say, let the paramilitaries fight it out amongst themselves and leave the rest of us alone. I just want to get on with my life."

"My father was blew up in a pub by the UVF," she went on. "He survived and I'm not bitter about it. We've all got the same blood, there's no difference. These days, the conflict is just about the paramilitaries, but for them I think it's a lot about money. Look at their homes: they've got fancy houses while we're living in heaps. There's lots of poverty, we've no leisure centre or nothing and everyone's on the 'bru' – the benefits."

"It's better than it was," she added. "There's places you can walk now. Protestants can live in Catholic areas, but not the other way around. I think Catholics are more welcoming – there's not as much hatred in the Catholics as there is in the Protestants."

She paused for a moment and took a drag on a cigarette.

"I went on a cross-community trip," she went on. "They told us about their lives, they had to give £5 per person to the paramilitaries – to me that was wrong. Catholics were never forced to do that. We're lucky to not have that kind of pressure in our community. They were nice wee girls, though."

"You could be a Protestant for all I know," she said to me as I left, "it makes no difference to me."

* * * * *

I couldn't help wondering whether my conversations so far, and the tour of inner-city Belfast with Ken, had focused too much on sectarian division, so when I met Anna Donaldson, a woman in her thirties who I knew didn't have any strong religious convictions, that afternoon, I tried to get a sense of the other big issues in Northern Ireland.

"One big problem is we've got no entrepreneurship," she told me, "and somewhere like Derry, there are insanely high levels of people dependent on the state."

"We used to be able to argue for extra money from Westminster," she went on, "but Cameron has no interest in Northern Ireland. There are huge cuts coming and we're really going to suffer – we've got higher numbers on the Disability Living Allowance than anywhere else in the UK. The main reason is depression, and, either way you look at it, it's sad – people are either using the system, or they really are depressed."

"And," she added, "there's a very high incidence of young male suicide here."

I asked her why that was the case.

"The young men used to have a calling and a purpose," she said, "but now they're looking in the mirror and thinking, 'We've got nothing'. But nothing gets done about it – we're so obsessed with the Nationalist and Unionist politics that we're oblivious to everything else. That means that someone like me doesn't have anyone to vote for."

"The problem is also religion's role in politics," she went on, "which is really, really unhelpful. A lot of the politicians are anti-gay, they will happily say on air that people will go to hell for being gay and people like me are disgusted that so many people accept it from the biggest political party in the country, the DUP."

"But there are good things, too," she went on. "Like the education system is way beyond the rest of the UK. The grammar schools have been phenomenally successful, they're like private schools. You've got to remember we're a tiny country – the size of East Anglia – but we hit above our weight globally. Just listen to the *Today* programme – the number of Northern Ireland people you hear… People do really well for themselves but that's very much a middle-class thing – the product of the grammar school system for the most part. It's like the Belfast Festival – it's great but it's only for the chattering classes."

"Social mobility is a major problem here," she added, getting ready to leave. "People have not only inherited the Troubles, but they inherited deprivation too."

On the table next to us a man was arm-wrestling with a boy while the boy's family looked on smiling. As we stepped outside, three students with pumpkins walked past ahead of Halloween. The city centre was very mixed, in contrast to the divided residential areas I had visited with Ken, but as I looked around I saw a few GAA jumpers and Rangers shirts, and it felt like, even in the city centre, sectarian division was not far beneath the surface.

23

Politics and Friendship in Belfast

The next day in Belfast, I met Robin Wilson, an independent researcher involved in the Platform for Change movement, which was lobbying for reform to Northern Ireland's political system. A lot of the issues I had discussed in Belfast the previous day seemed to be rooted in politics, so I was interested to hear more from him.

"We have a coalition government where power is shared out rather than genuinely shared," he told me, "and we also have a political class that is basically the same people who were involved in the Troubles, either politically or in a paramilitary faction, or both, who are looking backwards not forwards."

"There has been nothing significant that the devolved government has done since it was established in 1999," he went on, "whereas, by comparison, in the period of direct rule between 2002 and 2007, there were quite important policy documents produced, for example on community relations – the first time that any government had officially said we have a problem with sectarianism and we have to deal with it. But, when direct rule ended, that policy was ditched because neither Sinn Fein nor the DUP wants to break down the divisions on which they rely for their power bases."

I asked him how this affected ordinary people.

"There has been a huge drop in election turnout," he said, "and when people are asked in surveys 'What has the assembly achieved?' the big majority say little or nothing. When people are asked 'How optimistic do you feel about the relationship between Protestants and Catholics?' it's very telling because, in the first period of devolution, people became less optimistic, then they became more optimistic under direct rule and less optimistic when devolution was renewed."

"Those surveys are also very interesting," he continued, "because everybody talks in terms of the 'Unionist Community' and the 'Nationalist Community' like that's all there is to it. But when people are surveyed about their identity, 58 per cent say that they are some combination of British and Irish rather than exclusively one or the other. When they are asked 'Are you Unionist, Nationalist or neither?' the neither group is the biggest."

I thought back to Anna Donaldson the previous day, and suspected, on the basis of what Robin had said, that she was more representative of people in Northern Ireland than anyone else I had met so far.

"What you hope," Robin went on, "is that things will happen on the ground that the politicians lose control over, like migration into Northern Ireland by people of different nationalities. For instance, on Thursday nights I go to the Belfast Friendship Club, which is a way of people getting to know each other if they are newcomers to the city. Every Thursday night there will be about fifty people from different nationalities all chatting away. That's a sign of a new Northern Ireland."

He gave me the details of the club and suggested I went along.

"Another factor," he continued, "is that the lives of people here who are 'indigenous' are changing through globalisation and you can't keep saying in a globalised world, like the DUP does, 'Stop the world, we want to get off' because there are just too many influences which keep rushing in."

"The other positive," he went on, "is there are some fantastic non-governmental organisations who have done great work to promote reconciliation, like the Spirit of Enniskillen Trust, which was set up after the Enniskillen bomb in 1987 to promote exchanges between young people and they do some fantastic work with students. Another example is the Irish Football Association, which has been really successful in turning round the atmosphere at Northern Ireland games, which used to be the Protestant working class on its own with all the paramilitary/sectarian paraphernalia that went with that. That has all gone now – it's still mainly Protestant support but it has been turned into a carnival atmosphere. The GAA has pushed very hard towards more tolerant attitudes, getting rid of rules which would have been seen as excluding Protestants and there have been modest efforts in rugby, too."

"But, again," he added, "the three associations, football, Gaelic and rugby, were supposed to be getting a new stadium at the Maze Prison site, but the DUP and Sinn Fein couldn't agree on it – Sinn Fein wanted a bit of the site to be linked to the hunger strike but the DUP said it would be a shrine to terrorism so that's as far as it got."

"We're getting dragged back by the political class," he said, "but the hope is that the changes in society will gradually mean that they have to adapt or die."

I said it sounded as though he was pinning his hopes on social change rather than party politics.

"And also bottom-up political pressure," he said, "like Platform for Change has been pushing very hard for a proper community relations strategy. Since the election, a working group has been set up to look at the issue; but, while the other parties have nominated to it, the DUP and Sinn Fein haven't. They don't want to face up to it because if we had a non-sectarian society they wouldn't get into power."

Thinking back to Ken Robinson, I asked whether he felt the divided education system could perpetuate sectarian attitudes.

"Yeah," he said, "only 6 or 7 per cent of kids go to integrated schools but we know that they work. A study was done ten years ago that interviewed alumni from the first two integrated schools. It found two things that differentiated them from people who went to segregated schools: one was that they had random marriage patterns and the other was that they tended to show generally more tolerant attitudes towards diversity. But, yet again, there is no interest among the political class in integration, even though it is far more expensive to run it this way."

"In 2007, the devolved government inherited a study commissioned under direct rule on the costs of sectarian division," he went on, "and it concluded that, if you added up everything, the costs in lost tourism and lost investments and law and order as well as the direct costs of duplication of provision, you are looking at 1.5 billion pounds a year, but, at the same time, we still don't pay for water here because none of the parties wanted to be the one to say, 'Let's put a water charge in.'"

"Last winter," he added, "the whole system nearly collapsed because of underinvestment and we had to get bottled water in from Scotland like a developing country. But they still won't bring in charges, even after that."

As I left, I asked him if there were any reasons for hope.

"There are plenty," he said, "and people will vote with their feet given the chance. Just yesterday on the news there was a piece about the new footbridge that has been built in Derry to bring people from the two sides of the city together. Apparently a quarter of a million people have used it since it was built. And, again, if you look at the surveys, huge majorities say that they would prefer to live and work and have their children go to school in a mixed context. So, it's not as if you would have to engage in some kind of social engineering to make this place normal. It's more the other way round – it would be normal if it wasn't for the politicians."

* * * * *

The next day, I went to meet Breidge Gadd, a respected columnist with a local newspaper, to find out more about the political situation and some of the issues I had encountered in Belfast, particularly with the Protestant students who clearly felt under threat.

"Catholics saw education as a route out of poverty," she told me, "and put a huge emphasis on it. Now even less academically-minded

Catholics are doing well at school while the working-class Protestant population is falling behind academically."

"There's a great deal of disillusionment amongst the Protestant community," she continued, "and fear that a united Ireland is inevitable. Protestants feel so downhearted and many living in areas that used to be predominantly Protestant feel surrounded by a growing Catholic population."

I was really interested by what she said. The quality of life for Catholics and Protestants seemed very similar, but, from all I had heard, there was more optimism in the Catholic community than amongst Protestants – a sense that Catholics were 'on the up' while Protestants were looking back to a more secure past. The Protestant pessimism and the Catholic optimism seemed linked not to their present standards of living, but rather to where they had come from and their prospects for the future. I felt a clear parallel between the nostalgia I had heard earlier on my travels amongst the 'indigenous' British population and the optimism and energy amongst many of the migrants to the UK I had met.

"Everyone pretends there isn't a problem," Breidge went on, "but there is. The Protestant population is an ageing one, more young, middle-class Protestants leave Northern Ireland and those that stay have slightly fewer children."

She told me that the Catholic population was predicted to become the majority in Northern Ireland by 2030.

"The problem is that this information is like the elephant in the room," she said. "We need to start to talk about the increasing 'balance' in the population and, if we did, people would start to relax."

"There is the beginning of discussion about what percentage of the Catholic population would wish to remain within the UK," she went on, "and with the crisis caused by recession, and with the Republic being especially hard hit, it's possible that many Catholics here will let their monetary head dictate rather than their emotional heart and opt to stay within a more stable Britain."

I thought back to my discussions in Scotland. Again, fundamental questions about the future of the UK were being asked and there was clearly a large portion of the population that felt a separate identity from Britain, but, again, that didn't necessarily mean that everyone wanted complete political and economic separation.

"It's only a matter of time before we have a Catholic majority," Breidge continued, "and I think Britain knows that as well. All the ingredients are there for a Federation of Britain – there should be an English Parliament and then Westminster should be a Parliament of the Nations, but, until we start discussing these things, we're still going to have this dysfunctional system."

"Take the DUP, for example," she went on. "Their support for selection at aged eleven and retention of grammar schools continues to enable the middle-class kids and militates against poorer people yet they continue to be popular in poorer areas."

I asked why that was the case.

"Because people want to protect the Union with Britain," she said. "They don't think about who has the best education policy."

"While we are moving forward slowly," she added, "too much politics here is still dominated by religion and fear."

* * * * *

That evening, I went along to a cafe in south Belfast to visit the Belfast Friendship Club as Robin had suggested. There I met Stephanie Mitchell, the organiser, who told me the group had been set up in 2009 to give people from Belfast and beyond the chance to come together and meet in a neutral setting. There were thirty or forty people around, drinking coffee and chatting as I entered, and she suggested I talk to some of them.

"This is a great place to make friends," an Indian IT worker told me, "international people, any age, whatever their belief, they can make this link here. This night is just the start – I have done the hiking which was organised and I went on the holiday to Ballintoy. We had so many activities, like Bollywood Dance and I was teaching everybody. That was… How do you say? The top – the highlight."

We were joined by community workers originally from Somalia and Sudan, and they talked equally positively about the Friendship Club and how it helped them to build social bonds in the city. Across the table, I heard a member of the university staff explaining the importance of the handshake in British culture to a group of Japanese and Bulgarian students.

"The handshake with a smile expresses genuineness," he said, "so, in my classes, I shake hands with every student every week. It's a gesture to literally extend the offer of friendship."

As he spoke, Stephanie announced that there was to be a cycle ride to the town hall in memory of a young Polish woman killed by a lorry while cycling in Belfast and that there was to be a film night, where *The Jungle Book* would be screened.

When she had finished the announcement, she told me more about the club.

"We now have more than seven hundred members from eighty nationalities and all walks of life," she said, "and we work on three principles which form our DNA: Equality, Respect, and Solidarity. This isn't charity – it's all fuelled by goodwill. We create a safe space for people to come together, and, when you provide that, all kinds of things become possible."

Around us, people chatted and laughed, and as they left they hugged each other goodbye. Stephanie showed me the attendee list for the night's event – there were fifty-nine people from twenty different countries, including China, Syria and Zimbabwe.

"It provides a sense of family for people," she said, looking around, "and, once you meet people here, you'll see them again in the city centre and they'll wave hello and that makes all the difference. It's what we're all looking for at some level."

As I left, I thought about what Robin and Breidge had said about the failure of politics to better people's lives and how Stephanie was trying to achieve social progress not through politics but by building connections between people. A sense of disconnection had been common throughout my travels and it struck me that it would be good to have similar initiatives building those connections across the UK, focusing not just on migrants but on people of all backgrounds. As I continued my journey, I began to consider how such connections might be built without government funding, since my experience in Northern Ireland had reinforced my sense that party politics was not the best way to bring people together.

24

The Economy and the Farming Industry in Armagh and Newry

The next day, I decided to get out of Belfast and see how the economic situation in the UK was impacting on daily life in Northern Ireland. I headed for Armagh, a journey that involved changing trains at Portadown. It was a cold day and the train was late, so all the passengers huddled in a waiting room. After fifteen minutes, the station guard announced that the train was on its way and everyone filed out on to the platform. A few moments later, the guard appeared holding a rucksack that had been left in the waiting room and walked up the platform seeking its owner. Eventually he found that it belonged to a young man and returned it to him. The young man thanked him sheepishly as he was mocked by his friends, and I wondered if the same thing had happened fifteen years earlier, the station would have been evacuated.

* * * * *

When I reached Armagh, I went to an employment support project to meet the manager, Declan McKee. I asked him what the employment prospects were locally.

"Very poor," he said. "There's a lot of people out of work with no way to pay the bills. I don't know how they survive mentally, never mind financially – it's an awful position."

"Week in, week out you see jobs going," he continued, "and it's not just the Northern Ireland economy or the UK economy, it's the Irish economy, too – if something goes bang down there it has repercussions up here."

I asked if the people he worked with would think about going for jobs in Ireland.

"The type of people that we would work with," he said, "they don't like going too far from home. I don't think it would be in them to survive."

"Their families are in the area," he explained, "so, even if their relationships haven't been great, they stay nearby. For people we work with, even if there was a job in Belfast that they were qualified for, they wouldn't dream of going for it. We had a presentation day at Queen's University recently and I took a group in the minibus. It was amazing the amount of people who had never been down the motorway – some of them had never even been as far as Portadown, which is only ten miles away."

"The other problem," he went on, "is that it's all very rural, and the transport's not good here. Sometimes people have to take three buses to get here. Imagine having to take three buses to be at your work for eight in the morning. Some towns here, there are only two buses, one in the morning, one in the afternoon, that's it; whereas if you live on the outskirts of somewhere like Belfast there's buses everywhere and you just hop on and you're into the city centre."

I said it sounded like these day-to-day issues were more pressing for people here than the sectarian divide.

"The big issue now," he said, "would be trying to get into a good job and a house but it's not easy for anyone. Well-qualified people are just sitting at home, can't get into work, and it's not for want of trying. I feel an awful pity for them – they have worked hard all their life, have been made redundant through no fault of their own and that puts pressure on people – maybe there's a mortgage to be paid or you've a young family that needs money for school. So that's a big problem now, almost as big as the Troubles were mentally to people."

It seemed like a big statement and I asked him to expand on it.

"I know a lot of young couples who bought houses," he said, "and, the way the mortgage companies were going, you went in looking for ninety thousand and you came out with maybe one hundred and fifty thousand. They were throwing money left, right and centre at people and then the bubble burst, and now they're out of work the houses are being taken off them. The Troubles were hard times but now you are thinking, 'How am I going to survive with no work?'"

"Things politically have settled and are going well," he concluded. "People are starting to get on a bit better, but now the economy is falling apart and employment-wise things have gone downhill big time. But that's life I suppose: things go up and things go down."

* * * * *

From Armagh, I travelled to Newry, a market town near to the Irish border. A sign in a shop gave its prices in pounds and euros, while I saw many cars with Irish number plates. In the outdoor market, U2 was playing on the radio and clothes, bric-a-brac, and fruit and veg were on sale. A few other customers went round looking at the wares, but the market was generally quiet. I got chatting to a Pakistani stallholder and asked him how business was.

"Slow," he said. "Recession, it's hitting. Over here, it's worse because the cost to the customer is higher. Bringing things over on the ferries, you pay everything extra here."

I asked if the Irish economy was also having an impact. He nodded.

"They still come up to shop," he said, "but not many and only if the currency is good."

A customer appeared, and I went on, and found a woman and her husband on a stall selling bric-a-brac. I asked her what Newry was like.

"Tough times," she said. "I remember coming into the market thirty years ago – those were the good times. The money was there but not any more and I think the government's a lot to do with that – cutting back, making things dearer."

I asked if that was the British government or the Northern Ireland assembly.

"All of them," she said.

"What you have to know," her husband said, "is that it hasn't really had a chance to settle because the economy has been a mess. I think it is the only way to go forward, you know, the democratic approach, but, to be honest, people don't even talk about it here. It's more about the economy. Getting through, living, paying bills."

I asked him what he felt the future held.

"To be honest with you," he said, "I'd like to go back to the way it was in my day, but there's not a lot of my day left. I wanted a united Ireland, but, at the moment, it's just about getting through. I think most people would see it that way because they have to."

I left them to it and walked around the market, finally finding Nick, a farmer selling fresh produce, including huge pumpkins ahead of Halloween. I asked him how business was.

"Pretty poor," he said. "We haven't had this kind of stability in Northern Ireland for a long time but the world economy is battering us now. There's a rising population but no one wants our food."

I had been interested in food since my visit to Rotherham, so I asked why no one wanted his produce, which seemed to be of very high quality.

"People need education about how to improve their diets," he said. "Like these pumpkins, they scoop the inside, throw it away and it ends up in the landfill, but, if they knew how to, they could cook so many different meals out of it."

"I get kids coming past here," he went on, "looking at the sweetcorn and saying, 'Mummy, can we have that?' and mummy goes, 'I wouldn't know how to cook it,' and you think to yourself, where did it all go wrong?"

"I think there's a huge gap between rural and urban," he continued. "The urban people don't know about the farmers' work and they buy cheap, processed food and, if you look at the side of the box, the chicken has been sourced from Vietnam. There's nothing wrong with the chicken in the UK, but because all the stuff is cheap in Asia, they go for it. But then you think of the air miles to bring it in, the pollution, the CO_2, and then you have to refrigerate it… There's no need to do that, but big companies work on big figures. It's sad and, if it doesn't change, we're in trouble."

I asked whether he ever sold to supermarkets. He shook his head.

"I'd get absolutely thrashed on price," he explained. "They'd take it at whatever price, multiply it by four, and throw it out when it goes off. And, the next time you go back to give them an order, they say, 'It didn't last and we need to give you less for it next time.'"

"The sad thing," he continued, "is that this is only part-time – I've had to find other work to subsidise it. In November I'm going to Saudi Arabia to work because there's nothing here – I don't want to be separated from my family, but there's no choice."

"People say there's no work," he went on, "but, if you're prepared to travel, you'll get it. The last five years I've been travelling back and forward to farms in England because there's a huge gap over there and farmers can't get skilled operators."

I thought about what Declan had said about young people in Armagh being unwilling to travel to Belfast, let alone further afield, and wondered whether mindsets might have to change.

"The average age of a farmer in the UK is fifty-eight," Nick continued, "so I don't know where the new farmers are going to come from. A lot of young farmers, their friends are tradesmen and they work nine to five and they get a half day on a Friday; whereas for the farmers it's seven days a week, non-stop…"

I asked if there was anything the government could do.

"The government will just set up a committee," he said. "They'll have a meeting about a meeting, but nothing will happen."

A couple came over.

"You must have given them a lot of fertiliser, the size of these," the husband said, pointing at the huge pumpkins.

"No fertiliser," Nick said, going over to serve another customer, "just cow muck."

I got talking to the couple, Jane and Tom, and they agreed to be interviewed. It turned out they were on holiday from Belfast, and, over a cup of coffee, they gave me their view on the economy and the farming industry.

"In my youth," said Jane, "I spent a lot of time on my uncle's farm and it was a very happy time – I used to go up and down the drills of carrots and cauliflower and cabbage and gather them, but that's all gone now. Machines come in and harvest vegetables – it's a completely different system to my childhood, which was meeting people and getting your hands dirty and that was a wonderful feeling."

"What's driven that is finance," said Tom, "because it is cheaper to harvest carrots with a machine, even though it leaves 40 per cent of them in the ground. Those that are harvested are put in a truck and taken to England where they are washed and packed and then they're brought back here to be marketed."

"Now, for financial gain that may sound fantastic," he went on, "but what has had no value placed on it whatsoever is what Jane is talking about, the role of the community in harvesting these vegetables, where you end up at the end of the day sitting down with a lot of people in the farmhouse having tea and jam sandwiches and everybody would be having an awful lot of fun and feeling good about each other."

"What you have instead," he went on, "is a whole bunch of unemployed people who are feeling disengaged with the community and do not have a sense of responsibility, so the crime rate goes up, drug misuse or what have you, while 40 per cent of the carrots are left in the field. It just seems very strange that this whole process has been let rip in terms of money without any value placed on its impact on the community."

* * * * *

As I took the bus out of town, I thought about what I had heard. I wondered whether the value of traditional farming methods outweighed the need for affordable food and whether Declan was right that economic worries now were as big as the fear of violence during the Troubles. Again, I had found my conversations about modern life in the UK drifting into unfavourable comparisons with the past, and I began to feel that what I was hearing could not simply be dismissed as nostalgia.

25

Wealth and Class Separation in Hillsborough

From Newry, I travelled north to the affluent village of Hillsborough. I had been struck by disparities of wealth in Northern Ireland, and indeed across the whole of the UK, and wanted to get a perspective from those who were better off. In the pub on the high street, I got talking to a man in his sixties sitting by the open log fire.

"It's relaxed and friendly here," he said. "House prices are a bit more expensive than Moira or Dromara because it's just that bit nicer – that's not a snob point of view, it's just a fact of life. We've got a thriving school, community centre, pubs and there's a very good road connection between here, Lisburn and Belfast."

I said it sounded like life was good.

"Yes," he said, "but remember you're dealing with the middle and upper class here and we look at things through rose-tinted glasses – some people in Belfast are going to be struggling to heat their homes this winter."

I asked him how he responded to such disparities of wealth.

"At the end of the day," he said, "it's about your family, protecting them and providing for them. You just have to plough your own furrow."

He had to go, but I decided to stay around to find out how others saw things.

* * * * *

In a corner of the pub, I found a couple in their sixties who had been out walking, and they agreed to be interviewed. I asked them about society in Northern Ireland.

"What I find very interesting," said the husband, "is the mass movement of people from established terraced-housing communities out to new estates with the three bedrooms and inside bathroom. That was a middle-class solution to a working-class problem, and people, I think, have lost out as a result of that."

I asked what he meant by 'lost out'.

"They lost the fabric of the community," he explained, "the mutual support that was there. In the old days, if children did something wrong, they would be reprimanded not just by their parents but by everyone, and out of that emerged a feeling that they were part of a community. They knew where they stood. There were people in the community who mothers could look to for advice if the baby was having problems and, even if someone died, there would be people who knew what had to be done."

"The community was self-sufficient," he went on. "It worked like a traditional village. There was an order to it, and that order was completely dispatched by putting these communities into modern housing estates. And, as a result, huge demands were placed on public services because a lot of the services that were provided within the community were then demanded by these people from the state."

"People's expectations are so much higher now," he added. "They feel as if things are almost theirs by right. No longer is it that life has a metre and occasionally things happen and that has to be accepted; there's a feeling now that, no matter what happens, there ought to be a state solution to it."

I asked his wife if she shared that view.

"Certainly, in my role managing social workers," she said, "there are very few grandmothers around. Families have been split up, young mums have been moved into housing estates where they've got no family support and they end up having multiple partners. Each child has a different father and it turns into a very abusive situation."

"The skills of child care and running a home haven't been passed down from one generation to another," she went on, "and you end up with these really sad young people getting pregnant, one baby after another, and they cannot support themselves. And I'm now seeing the children of those children I first worked with in the early nineties coming into care – it's a spiral through the generations."

"I think it's part of the cultural change that has taken place here in the past twenty or thirty years," her husband said, "which I think has been too rapid to be assimilated by the community. There's been a great deal more money available and I'm not in any way devaluing the right of people to go on foreign holidays or have TVs, but the fact that all of that has become available very rapidly has been destabilising in my view."

I asked how people in middle-class communities viewed the problems in working-class communities.

"They wouldn't think it's anything to do with them," his wife said. "It would be a complete other world – unless they were in an area of work that drew them into those communities, I don't think they would be aware or consider it any of their business."

"There's also a very large section of the middle-class population that is very happy with the way things are," the husband said, "because the middle classes here are remarkably well catered for. Our children went to a very good mixed grammar school and they didn't know whether their friends were Protestants or Catholics. That's one of the greatest things – that middle-class young people no longer have any consideration about religious denomination, even when it comes to marriage."

"The cost of living here is also very low," he went on. "Royal County Down is a very nice gentleman's club – it's the third best golf club in the world. The sailing here is superb, you've got wonderful yacht clubs, all sorts of things. If you look upon it in those terms, as most middle-class people do, it's an absolutely idyllic place to be."

He didn't seem convinced so I asked whether he himself was content with things as they were.

"No," he said, "to the extent that I would move. I find the political situation really quite intolerable."

I asked him why and he told me about his frustration with many of the political issues I had discussed previously with Robin Wilson and Breidge Gadd.

"The place is stagnating," he said, "when there's so much that needs to be done and could be done in Northern Ireland if people were properly motivated up at that legislature. This country has such a lot going for it and it has the goodwill of the world behind it. But, as it is, it's a basket case…"

His wife clearly disagreed about leaving.

"My view," she said, "is that both of us are now in our sixties and, at this stage of life, you don't know how long you've got left; it may not be very long. We've a lot of people around who have been friends all our lives, and to leave all that… I know the frustrations here are great, but, for me, the upside is that we've got wonderful places to go, Strangford Lough for sailing, the Mourne mountains, so to leave and set up home somewhere else would be quite a risk."

"I just find the prospect of ending my days in a situation like this really, really frustrating," her husband said, and they continued the debate for a while. Finally, they had to go and they said goodbye, the question still unresolved.

* * * * *

On the next table, I found a couple who said they were happy to talk briefly before they returned to their home in the country. I asked whether they were farmers.

"No," said the wife, "we're just country-lovers. We came out of the city for the peace and quiet and the joy of having our own land. We never thought we'd end up with forty-five acres, but we always wanted to grow trees, so we've planted twelve acres of native hardwoods and we let out the rest of the land for grazing. Being able to walk over your own land is just a real pleasure and privilege. We're very, very lucky."

She told me they had seven grandchildren, and I asked what life was like for them growing up in modern Northern Ireland.

"I just think there's so much pressure on them at too early an age," she said, "and the speed of change is so dramatic. Huge opportunities – that's the good side of it – but also huge stresses in terms of getting through uni, getting a job, keeping up with the social side of things. It's just moving at an astonishing pace – strangely, my teenage years were much more peaceful in spite of what was going on over here."

I guessed she hadn't lived in one of the more violent parts of Northern Ireland during the Troubles but I was still surprised to hear anyone say that things were more peaceful then.

"I think the stresses were more concrete back then," she said, "and boiled down to whether you were going to get embroiled in a situation if you went to a certain area. The stresses now are happening so much earlier – children are being pushed to do well at such an early age now, not having the freedom of a childhood, like we had. For our grandchildren, the stress and pressure of doing well is building up from age eight or nine – it would never have entered our heads that you would have had to strive so hard at that age. It wasn't life or death as it seems to be now."

I asked why exams were so important now.

"Expectations are so much higher," she said. "People expect a job, a reasonable salary, a quality of life. I think the expectation of parents is that children will have more than they had themselves. But then there is the other side of the coin, the third generations which are not in employment, and there's no work ethic there at all…"

"One big problem we have here," her husband added, "is that the majority of people who are employed are working for the public sector; they're not making things. I'm not saying all civil servants are useless, but one hundred years ago, the Foreign Office had eighteen hundred people managing an empire. Now they've got thirty-five thousand people in Northern Ireland alone – it's crazy. If there'd been less money poured in, we'd be more self-reliant. When life's made too easy, it weakens that instinct."

We talked on about class and the sectarian divide.

"You need to have children educated together," she said, "so they regard each other as human beings first rather than being identified by your religion. But it's easier to achieve that here than in the centre of Belfast, because the whole thing is less pressurised. You haven't got the huge concentration of people living cheek by jowl, where feelings are much more likely to run high. It's much less of a pressure cooker."

I asked what she meant by a 'pressure cooker'.

"A lot of it is to do with space rather than wealth," she said. "I think feelings are less likely to run high when you can remove yourself from the situation. Everybody needs space to work things out and to be able to remove yourself, even a small distance, as you can in the country, is incredibly important. But for somebody right on the edge of a religious divide in Belfast, you're not able to get away from that."

"Children need space," she went on. "You're under constant pressure from your peer group – in school, walking home, living next door – compressed, compressed, compressed – and you haven't got any space for yourself to think differently, and it's very hard to break away from that unless you have parents who encourage you to think differently and, in the poorer areas, that's just not likely to happen."

"A huge part of the problem," she continued, "is that these kids don't get the opportunity to experience what we take for granted living out in the country. There is the greatest calm to be drawn from the natural world, and the odd school trip isn't going to do it."

I asked how it felt to be on the more privileged side of the divide.

"It feels unfair," she said. "It is the way it is, but it doesn't feel right that, because of where you were born, you have a life that is comfortable and cosy compared to the vast majority of the people. But I still would need to see some kind of endeavour from the less privileged people – if the help was there for them, I would still want to see some input from them, whereas I think there is now, because of the welfare state, a sense of entitlement. Not 'I'll go out and work for it' but 'Maybe I'll just take it.'"

"I don't say that from a superior standpoint," she added, "because I know how incredibly lucky we are, but, at the same time, I've got a strong work ethic, and that is something I'd appreciate in anybody, wherever they came from."

We talked on, and I told them about my visit to inner-city Belfast earlier in the week.

"You've seen more of those parts of Belfast than we ever would," she said, "because we just wouldn't go into those areas. You completely avoided them during the Troubles, and I suppose curiosity could take you there now, but then you don't want to go to gawp. I can completely understand tourists wanting to look at the peace walls, but it would seem for us crude to go and ogle at what they're living in."

"It's also maybe more comfortable for us not to go and look," she added after a moment.

When they had gone, I sat down for a drink by the fire and reflected on what she had said. Her last remark was one of the most honest things I had heard on my travels but her comment that things were more complicated now than in the Troubles also struck me. Even though what she had said clearly came from a fairly privileged position, it told much about the unsettling effect of rapid change that the husband of the previous couple had also talked about, and took me closer to understanding the sense of unease that I had encountered throughout my journey.

26

Sectarianism, Class and Britishness in Belfast

The next day I returned to Belfast and headed to the north of the city to meet Issac, a former Loyalist paramilitary, and G, a former British soldier, who were now youth workers on the interfaces between Protestant and Catholic communities. They met me in their office, a portacabin in the heart of North Belfast, and told me about the communities they worked with.

"Northern Ireland communities to this day are still in a conversation about what happened during the conflict," Issac told me. "Young people are growing up and continuously hearing about the past. Some young people are actually saying they felt that they missed out because all they were hearing were romanticised versions of the conflict, and not the true realities of it. We try to get them away from that."

"G and I have been working on the interfaces for a long time," Issac went on, "and we never want to see anyone having to go through the conflict. The worry is that there is people wanting to go back – some organisations and groupings, they're using young kids as cannon fodder. Some evenings here, it's been nightly riots and the media and politicians were using words like 'recreational rioting' – but it's not."

I asked why he thought people rioted.

"Because they're not seeing any benefits of the peace process," he said. "Their areas aren't being regenerated, there's lack of employment, there's lack of good education, and there's no money getting pumped into it."

"There's massive deprivation around us," said G, "and, when you look at conflict, you always find that the social/economic situations in communities are extremely bad because, if someone is quite well off, has a job, the kids are getting good schooling, it eases the factors that can cause conflict. Within these communities, there is no help from our government at all. What you have is community workers like us trying to put micro peace processes on but with no help, no money. It gets quite difficult because you've got people in a conversation of 'I hate the other community, the other community's getting more than me.' But both the communities, if you'll excuse the language, they're in exactly the same shit."

"A lot of positive things are happening, too," said Issac, "but our main thing is we need a relationship with our political parties. There's this old perception within Unionism, in Britishness, that you should always tip your hat to the man at the top of the hill – whatever they say goes – and sometimes, in Loyalist areas, there's a pride so you don't ask for anything. But, for me, it's about creating a better relationship with the Unionist parties so they're actually working with the working class, not talking down to them."

"I would sort of disagree with Issac," said G. "Our politicians have always been middle class and the only people they've done anything for is the middle class. I have no love for Sinn Fein, but at least they are a working-class party."

I asked whether the attitude of 'tipping the hat' still persisted.

"To a certain point," said Issac, "so, within the Catholic community, if somebody got a washing machine off the DHSS, they would go out and tell everybody 'Here's how I got that...' and, the next thing you know, they would all have one. In a Loyalist-Unionist area, if somebody was to get one, they wouldn't tell anybody."

"That's around shame as well," G said. "That whole Britishness thing – no matter what's happening, stiff upper lip. Don't ever ask for anything, because that's just begging. Don't tell people when you're in trouble. It'll be OK because you're British."

Issac had to go, but he had a few words before he left.

"Gerry Adams' famous words," he said, "was that 'They haven't gone away.' Well, I believe they have, and that's what's causing the problem. Because what you've got in Nationalist areas is groups coming in to fill that void. They say that they're the true IRA; that all this violence wasn't supposed to get Sinn Fein into Stormont, it was to get a united Ireland. And then you have Martin McGuiness, fair play to him, what he said after the two soldiers and the young police officer was killed, he said 'These are traitors of Ireland,' but, unfortunately for me, that just hardened it within them groups."

"I believe it was all totally wrong," he went on. "For me, personally, it was sectarian – I had no interest in politics. It was, 'If you're going to do this to me, I'm going to do this to you,' 'If you're going to bomb my community three times, I'm going to bomb your community ten times.' Sinn Fein says their work was against the state and, even to this day, they won't say the word 'sectarian', but there was bombs planted in pubs, shopping centres, babies blew out in the Shankill Road, people took out and shot simply because they were Protestant, so they have to admit that what they were involved in was sectarian. But, in their eyes, you can't criticise them, because once you criticise them you're a dissident, you're against the peace process."

"So, from a perspective of a Unionist or a Loyalist person," he went on, "it's more and more one-sided, and the more they see it that way, the more you have the possibility of people wanting to go off in another direction, but I still believe wholeheartedly that the organisation I used to belong to is totally behind the peace process. I don't believe that we will ever come back to how it was, but my worry is, if one of these dissident groups were to have a bomb somewhere, in a parade or something, they may get the reaction they're looking for."

He apologised for having to leave, and he was gone. I said to G that it seemed hard to completely move on from the past.

"Northern Ireland is filled with victimhood," he said. "Everybody's, like, 'I'm a bigger victim than you are – we need to hold an inquiry.' I don't know how many victims of the Troubles there were, there were that many that you couldn't even count, but if we had inquiries into all of them it would just drag the country down."

"I've had a lot of hurt from the Troubles," he went on, "but if people's been killed, they're dead. And maybe that's a bit harsh, but, no matter how much money you spend, you're not going to bring them people back. I think we worry too much about the people who are dead, rather than the people who are living. There's pensioners who can't heat their house, and, OK, it's sad that people lost their life, but the money for all the inquiries we've had could have gone into giving pensioners a few quid in the winter."

Our conversation moved on to poverty in Northern Ireland.

"When you have deprivation," he continued, "and there's a lack of education, young fellas about the street with no hope, and somebody comes along with some drugs, some money and says, 'You're looking for identity – we'll give you this big romanticised identity.' In the Catholic community you have dissidents running around and people think, 'I want the respect he's got.' That's how they prey on the young people; they think, 'That's for me; I'll be part of something.'"

I asked if he had any final thoughts about the interface communities.

"Within the communities I work in," he said, "I do see positive things. Children now aren't getting caught up in explosions, they aren't hearing shootings on a nightly basis, and they aren't getting conditioned to all that, and that's a good thing, so it is. I can remember as a child seeing dead bodies, getting woke up at three o'clock in the morning by the army, getting taken out of my house because there was explosions in the area, army getting shot at. I remember there was people shooting from each side, a Republican RPG-ing a police land rover and it was just complete mayhem. That was just mental, but, at the time, it was just like normal life. But that community now, you walk around it at night and hear a pin drop."

"It's all about creating relationships," he went on. "When I was young, I was told, 'Don't speak to people on the other side, they worship the anti-Christ, they're the devil' – all this crap from church. When I see people across the road, I didn't see them as people; I see them as all IRA men – it might have been a child, it might have been a woman, it might have been a priest – I just see everyone on that side as IRA. I had a lot of hate for them but I think the more the people talk to each other, the more they'll see they've got a lot in common. I'm thankful to be able to do this work, and it gives me a lot of gratification when I see Protestants and Catholics building relationships, seeing each other as human beings after years of dehumanisation."

"We've got a cross-community staff in here," he continued, "and, for Halloween, they're going to a Catholic area and a Catholic pub, but half of them's Protestants. If the community leaders are being seen to behave like that, then that sends a strong message to the normal people in the community – 'Well, if they can do it, why can't we?' The more them relationships get created, and the more the trust is built, the harder it is to go back. The peace we've got now gives young people respite so that they might be able to see the people who live on the next street as human beings. While there is still sectarianism going on, they're also integrating more and they're on the PlayStation networks talking to each other. They might go out and knock seven bells out of each other now and again, but generally there's no body bags getting filled."

Before I left he told me he had one thing he wanted to say.

"Just something about Britishness," he said. "I come from a military family, my grandfather, my father, my brother, very loyal to the Queen, very proud of being British – the best nation in the world, the best army in the world. But lately… You're disappointed when you hear that the security services, MI5 and MI6, were working with the Provisional IRA, so that knocks a bit at your Britishness, that people were able to play games with people's lives."

"People also get used by the whole idea of being British," he went on, "like when they say, 'We're going to be in a recession, but never mind – *we* can all get through this.' David Cameron, living in Downing Street on a fortune, but it's still that Britishness – '*We* will all get through this'; sending young lads to Afghanistan – '*We* have to do this.'"

"I was a soldier," he went on. "I understand that to sign up means you might not come back, and I had a lot of friends killed, but it just sort of grates on you, when a young lad's got his legs blown off, or a family's got their son killed, that the pension isn't great. Do you know what I mean? You've got footballers on one hundred thousand pounds a week in England, you've got bankers getting bailed out even though they made a complete horlicks of the system, and then you've got young lads running about Afghanistan, with IEDs everywhere, for thirty pound a day."

"I'm still proud to be British, though," he concluded. "I think being British is about the people in Britain, know what I mean? People always jokes when they're down, no matter what the situation is. We always try, although sometimes we're not in the best circumstances. I think rather than the monarchy, I think it's more the people that makes Britain a great place to live."

What he said stayed with me: he was losing faith in British institutions and, indeed, the very notion of Britishness, but he still had faith in his fellow citizens. It seemed a very important distinction to make, especially when there was so much mistrust of politicians and others at the top of British society. From my travels so far, I felt that G was justified in believing in the decency of British people and that if that decency could be better harnessed, it could be very powerful indeed.

27

Moving On from the Past in Belfast and Derry/Londonderry

With just a couple of days left before I was due to return to England, I got talking to a man standing outside a pub in south Belfast. I told him about the book and the conversation turned to how Northern Ireland was moving on from its past.

"There'll always be that element who want to go back to the way it was," he said, "but the majority definitely don't. Unless you're from here, you can't grasp what it was like – bombs going off the whole time, people getting murdered…"

"I was on holiday when Omagh happened," he went on, "and it was only when I seen the news, the scale of it… And whoever is responsible is still walking our streets. And then you've got Martin McGuiness as Deputy First Minister…"

I asked him how he felt about that. He looked me straight in the eye with an expression of deep anguish and pain.

"I accept it," he said, "but it's a sin."

"It makes me angry," he went on after a moment, "but it's the price we have to accept for peace and to make the next generation safe."

"I hate him," he added, "but I just hope he doesn't get whacked. Forget about Afghanistan – that would be World War III."

He was heading back in to the pub so I thanked him for his time.

"My pleasure, my absolute pleasure," he said.

As I walked on I felt that his pleasure had not so much been in meeting me, but in being able to talk about a pain he clearly still felt.

* * * * *

The next day, the question of moving on from the past still in my mind, I met Reverend John Dinnen, the former rector of Hillsborough, and I asked him how people were able to cope with the grief caused by the Troubles.

"There is no pat answer to that," he said, "and some people just can't. I know people today who are still very bitter and when you hear their story you can understand why: they have been deprived of a father, a brother, a husband, and life has never been the same. On the other hand, there are people who have said, 'This is the worst thing that could possibly happen and I wouldn't want it to happen to anyone else – I'm not going to let it beat me or poison the rest of my life.' And they have picked themselves up and some have actually got involved in reconciliation work."

I asked how those people were able to deal with such pain.

"I wouldn't underestimate the faith dimension in both sides of the healing process," he said. "I think that both traditions here, the Catholic and Reformed, have played a major part in the healing. I know the Church was also part of the problem, and to some degree still is part of the problem, but I also think that there was a mellowing effect which a lot of people in churches of both traditions worked very hard to maintain."

"I also just think that there is a maturity about today that there wasn't in the past," he went on. "Everyone knows you don't win people to your point of view if you shoot them. Obviously, there is a minor element who feel that is still the way to go, but it is also remarkable to see people take their place in politics who would have endorsed that violent approach ten or twenty years ago."

I asked how people perceived former paramilitaries now in power.

"I think, at first, they were tolerated," he said, "and, increasingly, they are accepted. Paisley and the Provisional leadership sitting down together was a big jump and the stories, at first, were that they wouldn't shake hands or sit in the same room. That has all gone now and that has changed the whole atmosphere and trust has been built up."

"Again," he went on, "I don't think that the faith dimension has been totally absent, because there must be an element of forgiveness in there somewhere. How can you go from what has been in the past to where we are today without saying, 'We've got to leave that behind?' That is the 'pin' that they try to get people to stand on, asking people to apologise and express regret, but that isn't going to change the past. I think people in the present will be measured by their actions and their deeds, and, at the moment, I think there is a fair wind on that."

I asked him about the faith dimension he had mentioned.

"Faith can offer people grace," he went on, "and, by that, I mean that it can offer people forgiveness. It isn't the easiest thing to do by any means but I have seen clear evidence that where forgiveness happens there is a better future. All of us can think of personal situations where, if forgiveness was on the agenda, the whole situation could change; or political situations where, if only people could sit down together and say, 'Let's accept that we have done things wrong in the past,' they could start again. Being able to forgive is key to all human relationships, be they personal, political or religious."

* * * * *

The next day, my last in Northern Ireland, I decided to go to Derry/Londonderry – known as Derry to Nationalists, Londonderry to Unionists – to see how ordinary people felt about the future. When I arrived, I decided to head to the 'Peace Bridge', the footbridge across the river that Robin Wilson had mentioned linking the mainly Protestant community on one side of the city to the mainly Catholic population on the other.

The bridge was stunning, curving and arcing across perhaps one hundred yards of water. It had been raining but now the sun peaked out from behind the clouds and a steady stream of people walked across: couples, families, groups of friends. It was a happy scene, but, when I looked at the glass panels lining the side of the bridge, I saw that one had been smashed. An elderly lady walking past saw me looking at it.

"It would have taken a lot of effort to do that," she said. "You'd need something heavy to do it, a sledgehammer or something."

"It's sad," she added. "Some people always want to go back."

She walked on and a group of young people walked past, two hand in hand, one with a dog wagging its tail. Behind them was a man with a goatee beard and we got talking.

"It's a great city," he said, "but it always gets left behind. Belfast redirects all the funding away from it – they fear if we ever developed we would be a big threat to them. They even tried to stop us getting the City of Culture in 2013…"

I said that it seemed he was more focused on the divide between the two cities than the sectarian divide.

"The sectarian thing," he said, "I've worked everywhere and I don't give a shit – I don't care. The only way to stop sectarianism is to get people jobs, get them money, and then they won't be rioting on the streets, they'll be in the pub. The peace process finally got going when the economy got going, because people were content and they thought, 'I can't be arsed to go out and fight.'"

He looked at the people walking past.

"It's all bullshit," he said. "They don't go to church, they don't know anything about their religions – the politicians just keep it on edge because it keeps them in a job. The whole thing's just a myth but as long as people buy into it there'll be trouble."

He went on his way and I thought about what he had said about myths being damaging, whether or not they were true, which seemed applicable for the UK as a whole.

A wedding party walked by, the bride and groom, bridesmaids, ushers and flower girls, to take some photos on the bridge. A man walked his dog, families with children walked past.

A woman walked across the bridge and I got talking to her about the future.

"My family have never moved away from their little town," she said, "and you have all these silly little fallings out because your eyes aren't opened that bit wider. It's a bit the same in Northern Ireland. I know it's hard to forgive but I think there comes a point where you just have to get on with it – we have all sorts of inquiries going on here and it's stopping people from moving on because it's always there facing them."

"I think a lot of it, as well, is to do with the upbringing," she went on. "You have to snap away from the traditional upbringing of some people. There should be a lot more community integration – if you start from primary school, hopefully, you'll break them out of 'I hate that one because he's a Catholic or I hate that one because he's a Protestant' and all they'll see is a friend from school."

I asked how people found it within themselves to move on from the past.

"I had friends killed," she said, "and I've known people who've killed other people. Ultimately, you have to think it was another time and you can't judge a person on the basis of that forever."

"It just takes time," she added. "Trauma takes generations to work its way through."

The new husband and wife walked back across the bridge hand in hand, with the ushers, bridesmaids and flower girls behind. As I began to make my way back to the station, a couple walked past and I got talking to them.

"We're just having a day round the shops," the husband told me. "It's nice to see it so calm and peaceful – that place used to be a beehive for helicopters."

He pointed to what was once a barracks, and was now being turned into a piazza. I asked where they were from.

"From Omagh," the wife said.

"We're known for all the wrong reasons," said her husband. "We had that big bomb all those years ago."

I asked how the town was now.

"They fixed it up as best they could," he said, "but then we had that young policeman killed this year as well. Unfortunately, you've still got the odd lunatic running around. But everyone else has had enough of all that."

"I'm just worried about the recession," he went on, "young people out of work. Idle minds can cause problems. That's the same everywhere, but with what we've been through it just makes you more concerned that we could end up going back... But hopefully not, hopefully not..."

They wished me luck and were gone.

As I made my way back to the station, headed for Belfast and then back towards England, I reflected that he had captured perfectly my biggest concern about Northern Ireland – the danger of slipping back into violence in a difficult economic time. Otherwise, many of the issues I had found were similar to those I had encountered across the UK, though often heightened in what seemed a tightly compressed place: social and economic inequality; mistrust of politicians; fracturing of social bonds; difficulty in dealing with a rapidly changing world; prejudice and fear between communities exacerbated by the sense that for some the best days were in the past while for others the best days lay ahead; and, in amongst it all, decent people trying to make the best of things but somehow held back by myths and memories of the past.

28

Wealth, Inequality and Class in the North-East

As I returned to England, I realised that it had been a month since I had been in Rotherham, and Scotland and Northern Ireland had raised a number of new issues I wanted to investigate in the final weeks of my journey. I didn't want to look any further into ethnic or sectarian division, which I didn't feel could be any more pronounced than in Belfast. Instead, I wanted to look more at money – class, poverty, the impact of government cuts – as well as looking at institutions that brought people together as I sought to focus my thinking on what I wanted to do when I completed my journey. I decided these would be my priorities as I travelled down through the North-East into Yorkshire and then towards the North-West.

My first stop was Newcastle, and in Times Square I got talking to Chris, a student who was back for the weekend from Glasgow, where he was studying.

"People in the North just feel they have nothing to do with what happens in London," he told me. "It's just self-perpetuating – it comes from unemployment and lack of aspirations. There's complete under-representation at Westminster; our voices are never heard."

I asked about prominent MPs, including Tony Blair, who had represented constituencies in the North-East.

"But he was just parachuted in," he said, "he went there because it was a Labour safe seat. He couldn't have been more distant to the working class."

"I think class is one of the most core parts of where people feel their identity lies," he went on, "and where people think their allegiances lie as well."

I asked whether he felt class had changed at all over the years.

"It definitely still exists," he said, "but now you have this white collar working class who work in call centres or for next to nothing in offices. You might not have the industrial working classes of yesteryear but you also have this new class, the dependency class, who just live on handouts and don't aspire to much at all."

"You couldn't have had it in the eighteenth and nineteenth century," he went on, "because you didn't have the welfare state to support them, but you do have people who aren't born with aspirations so when it's the option between working seventy hours a week to bring home the minimum wage or go on benefits, some people will choose to go on welfare rather than putting themselves out there."

I asked whether he thought things had progressed at all.

"They have," he said, "and I know, for example, that if I had been born twenty years earlier there's no way I could have gone to university and fulfilled my potential. But I also know there are people now who don't have that aspiration. I suppose, even on a basic level, I feel alienated because I have to pay tuition fees whereas the Scottish students at Glasgow don't."

"My parents are both public sector workers," he continued. "My dad works with adults with learning difficulties, my mam's a nurse, and my sister is going to go to university after the tuition fees rise. She's going to get into twenty-seven grand of debt and that's before a mortgage or a family or anything else."

"Debt isn't a class thing," he went on, "but your capacity to pay it back is. Somebody from a poor background can't afford to have that risk of being straddled with twenty-seven grand's worth of debt and not getting a job at the end of university. To me, that's discriminating on the basis of capacity to pay, not capacity to learn. Class is the most acceptable form of prejudice in society today."

* * * * *

The next day I headed south to Northallerton and walked into the centre of town. I knew it was an affluent market town, so this seemed a good opportunity to look at the questions of inequality and class from the perspective of people in a wealthier part of the country.

"I think it has become too unequal," a man who was visiting Northallerton with his wife told me.

I asked him why he thought that.

"It's the obvious reasons," he said, "bankers' bonuses and such like. Tyneside, where we're from, it's a different kettle of fish, and there's pretty gut-wrenching poverty amongst the farmers."

"Social mobility has gone down the creek," he went on. "In cities things might have changed but we still have the class system round here."

"Don't get him started," his wife said.

"She's right," he said. "I'm just a grumpy old man."

They wished me luck and moved on.

Two women walked past, and I asked them if they felt the UK was too unequal. They both said that it was and I asked them asked why.

"Because we've got a massive underclass," one said, "and we, the rich, seem to put all our money in tax havens."

"I don't think it'll ever change," said her friend. "The rich get richer; the poor get poorer."

Her friend disagreed and thought there could be change one day.

"But when it changes," she said, "it'll be a global thing – there'll be some cataclysmic event, like the collapse of the euro. I think we're at the beginning of a very difficult ten years."

"And it's going to hit the young the hardest," her friend said. "Our generation had to wait for things – this generation, it must be now and it's all about them. They're going to have to wake up."

Her friend agreed.

"I've got grandchildren and they're lovely but it's just that way with them," she said, "and it's not their fault, it's the world around them, their friends, the TV…"

"The art of conversation seems to have gone," she went on, "but, when it comes to employment, not being able to string a sentence together is not a good look…"

I talked with them for a while, but others were less forthcoming, and few wanted to stop and talk. After some time, I finally managed to find a couple who seemed interested in my questions.

"There's too many on benefits," said the wife. "They don't have the slightest intention of working."

"And it's because of *their* choices," said the husband, "for example, if they choose to have a baby as a teenager…"

"It's far too easy to get benefits," he went on. "Young people have lost the incentive to work."

I asked whether people in the UK had a responsibility to one another.

"No," he said. "If they're richer and they earned it and they haven't broken any laws or harmed anyone along the way, then why should they? I've not got the slightest bit of guilt. I worked my whole life and so did she, we never missed a day's work in our lives, we both come from a working-class background – terraced housing, the lot. I take a good pension, but I've earned it."

"We have a responsibility to people who are genuinely ill," he went on, "but, too often, benefits are just a nice, soft option."

"I think we should have a responsibility to each other," his wife said, and then looked around at the shoppers going past, "but, even here, it's all me, me, me."

They moved off, wishing me well with the book, and behind them two women walked past. I asked them if they felt that the country was too unequal.

"Yes," said one, "because I feel that I have quite a lot and I work with people who have very little. But that could change if the right policies were put in place."

I asked if she would support those policies.

"I would," she said, "up to a point. I wouldn't want to lose too much."

"I don't want to pay any more tax," she went on. "I'd like to see them using the tax more wisely instead of wasting it on inoperative computer systems."

"And," she continued, "it sounds terrible but I'd much rather give to people who are actually working for it – not those who are fiddling the system."

They went on their way, and I found a woman who held a similar view.

"I know some people are vulnerable," she said, "but sometimes the people who you think don't have money actually turn out to have a lot. I know from working with offenders that they'll take the money and then spend it straight away down the pub or on drugs but they still expect us to look after them."

"People talk about fairness," she went on, "but I know of a drug dealer who was found claiming benefits while he had £25,000 in cash on him – that's not fair, either. People need to take more responsibility for themselves."

It was getting late but when I found a man waiting for his wife outside a shoe shop, I decided to try for one last conversation.

"It probably has become too unequal," he said, and then added, "I just wish I was one of the unequal ones."

I asked him what he meant.

"At the top end," he said, "that's where I'd like to be. And, if that was the case, I'd be saying it's not too unequal, I'd be saying it's fine."

I asked him if his position would really change if he was richer.

"My prime consideration is my family," he said. "I don't give a lot to charity, but I always make sure I look after them."

His wife came out with her new shoes and they went on their way.

* * * * *

From Northallerton, I headed to Darlington, a less affluent town, and stopped for a drink in a little cafe across the road from the station. Inside, I got talking to Susy, the owner, and Fran, a regular customer, who said they would give me their perspective on inequality in the UK.

As we waited for Susy to join us, Fran told me she had recently moved to Darlington from the South-West.

"I'm used to living in university towns," she said, "and I just found it incredibly difficult down there. The average conversation in the pub was 'I work in a quarry' or 'I'm a garage mechanic.' And I'm not the kind of person who likes to go to the Conservative club for a tea dance – I'd rather go to a rock club and watch a band."

Susy came over and we started talking about inequality.

"Obviously, there are lots of forces in the country," she said, "that would like to go back to the nineteenth century when it was just the relentless pursuit of profit at any cost, and poorer people just have to survive on the charity of the rich…"

"There is a tendency to blame," said Fran. "You blame the underclass because it's their fault they're on benefits…"

"I think right-thinking people are blaming the bankers," said Susy, "but *The Sun* and the *Daily Mail* are encouraging people to say it's the immigrants and the scroungers."

"It's the newspaper owners who are the real problem," said Fran, "like the coverage of the protestors at St Paul's – the media streams haven't got a clue what to do: if they highlight the problems of capitalism, then they run the risk of harming the fat-cat capitalist moguls who are their paymasters. But if they attack the protestors, they risk alienating their audience and losing their market share."

What she said interested me a great deal: a few days earlier, a group of protestors from the Occupy campaign had pitched tents outside St Paul's and in other parts of the country, provoking a great deal of media attention and debate.

"It's like Canary Wharf and Paternoster Square," said Susy. "They already have injunctions out in case the protestors go there, and it's like 'Paternoster Square's income will go down 90 per cent' – my heart bleeds for them."

"It just seems to me," she went on, "that there's a massive mismatch between people's attitudes and what they actually do – half the people in the country don't vote because they don't see the point, but they aren't prepared to do anything about it except complain. It's like in Darlington the council is universally hated, but you could put a red rosette on a donkey and they'd vote for it."

I asked why that was the case.

"People think that they have no control," said Fran, "and that's reinforced by the media, so they do complaining, but they don't do politics."

"The British public is also very 'small c conservative'," Susy said. "We're not forward-looking, we're backwards-looking. We're a country after the decline of empire, and there's this thing like the good days are behind us; everything is just horrible now and most people want to get out."

"But that's not new," said Fran. "There's always a fear of change and difficulty with it, these things always cause societal panic – people find it difficult to cope with change, it's human nature."

Their discussion struck a chord and reminded me of many of the other conversations I had had on my travels. I felt that what Susy had said about people being backward-looking was borne out by many of the opinions I had heard, but I was also interested in what Fran had said about people struggling to cope with change: that also seemed from my conversations to be true, and while it didn't seem to have caused the panic she had described in the people I had met, it did go a long way to explaining the sense amongst so many people I had met that things were not quite right.

"But whether or not history is repeating itself, things are bad," Fran continued. "I read the other day that one of the top five items being shoplifted at the moment is cheese. You know that you're in a society which is in deep shit if people are shoplifting those basic foodstuffs. You imagine people steal stuff to sell in the pub, make a few extra coins under the table, but it's not perfume or even cigarettes – you're talking cheese…"

29

Tradition, Charity and Commitment to the Armed Forces in York

My next stop was York, which I planned to use as a base for the next few days to explore the surrounding area. My first planned destination was Scarborough, but, at York station, I saw a man collecting for the annual British Legion Poppy Appeal, so I went over as it seemed a good opportunity to understand more about the generous things British people did and why they did them.

"It's the negative things that get all the publicity," said George, the volunteer collecting for the appeal, who was in his seventies and wore a flat cap and a number of medals on his chest.

"It's one terrible tale after another," he went on, "but I must say that we have found people most generous with this appeal. About ten years ago, around the time of the Iraq War, the armed forces were quite unpopular but that's all changed now. This appeals to the innate good nature of people – it raises about £80million a year you know…"

A man walked by, made a donation and took a poppy.

"Did you see that?" he said. "There was an ordinary working chap who put in £10 – a lot of paper money goes in there these days."

People queued patiently, made their donations, shared a few words with George and then moved on.

Two women approached.

"Such attractive people in the North," he said to them. They smiled, made donations and moved off with their poppies.

When they had gone he turned back to me.

"I like to indulge in a little bit of banter," he said.

I asked if the banter helped with the sales.

"We don't actually sell anything," he explained. "We'd have to have a trader's licence and be liable for VAT so we just ask people to make a donation, which they do most generously."

"It used to be just the poppy," he went on, "but we live in a marketing age now so there have to be all these options – big poppies, small poppies, pins, wristbands... The big poppies are the ones the Queen Mother used to wear so they're popular with women of a more mature generation..."

As we waited for people to appear, I asked how long he had served in the armed forces.

"Four decades," he said. "All the usual trouble spots – Korea, Malaya, Northern Ireland..."

I asked him if, in his experience, soldiers felt they were fighting to uphold British culture and values.

"I don't think they have that aspiration," he said. "That's a bit too grand for your average squaddie. I think they see it as an adventure, and, of course, it is – a very dangerous adventure but they don't mind that. I don't think there's any aspiration of fighting for British culture."

Another veteran from Korea came over, and they compared medals.

"Two GSMs," the man said, "that's greedy! I already had mine from Palestine."

George smiled.

They shared stories for a while and then the man continued on his way, leaving George to keep up his patter with the women making donations.

"At the risk of getting into trouble with the health and safety police," he said to one woman who took a poppy, "may I invest you?"

She seemed unsure of what he meant by 'invest', but soon found out as he put a pin into her coat and lodged the poppy in.

"I hope I don't ruin that Armani number," he said to her.

"It's not Armani," she said.

"Oh, very well," he said, "Primark, then."

She went away and others came, and they all got the same routine or variations on it. Large numbers came and made donations, and it was clear that George was happy with how things were going.

"Look at all those notes which have gone in," he said, "and from the most unlikely people."

The people making donations were certainly being very generous so I decided to stay around to talk to them.

"I'm just back from Afghanistan," one man told me, "and we shouldn't forget the sacrifice that everyone's made. I've got three or four poppies in different jackets – you almost feel embarrassed not to be seen with one."

I asked whether, as a soldier, he felt he had been fighting to protect British culture.

"The younger lads just go where they're sent," he said, "but the older you get, the more you pay attention to *why*. But even when you're older, that's not really what you're thinking about – you're just thinking about getting through."

He moved on, and I asked a student why he had donated.

"It's a tough one," he said, "I guess it's just the done thing. My grandparents were in the war and I'm not sure it's something I could do myself so you've got to admire it."

"It's not so much giving the money," he said after thinking about it for a while, "it's showing respect. And everyone wears them on the news – it shows it's a big deal, probably the biggest deal there is, so you know you have to do it and you have to show other people that they should do it, too."

He went on his way, and behind me an elderly lady approached George to make a donation.

"My dear lady," he began, and then corrected himself, "I'm sorry, my dear *young* lady... Any contribution would be much appreciated – dollars, yen, we're not so sure about the euro at the moment..."

"Flattery will get you everywhere," she said, made her donation and moved off.

Behind her, a young Asian man came past and made a donation.

"My granddad's older brother served for the British army," he told me. "A lot of people don't realise you had about three hundred thousand Indian soldiers who served for the British Empire, and I guess that's why it's so important to me."

I thought back to Jatinder in Greenwich, remembering that he had said his father and grandfather had served in the British army too.

"It's a unique campaign," said George as the young man went on. "There are boxes in just about every pub, club, shop, hotel in the land. And we get four days of street collections – all other charity appeals only get one. And it's been going like this for ninety years…"

A young man in an England football shirt approached. I asked him why he had donated, and he looked at me blankly.

"Because everyone's fought for what we've got now," he said after a moment, "but if you look a bit deeper, there's lots of employers who won't let their employees wear them to work because it might offend the foreigners, but those foreigners wouldn't be allowed here now if it wasn't for the armed forces – we'd all be run by Nazis."

Behind me, a woman had approached with two dogs, a Labrador and a Golden Retriever, and George had put poppies into their collars.

"They'll be the talk of the town," he told their owner.

"Oh, bless them," said a woman in the queue and she and the dogs' owner got chatting. I told her about the book and asked why the appeal was important.

"Lots of reasons," one said. "My family were all in Gibraltar and we were all evacuated. And I was in the army and the air force, and this is just for all the soldiers out there – it's a bit sentimental I guess."

"England's good like that," she went on. "It's a bit underrated – but that's not to say it couldn't be better."

They walked away and an older woman with her daughter in her twenties approached. I asked them why they had donated.

"I don't know," said the young woman, "it's difficult to say – it just feels like the right thing to do."

"It's a thank you," said the older woman, "for all the people who fought for us and are still fighting now."

My train was due imminently, so I asked George why he gave up his time to stand in the cold taking donations.

"It's hard work," he said, pushing tobacco into his pipe, "but it's very rewarding. We've lost a lot of people in two world wars, and the wars since, like Afghanistan. And it's not only for them; it's for their families, especially those who were injured. They've got to be looked after – and this is a way to show solidarity with them."

As he said 'solidarity', my mind went back to Stephanie Mitchell and the Belfast Friendship Club which, she had told me, was based on solidarity rather than charity. I had always associated the word 'solidarity' with left-wing politics but I didn't think that either George or Stephanie meant it in a political way; they seemed to mean it almost as the French used the word 'fraternité' – brother- and sister-hood. The poppy seemed a very simple way to show that solidarity with the armed forces and had certainly struck a chord with the people I had met. Indeed, it seemed that the gesture of solidarity, symbolised by the poppy, was almost as important as what the money raised by the appeal was actually spent on.

I thanked George for his time and was just moving away when two men walked past and one realised that he had left his poppy in another jacket. He slipped a five pound note into the collection tin. I asked him why he had done so.

"I've always done it because of my father," he said. "It's just what you do – carry on."

* * * * *

On the train I reflected on the contrast between the often negative views about British society I had heard around the country and the generosity and commitment to the armed forces I had just seen. I wondered if what the country needed was to find ways to enable people to show their solidarity with others in society beyond the armed forces, and whether that could be done not just through annual appeals, but all year round. I thought if that could be done, then it would help to build a sense of common citizenship in the UK that went beyond people simply holding the same passports.

I headed to Scarborough, and it was there, that evening, that I learnt that a British soldier had been killed in Afghanistan earlier in the day.

30

Ethical Dilemmas, the Media and the Past in York and Leeds

In a cafe in York the next day, I met Lisa Mellor, a civil servant and mother of two young children. We talked about parenthood in modern British society and she started by telling me about a television programme she had watched a few days earlier.

"It was about films that had been banned like *A Clockwork Orange,*" she said, "and I thought how that's changed now, with these ridiculous porn-horror films like *Saw* and *The Human Centipede.* I think *A Clockwork Orange* is more dull than anything, but people were banned from watching it, and now you see what's deemed fit for human consumption, there must be some impact of kids seeing it."

I asked her view on where the line between freedom and censorship lay.

"People talk about freedom, don't they?" she said. "But what's good about having the freedom to watch whatever sick horror you want?" And you have to ask, what is the ultimate end of that freedom? That I might get mugged in a few years' time by someone who's been desensitised by watching that kind of sick stuff?"

"I know it sounds like a Mary Whitehouse argument from a different era," she went on, "and that's really been slapped down now. She was portrayed as a figure of fun for trying to curb people's freedoms and we don't question it any more but I've seen some things on TV which I've had to switch off because it's made me feel sick. That's me as an adult, so what does it do to impressionable kids? It must be part of the reason why kids are more violent and disrespectful now."

I asked if she saw that violence and disrespect as she went about her daily life.

"My cycle route home from work goes through the Tang Hall area, which is quite rough," she said. "You get abused by little kids on the cycle path. They use their bikes to stop you getting past. I was even pushing my daughter along one day and a little kid, he could only have been eight or nine, cycled straight at the buggy and then turned at the last minute – deliberately intimidating us. When things like that happen you do question, as a parent, where it's all going."

"I even moved my son's school this year," she continued. "He was in a school which backs on to Tang Hall, and there's something about the kind of area that it covers, some of the parents at the school, and I just didn't want him exposed to that."

"It sounds like a bit of snobbery," she went on, "but one day when I dropped him off at school, some of the parents were continuing on to a hen do straight from the drop-off, and they had inappropriate slogans on their T-shirts, and I just didn't want him in that catchment area with that exposure – they grow up fast enough as it is."

"It feels like a betrayal of your own roots," she continued, "especially when you grow up in a working-class area, and it does feel a bit hypocritical, but when you're a parent, that's what you've got to put first. And if that means sacrificing a few principles, that's what people do, isn't it?"

We talked about her own childhood in Barnsley.

"It wasn't a golden period," she said. "There were problems, but the men all worked in one place and they all drank together… I sound like some kind of old granny, but we did have a community and everybody knew each other and looked out for each other. It creates a bit of a vacuum in those areas when there's an expectation that you're born there, you'll work there and you'll die there, because once you start closing the main places of work, that expectation can't be met. People get depressed and that just permeates through everyone – you feel that even as a kid, even if you can't articulate it."

I remembered a similar feeling in Rotherham and wondered whether it might have been exacerbated by people leaving the town looking for opportunities elsewhere. I asked Lisa whether she would to go back to Barnsley.

"No," she said. "It sounds awful, but in my defence there aren't any government departments there for me to work in. There are more opportunities in York and it's a better place to bring up children."

I asked if she had any potential solutions to the problems we had discussed.

"I wish I did," she said, "but I don't. The saving grace for me was always my teachers and the school. In the absence of a strong parental situation, you've got to put those structures in place somewhere else and school seems an obvious choice."

"I don't know," she went on, "I just see that things are going to get worse. There's too many reasons for why things are the way they are, and there's no one solution. And while we bail out the bankers, my pay is being frozen for two years, youth clubs are being closed – we're going to get what we've asked for, aren't we?"

I asked what her personal response was to all the societal problems she had described.

"Everybody can bleat on and expect the state to take control," she said, "but everyone's got to contribute. It's hard because I work full-time and I've got two small children – and I know that sounds like the ultimate excuse, but long term, once the kids are older, I'd like to get involved in local politics. In the absence of anything else that's all you can do – make a contribution that's meaningful to you. That'll be my small payback, I think."

"In the meantime," she went on, "I'll try to bring the kids up well, let them watch TV but watch what they do and discuss and challenge what they're seeing, and make sure they're not just a passive recipient.

Those are the small things I can do for my family, but you can't tell other people how to bring up their families."

"Maybe that's one of my easy cop-outs," she went on, "to put my son in a more middle-class school. Because it's next to the university all the children are from academics and it's the most multicultural school in York. They speak twenty-five different languages there – that's a great exposure for him."

"That's my defence," she added, smiling.

I said I hadn't been trying to criticise her decision.

"Oh, I know," she said, "but it's easy to go on about society but I think you should either do something about it or shut up. We're all time poor, so you've just got to do what you can. I'd love to put up a tent outside St Paul's and rail against capitalism. If you've got the time to shout out your political beliefs that's great, but if you've got two kids and a full-time job, you can't be as active as you'd like to be."

She had to go, so we got up and headed for the door.

"The more I talk to you," she said, "the less I think I've got to say. It's easier when you're younger – the older you get, the more confused you become. When you're at university, you know what's what, and how things should be, but as you grow up you realise that nobody really knows."

I thought back to Ann Courtney in Malvern, and the challenges of living in a world where the idea that you could look to people in power for answers had been shattered. Lisa had talked about a 'vacuum' in Barnsley, and that seemed to capture the feeling well.

"You think that the powers that be are there for a reason," she added as we said goodbye, "but the older you get, the more you realise that everyone's just winging it."

* * * * *

That afternoon, I headed over to Leeds to meet Gavin Emmett, a sports journalist in his mid thirties. We met in a cafe and, over a cup of tea, he told me about his perception of life in the UK, having lived abroad.

"One of the things I found coming back from Spain," he said, "is that people have got quite a bad opinion of what they've got here but if you've lived abroad then you notice that it's not as broken as people try to make out. You'd pay more taxes in most European countries, you've got a worse standard of living and the bureaucracy is incredible."

"In one way it makes you proud," he went on, "that we've got a society which, in general, works. I know there are things people have gripes about – like here in Yorkshire, where it rains all the time, the reservoirs ran dry – and it's quite a British thing to moan, but generally it's not as bad as they make out, and a lot of this Broken Britain stuff really gets my goat. I've been to South Africa, I've been to India, and you see people who have nothing. I know people here expect a certain standard of living but I think people need to take a step back."

"But having said that," he added, "appreciating something for what you've got is really hard because people always want more – I'm party to that and I think everyone is in this country because it's the culture."

I asked what he meant.

"It's all linked into the media," he explained. "Everyone's got forty channels and with the power of the Internet, it has this attack on the senses. For me, it all comes back to the media portrayal of society: is it a story they're telling rather than a reflection of the society we're actually in? Like the riots, it's such a minority of people involved but it becomes a vehicle to say the country is broken when 99 per cent of people in this country just want to have a decent life and do what they've got to do."

"And people say they're marginalised," he went on, "but I worry they might feel marginalised from the society that's depicted, rather than the actual society. You get this portrayal in the media of this being a bad place to live, and people feel marginalised because they don't want to be part of that. I think there's a discrepancy between the people in this country, and what we're told the people are like."

It was an interesting perspective, and contrasted with the view I had heard that young people had looted during the riots because the media had raised their expectations so much that they felt left out if they didn't have the latest gadget. It also echoed my own experience that, while I had discussed some serious concerns with people, I had found them overwhelmingly kind and generous.

I asked Gavin how he felt the media should deal with an incident like the riots.

"It has to be reported," he said, "but *responsible* reporting. It was just the way hysteria was created – 24-hour rolling news, all the time, everywhere – it was just a barrage. I'm not saying the past was better; I think it's great that people have access to all these channels – it's the industry I work in and it's a cheap way for people to pass the time, but people are really easily influenced by media and there's a lot of responsibility that's not being taken, like with the *News of the World*."

"Northern Rock is another example," he went on. "Of course people were going to queue if you report that this bank might go to the wall. There's always an argument from the media, 'We have to report it, people want to know,' but sometimes I get a sensation that the media is telling us what people are thinking, not the other way around."

"I know one thing I'll never do," he went on, "is believe anything I see or read – I'm a complete cynic. If I see something in the paper, I'll try to read two or three different versions, find out the whole story. I won't ever touch the *Daily Mail*, I won't go near it. *The Guardian* is a paper I would probably read, but even with that I find myself really cynical and that's when I think I'm just going to jack everything in and live for peanuts in some far-flung corner of the world – get completely off the radar."

"I went to public school," he continued, "but I'm from a working-class background and I'm definitely at heart a lefty-liberal, but, when you earn a decent living, it's hard to keep that philosophy going and have the life that you want, going out for a couple of nice dinners a week and shopping at the shops you want to. I think a lot of people have that conflict where they want to do more for charity, but I find I don't actually have time – I think a lot of people are caught in that middle-class bubble, where they think 'I'm not as bad as that banker or whatever,' so you end up shopping at Sainsbury's, not your local greengrocer, and that's like 'the man' is getting his way."

"You're caught in a kind of paradox," he went on, "of knowing that I don't want anyone to be poor or have to suffer but also wanting to be successful in my own life. For me, it's not about money. I could have stayed in Spain where I was on the board of a big company and yet I came back, decided to do the journalistic thing, and have less money but a better standard of life, but yet I still find myself subscribing to all these aspirational things of wanting a house or a car. I would love to be a paragon of virtue but, by the same token, that would mean giving up a lot of the things I like and enjoy."

"This is completely unrelated," he went on, "but I saw this programme the other day about social structures, and there was a time when you were either aristocracy or you were a serf, which meant you were in service to somebody, or you were a freeman, which meant you had a trade or you had your own business, and I know it was a long time ago but it's still quite relevant. Emancipation has got to be a great thing, because people start to think for themselves and value their own lives, but, in the past, it probably just worked a bit more. Everybody had some part in society, their place."

"I sound like a dictator now," he continued. "What I mean is that everyone had a role to play. And, yeah, I'm sure it was really cruel and it's great that people don't live like that any more but, by the same token, it's a system that worked, not necessarily the right way but it all comes back to that thing of people recognising what they actually need to survive. It also links to the sense of community – community in this country has dissipated a bit and I think it comes from a lack of trust. I think our trust in strangers has diminished massively, even in my life. I don't mean to sound like an old fogey, but it's true. I'm guilty of it; even in my block I don't know anyone."

I asked where he felt that mistrust came from.

"I think it's because we're constantly told about bad things," he said. "The media is a small part of society but it's so influential in every aspect of our lives. It scares me that it can be that influential but then I work in it... In a completely different side, obviously – what I do is sport but if you were cynical about it you could say it's the same thing, selling sponsorship or adverts, but I see it as just entertainment, really."

As we said goodbye, his point about the serfs and the aristocracy stuck with me, making me think again about what it said about the country's relationship with its past and how uncomfortable many people felt in modern Britain. He had to be right that things were better in the UK both than in the past and in most other countries, but that didn't seem to have translated into British people feeling happier and more secure. If anything, it felt quite the opposite, with Gavin's worries about the way society was portrayed in the media and Lisa's concern about the lack of role models in society seemingly part of the reason why. As I headed to the North-West, I wanted to look at initiatives and institutions that could support people as they sought to navigate their way in this complex, challenging world.

31

Cultural Institutions and Nostalgia in Carlisle and Blackpool

In the Lanes Shopping Centre in the heart of Carlisle, there was a buzz around as the *Blue Peter* crew prepared to start filming a bake sale in aid of Children in Need. Having heard that the sale was on, I had come along hoping to learn some lessons from successful British cultural institutions.

The sale started at four p.m. and, as children from a local school went around the crowd, selling cakes and taking money in a small Tupperware container, I talked to the crowd of people watching on – shoppers passing by or parents of children taking part – about what *Blue Peter* meant to them and how it contributed to British society.

"For me," one woman watching on with her young daughter said, "it's the same things that I did when I was young – bake sales, volunteering..."

"It's just childhood, isn't it?" she continued, and then gestured to her daughter. "And even though I'm grown up, she still likes it. Though we would have liked a bit of Barney here today, wouldn't we?"

She looked at her daughter, who seemed embarrassed.

"Barney is the other presenter," she explained. "He's a good-looking young man."

Another mother standing nearby had brought her son along and I asked her what she thought.

"You're better off asking him," she said, gesturing towards her son. "He's the one who watches it."

"It's just a nice programme," the boy said, smiling, "and they're always doing something nice – like now they're raising money for Children in Need."

I asked him why that was important.

"Because you're raising money for people who need help," he said.

They went on their way, and I got talking to a couple walking past. I asked them if they were *Blue Peter* fans.

"Tracy Island," the man said with a smile, "years and years ago. They always used to make things."

"Here's one I made earlier," said his girlfriend, "like the *Thunderbirds*."

"That's what I meant about Tracy Island," he said and they both smiled as they realised that, while they had met in their twenties, they had watched the same programme as children.

"It's a bit of an institution," the man went on, "one of those stable things in life."

They decided they wanted to make a contribution so they went to buy some cakes, and I found a woman and her daughter watching on. I asked the mother why they liked *Blue Peter*.

"It's one of those things," she said. "It's something I identify with because I watched it when I was a child, so now, when she watches it, it feels like a family thing. It's something that's always been there, and they're always doing something for the community – it was never just the telly."

Her husband came over.

"It's just childhood memories, isn't it?" he agreed. "It's important that things which were going when I was young are still going now. And what it stands for too – good rules for life: it helps kids raise funds, helps them make things… Fairy Liquid bottles, sticky-back plastic – that's a phrase in our language now, isn't it?"

"It just teaches good moral values," he concluded, "a genuine caring approach."

I thanked them and moved on to a couple with their young son.

"It's just an institution," the husband said, smiling. "Everybody knows *Blue Peter*."

I asked why that was important.

"It's just something we all share in common," he said.

"It's straightforward," his wife went on, "not like things these days. It's nice, in this modern world, to have something from the past – you don't want everything new."

The sale was still going, and someone had given a megaphone to one of the girls. "Buy for Children in Need," she whispered cautiously into it, before being overtaken by nerves and returning it to one of the crew.

I found a couple in their fifties looking on.

"It's just childhood memories," said the wife. "Monday and Thursday, wasn't it?"

"John Noakes, Shep, Peter Purvis, and Val..." said her husband.

"The incident with the elephant..." she said.

"I just loved it," he said, laughing to himself.

"It just gives you a really nice feeling," she said, "nice and bright and safe."

I asked what she meant by safe, but she struggled to explain.

"Even when they had that fire," she said, "they were so cool about it. I can't put it into words... It's that feeling of normality – of how the world should really be."

"When you have kids of your own," her husband added, "you're concerned – all the things going on in the world. But when your kids are watching *Blue Peter*, they're home, they're safe."

"It's how it should be," his wife said, "but we know it can't be."

As the sale came to an end, people hugged each other goodbye. Some of the cakes were left over, so I bought some for the journey to Blackpool. As I walked to the station, I felt that it had been a nice afternoon with good lessons about what made *Blue Peter* successful: shared experiences, reliable role models, strong but not overbearing values encapsulated in actions rather than words. But there was a feeling of sadness around, too, as if *Blue Peter* showed how far modern British life was from what people wanted it to be.

At the train station, I looked into the bag of cakes I had bought. Wrapped alongside them was a piece of paper with a note in a child's handwriting:

'Show a child you care; by helping Pudsey Bear; and buying what we bake; fancy a spot of Cake?'

* * * * *

I had organised to stay near Blackpool with James Bamford, a physics teacher in his thirties, and the next day, a beautiful Saturday, James, his brother Andrew and a couple of their friends took me to Blackpool Tower. Having never visited before, I was struck by the Tower's size, and, as we made our way to the top, we were told that it was made from two thousand tonnes of iron and ninety-five miles of cast steel. It had been built by the Mayor of Blackpool who had seen the Eiffel Tower and wanted his home town to have something similar.

We reached the top and stepped on to the viewing platform. One side had a glass floor looking straight down over the people on the street hundreds of feet below. One of Andrew's friends had a fear of heights, and stayed well clear of the glass floor.

"It would be OK if I couldn't see the people," she said, "they're so small."

A woman walking past touched her arm.

"Don't think about them as people, love," she said, "think of them as dolls."

I looked down and was surprised to be able to read the words 'Nice to see you, to see you nice' inscribed on the pavement far below. It turned out to be part of the 'Comedy Carpet', a series of quotes from performers who had performed in Blackpool over the years inscribed into the pavement opposite the Tower.

When we came down from the Tower, I decided to go out on to the Comedy Carpet. Around the edge were the names of comedians and singers who were part of Blackpool folklore: Vera Lynn, George Formby, Cilla Black, Ken Dodd. Some of the UK's most famous comedy quotes were inscribed on the pavement, from Tony Hancock's blood donation to Monty Python's 'Always look on the bright side of life'.

'I was born in the town of Erith in Kent,' one joke read. 'It's not twinned with anywhere but it has a suicide pact with Dagenham.'

'Did I ever tell you about my first house?' read another. 'They tore it down to build a slum!'

'I'm not a snob,' a third read, 'but I wear a bowler hat in the bath because you never know who might call.'

I reflected that the quotes seemed to have been carefully chosen to ensure that jokes from the past that might have been considered offensive in a modern context were not included and decided to talk to other people on the Carpet to see what they thought.

"It's different," said a woman standing next to me, "and it definitely takes you back. It's good for Blackpool to have something like this."

"Have you ever seen so many people looking at their feet and laughing?" another woman said. "It really gets people talking to each other; it starts a conversation…"

"We came specifically to see this," she told me. "We thought we'd see what all the fuss is about. And it's good – to youngsters this won't mean a lot because they won't know the jokes and the phrases but it's very good in my view."

"For us older ones," another woman said, "it's quite a trip down memory lane; it takes us back. It's interesting to watch people; they've all got silly grins on their faces."

I asked whether Blackpool and its comedy were culturally important to the UK.

"It is in a way," she said, "but as we older ones die off, these jokes will mean less to people. Like Arthur Askey – he was very famous."

I said I hadn't come across him before.

"Sid," she said to her husband, "this young man doesn't know who Arthur Askey was."

Her husband came over.

"Oh, he was very famous," he said, "from the late thirties, through the forties and fifties… His catchphrase was 'Hello, playmates' – small guy, wore big glasses…"

He looked around at the people smiling and laughing and looking down at the pavement.

"There's definitely a feel-good factor," he said as the sun set over the sea behind him.

I walked around for a while, and he was certainly right about the feel-good factor. People laughed and smiled and talked to strangers about the jokes. As I left, even though the sun had set and it was getting cold, people were still walking around, looking down, laughing and remembering. Hundreds of swallows swept across the sky as the lights came on at the Tower.

* * * * *

In the car on the way back to James's house, I asked James, Andrew and their friends Laura and Chris for their thoughts about life in the UK.

"I hate it here," said Andrew, "and I want to leave. I don't like all the people that are around nowadays – there don't seem to be any decent people around and there's so much chaviness."

I asked what he meant by 'chaviness'.

"Look out the window," he said. "It's literally everyone here. The way that they are all stupidly young and have children, the way they scrounge off benefits…"

"Daytime drinking," added Laura.

"Yeah," said Andrew, "like the guy we saw."

While I had been speaking to people on the Comedy Carpet, they had seen a drunk man shouting abusively at his child.

"It's common in Blackpool," Andrew added.

"Not just Blackpool," said Laura. "I used to work in an off-licence in Cleveleys and I remember one woman used to put everything down on the till and, when she realised she couldn't afford it all, she'd put the dog food and the kids' food back and the cans of beer would still go through."

"Nice selection process," said Andrew.

"The dog food went first…" said Laura.

I suggested that the majority of people weren't like that.

"No," said Laura, "but I do think everyone's just a bit fed up at the moment and in a bit of a slump – I just think there's a nationwide fed-up-ness."

"It's the time of year as well," said Chris. "You're getting close to Christmas and you're expected to buy a lot of things and, if you can't afford them, everyone seems more depressed."

They started talking about whether it would be a white Christmas, and the conversation moved on to snowball fights.

"We had a great one in the forest behind our barn with those local kids," said James.

"We always end up having fights with random people," said Andrew.

I said it reminded me of the Comedy Carpet, where the jokes had got people talking with one other.

"A woman once bought me a cup of tea on the train," said Laura. "We were just having a nice chat. I hadn't got any money and she wanted a coffee and felt bad about just getting one for herself so she got me one, too. We just carried on talking."

"Unless you're in the train," said Chris, "you don't tend to just start chatting to someone. The art of conversation just seems to have gone. Even on a night out, where you think it's a sociable environment, if you go up to someone they look at you like, 'What have you come to talk to me for?'"

"Do you remember when we were kids?" Andrew said to James. "We would always play out, cycle around… Nowadays, you don't see that. And you can't leave your door open."

"That's a common thing that everyone says," said James, and, though it was something I had heard a lot as I travelled, I was surprised to hear it from someone of Andrew's age, twenty-two.

I asked him why he thought it was the case.

"They've got other things to do," he said, "computer games and the Internet."

I asked whether he thought technological advances were a good thing.

"Yeah," he said as we parked, "but they stop other things from happening."

* * * * *

Andrew's words stayed with me that night as they took me to a club in the town of Poulton-le-Fylde, near where they lived. I thought back to my conversations in York, Leeds and Carlisle, as well as in Scotland and Northern Ireland, where I had again and again encountered the sense that things weren't as good in the UK as they had been in the past. I realised that, in the early part of my journey, I had been quick to dismiss these feelings as nostalgic but it was becoming increasingly difficult to do so, coming as the views did from so many different people from a range of different ages and classes. While there might have been some nostalgia around – for example, at the Comedy Carpet where jokes from the past seemed to have been carefully edited – it appeared there was also a real sense of loss and confusion around. I hadn't found the societal panic Fran in Darlington had described, but there was a feeling of sadness and uncertainty, and I wanted to understand more about that before my journey ended.

As James, Andrew and their friends enjoyed their Saturday evening, I walked around the bar, taking in the atmosphere.

"Football's no good any more," someone said. "They're all gays diving everywhere."

"My heels are fine," said a girl, "it's just the balls of my feet that are fucking burning."

"Some more whores over there," said a man to his friend.

"There's so much tail out tonight I can't cope," his friend replied.

"That's a fucking painful bird," the first man said, gesturing at a woman across a bar.

"That's my fucking cousin," his friend said.

We left an hour later, heading for another bar down the road, and, as we walked, a man retched in the bushes. Further down the road, a police van sped past in pursuit of a car and, outside the bar we were heading to, there was another police van waiting.

"What the fuck is going on with Poulton?" someone said.

"My friend's brother got bottled in Kendall of all places," his friend said. "Everywhere's getting like this now."

While the others headed into the bar, I stayed outside. It was midnight and people were drunkenly milling around. Beside me, the police patted down two young men, eventually cuffing them and leading them away. A couple staggered past me, arm in arm, the man holding the woman's purse. Behind them, a man asked a woman for a cigarette and an argument developed between them.

"Fuck off," she said. "I fucking hate people like you."

"Do you think you're better than me?" said the man.

"Do you want me to answer that honestly?" the woman asked sarcastically.

"Well you can fuck off then with your fucking Chihuahua," said the man. They almost came to blows, the woman's boyfriend having to hold them apart.

"You better keep your fucking bitch in order," the man shouted.

Around the corner, a woman approached a police officer and told him her bag had been stolen with her phone inside.

"I've got a sixteen-year-old daughter at home without a key," she said.

The police officer said he was unable to help.

"We're not miracle workers," he said. "Have you seen how chaotic it is tonight? There's nothing we can do."

"It's not chaotic," the woman said.

"OK," the police officer said, "I'm walking away now."

"OK," she said, "I'm going to call 999."

"You call 999," he said, "and I'm going to arrest you for wasting police time."

"Prick," she said.

"You call me prick one more time and I'll arrest you," he said.

For a moment, she seemed to contemplate opening her mouth again but eventually she thought better of it and went.

Behind her, a woman fell in the street and a man stumbled over and was led away by the police.

"Probably because he got his helmet out," another man explained to me. "I saw it but I didn't ogle it."

As they cuffed him, bouncers chased another man down the road.

I asked the man standing next to me why people drank so much.

"Why not?" he said.

32

Body Image, Self-esteem and Celebrity Culture in Thornton and Manchester

The following evening, I went to meet Sophie Meredith, a woman in her twenties who had set up a project for children and young people that focused on media literacy and self-esteem. Over a drink in a pub in Thornton, a village not far from Blackpool, she told me how the project had developed when she had studied sociology at university and become interested in feminism, gender and the perceptions women and men had of themselves and of others.

"My research began with me going into primary schools," she said, "and talking to the children about how they saw themselves, what they wanted to do when they grew up, how they viewed their peers, who their influences were and what kind of media they came into contact with. It was shocking how many girls told me 'I want to be a glamour model' and I found the number of children under the age of seven who knew what a Page Three Girl is really unsettling."

"I asked under-tens to list three things they wanted to achieve when they grew up," she went on, "and all of the girls said that they wanted to be 'pretty' while the majority of boys said they wanted to be rich. You couldn't get two more stereotypical answers."

In response, Sophie told me she had set up an independent educational organisation called SEE – Self-esteem and Empowerment through Education – that visited schools and colleges around the country delivering classes and workshops looking at the connections between media literacy, body image and self-esteem.

"I devise and deliver media literacy classes," she said, "to help my students understand what they're engaging with. You can't control the media – it's everywhere and it influences everything – but what you can do is teach people how to engage with it critically. It's a key thing that's missing from the curriculum."

"So you open up a women's magazine," she went on, "and it uses a dialogue which says 'You can be the best you that you can be' but the real message is 'You can be the best you that you can be if you buy all the products that we've been paid to advertise.'"

We talked on and the conversation moved to celebrities. She mentioned Lady Gaga, who she felt used a 'pro-equality' agenda to achieve commercial success.

"She uses a language that appeals to children and teenagers particularly," Sophie said, "because it communicates 'I know what you're going through, I've been there', but at the same time she's putting out this hyper-sexualised, available, damaged, 'it's cool to be broken' kind of attitude, which isn't particularly positive."

The conversation moved on to body image.

"It's a big issue for girls, and for boys increasingly," she said. "Working with children opened my eyes to how much pressure is increasingly on men and boys. I spoke to a boy who was twelve, and he was counting down the days until he was old enough to join the gym, because his dad weight-lifted and he wanted to lift weights, too…"

I thought of the young men in south Wales Howard Williamson had told me were obsessed with sunbeds and steroids, but before discussing male body image I wanted to finish the discussion on young women.

"There are so many requirements which make up the ideal that women never feel like they tick all the boxes," Sophie said. "If you're not skinny you're not beautiful, if you haven't got big breasts you're not beautiful, if you haven't got a tiny waist you're not beautiful, if you're not blonde you're not beautiful… The definition of perfection is constantly changing, so ideas of what is right and what is wrong are constantly changing. If you're a young person trying to figure out who you are, and you're being told 'Be this way', 'No, don't be that way, be this way but also be a bit like this and while you're at it, try to be a little bit like this, too', you're never going to feel like your feet are on the ground – you feel like you need to be everything all at once."

We moved on to talking about airbrushing, and she told me that her media literacy classes looked in great depth at the digital manipulation of body images. She said that not only did models in airbrushed photos go through hours of professional make-up, but they also posed in an environment that was conducive to flattering photography, and then images were digitally enhanced.

"That's three hits of fabrication in one image that is supposed to communicate a reality," she said, "but that image is in fact a complete lie."

I asked about the digital changes that could now be made to photos, and she gave me a long list that included airbrushing out of blemishes and wrinkles, thinning women's waists, extending the length of legs, stretching the whole image to make the model appear taller, adding gloss to hair and plumping lips.

"I show my children a video that Dove produced, which goes through the airbrushing process step by step," she said, "and the picture at the end is completely different from the initial photograph. My children sit there stunned and I hear an unbelieving 'Whoa, is that actually the same person?'"

I asked what the effects of all of this were on the girls she taught.

"Self-doubt, self-hatred and a real preoccupation with self-monitoring," she said.

The discussion of photo-shopped images made me think of Ann and Alan Courtney in Malvern talking about myths of a happy past and Issac and G, the community workers in Belfast, talking about a romanticised view of the Troubles in Northern Ireland. They were very different examples, but in each case it seemed that the line between reality and myth had been blurred, and there was the potential for harm to be done as a result.

I asked her about whether eating disorders and self-harm were also issues she encountered, and whether they were linked to the issues we had been discussing.

"Oh, yeah," she said, "absolutely, without fail – in fact, they're increasing amongst boys and girls. It's very rare that I'll go to a school and not meet someone who is suffering an eating disorder."

We moved on to talking about boys and young men because she had mentioned both anorexia amongst young men and children wanting to join the gym and become muscular like their fathers. I asked if there was not a contradiction between wanting to be thin and wanting to be muscular.

"That relates to what I was saying before," she said. "As a woman you've got to be thin, you've got to have large breasts, you've got to be curvaceous – there's no 'correct' way and it's the same with men."

"As a woman," she went on, "you're taught from a very young age that part of your job as a woman is to look a certain way, and not for your own benefit, but for men, and there's this definite idea that still exists now that you're not successful unless you're attractive to men."

I asked if she had any last words about the children she had spoken to and why this issue was so important.

"It's so important because individual identity is so important," she said. "There is so much pressure on young people to behave or look a certain way that the joy of life, quite simply, is extinguished."

As I left, she wished me well with the book and I reflected that the work she was doing was highly valuable in helping children to negotiate an increasingly complex world. From my travels, I felt that, in addition to rebuilding social bonds, the UK clearly needed to do more to help people – not just children, but adults, too – to find their way in this difficult world.

* * * * *

The next day I travelled to Manchester on the next stage of my journey and, while in the centre of the city, I passed a group of teenagers waiting at the back entrance to the Manchester Evening News arena. One wore a T-shirt that read 'OGD – Obsessive Gaga Disorder' while another had brought a homemade sign: 'We love you Gaga', it read.

The conversation with Sophie still fresh in my mind, I went over to see what was going on. There were about thirty or forty young people taking photos with their mobile phones by the gates at the back of the Arena, and it turned out that this was where celebrities were arriving for that evening's Children in Need concert, with Lady Gaga the headline act.

A car pulled in and there was much excitement.

"Is that definitely her?" someone said, peering through the gates.

"Yeah," said someone else, "it's her car."

"No, it's not her," said someone else. "Her security's not with her."

On tiptoes they peered over each other's shoulders to try to catch a glimpse.

"Gaga!" they shouted, "Gaga!"

"I wish she'd get out of the fucking car!"

They edged into the street, blocking traffic as they tried to see if it was indeed Lady Gaga and singing her songs to try to attract her attention.

"You'll get run over," said a steward who was manning the gate.

"Then I'll get run over," a girl said. "I've been elbowed in the face for Gaga before so I don't give a shit."

People walking by, including a mother pushing her pram, had to walk out into the road as the fans pushed towards the gate, trying to get a better look. It soon became clear that it hadn't been Lady Gaga, and the fans went back to taking photos of each car that drove in, even those with blacked-out windows.

I approached a group of two young women and a young man and asked what motivated them to stay in the cold waiting for celebrities.

"It's the thrill of seeing them," said the young man.

"When you meet them, they're really nice," said one of the young women, "and it's just a nice day out."

"It's more fun than it looks," she added, seeing me shivering in the late afternoon cold. "We've been here since eleven."

I asked how their college felt about them being here.

"I just walked out at lunchtime – they don't check on you," said the young man, "and it's only psychology."

I asked them why Lady Gaga was such an icon for them.

"She's brilliant," the young man said. "She fights for what she believes in."

"She basically says you can be who you want to be," said one of the young women.

I asked them about photo-shopping and celebrities setting unrealistic expectations for young people.

"Gaga's not photo-shopped," she said. "My cousin's friend met her and she's just really normal."

Next to them were another two young women and a young man. I asked why they were here.

"It was her idea," the young man said, pointing to his friend.

"It's not every day Lady Gaga is in the UK, is it?" the young woman said, looking out over the railings.

"She's an icon," agreed her friend. "Everyone can relate to her because she represents everyone."

"You feel like she understands you personally," said the young man, "and she has a lot of time for her fans."

A coach full of young people pulled past, and they began making clawing motions at the fans I was standing with, who in turn responded with the same motion.

"That's the 'Lady Gaga wave'," the young man explained. "It's called 'Paws Up' – it's from the *Bad Romance* video, and it really caught on."

I asked him what he thought about the celebrity airbrushing debate.

"That's the controversial one," he said, "and I think it's important not to get caught up in it, but every now and again I think it's OK to just get swept up and say, 'Oh my God, it's Lady Gaga!'"

I asked whether celebrities set unrealistic expectations for young people.

"But that's exactly what Lady Gaga is saying," he said. "She was going to watch Madonna in concert and wondering if she'd ever get there herself. It shows you can achieve the way she has achieved in whatever you want."

A car drew up with blackened windows, and they got excited for a moment. The excitement faded as a woman got out.

"Just another stylist…" he said.

I asked if Gaga was an inspiration.

"Absolutely," he said. "I know why you're asking but if you asked anyone here if Lady Gaga made them feel bad about themselves, they'd say absolutely not."

It got darker and colder. A young man ate pasta out of a Tupperware container; some of the young women texted and tweeted on their phones. Expectations rose every time a car with darkened windows appeared, but Lady Gaga was nowhere to be seen.

"I'm the smallest but I'm at the back," said a girl to her friends.

"But you came last," said someone else. "Remember how much you complained at One Direction…"

"If anyone else comes out you can go forward – I just want to see Lady Gaga!"

Suddenly, they began screaming: a group of cars had pulled in, and there was speculation that Lady Gaga had been in one of them. Once the cars were through the gates, the steward came out.

"That's everyone in," he said.

"What, Gaga's in?" someone asked.

"Yeah," he said, "she just went in."

He closed the gates.

"She wouldn't just have gone in," said a girl. "She would have waved or something."

"Seriously, that's it," said the steward. "I swear on my kid's life."

"He doesn't have kids," someone said. "He's lying, we would have seen her."

"He's chatting shit," someone else said.

"What way was her hair?" another asked.

"Her hair was in a bob," he said.

"Bullshit," someone said.

"He's chatting absolute shit," someone else added.

Soon they began to believe him, however, and started sending messages to Lady Gaga via Twitter.

"Keep tweeting her," someone said. "Tell her to come out."

"I'm tweeting her," a girl said. "I'm saying 'Please come outside, we're freezing.'"

I waited with them for half an hour, but she didn't appear. After a while, a father arrived to collect his daughter but she refused to go with him.

"I'm not going anywhere," she told him. "If we missed her on the way in, we'll just get her on the way out."

33

Community Division, Government Investment and the UK's Future in Rochdale

I headed east from Manchester to meet Eric Noi, a father of two who ran a boxing and personal development centre in Oldham. We met in the cafe of a leisure centre near to where he grew up – the Langley estate in Rochdale – and I asked him how he felt things were going nationally.

"We haven't seen anything yet," he said. "We're on the tip of a big iceberg. The cuts are going to go very deep and, as always, it's the most vulnerable who are going to feel it. I just think we've attempted to continue to provide a lifestyle which financially we are not capable of – if you look at each country as a business, the bottom line is that you need to sell more than you bring in to balance the books, and we haven't been doing that for a long time."

"Just look at football now," he went on, "which at one time was the sport of the working class – it's not the same crowds who were going thirty, forty, fifty years ago. There's been a massive demographic shift and it's highlighted by the unrealistic pay packages the players get. My sport, boxing, is one of the last sports of the true working poor because the barriers to entry are very limited."

I asked what fuelled his passion for boxing.

"I'm a cliché," he said. "You know, dad died when I was two, I was one of nine with a chaotic upbringing, but three nights a week I knew where I was going – to the gym. It instilled self-discipline, but more importantly it instilled self-respect and self-confidence and that enabled me to be myself. And that is what I say with young people I work with – be yourself. A lot of the time, just out of survival, they can't be themselves because up in estates like the Langley you've got to be tough. Qualities like intelligence and creativity attract unwanted attention. So, the whole hoodie thing; that's a tribalistic sign to say 'Don't mess with me, I'm a bad boy.' So the first thing I say to young people is to take their street armour off."

I asked what he meant by street armour.

"The mannerisms," he explained, "the attitude, the way they speak, the abrasiveness, the adversarial culture. To be yourself is the hardest thing for everyone that we work with."

I asked if he was talking specifically about young black males.

"It's a *male* thing," he said. "In Manchester, where I'm from, it can become a self-fulfilling prophesy, the media and the hip-hop videos – a lot of young people do buy into that and try to live that stereotype. I had it – you're black so they expect you can dance and everyone feared the black boxer. So you use it – if people want to think that and it can gain you some prestige, some advantage, then I'll buy into that."

"It's changing now," he went on, "because the world is changing and, thankfully, the media is evolving and realising that we have, for example, a black president of America. But I'm seeing it now within the Asian community in Oldham – this lost generation of young men, they have the old-world culture and the new Western culture, and mixed ideas about who they are. So what they have done, in my opinion, is looked at the black experience. The levels of racism which existed in Britain were unbelievable, and young black men were very confrontational about it and they beat it down. You know, the Notting Hill riots, black power... Eventually it was a kind of 'Fear us and then you'll respect us' type of thing and I think the Asian experience is wanting to have some of that."

"I remember in the seventies and eighties 'Paki-bashing' was a sport in poor areas," he went on, "and they've looked at the black experience and thought, 'That's what we're going to do' –'Paki-pride', call it what you want, but they've aped the gang culture. When I see them acting like that, I say, 'You ain't ghetto, you ain't never gonna be ghetto; there ain't no ghetto heaven, it ain't like that – when you go home you've got two parents at home and you've got your nice curry on the table and I bet you go to mosque on a Friday where you're instilled with ideals and morals.' It's hip-hop culture being sold for people to make money. 'Let's sell the ghetto, package it'. But young people are not realising that it's not real."

It seemed to be another myth having a real impact, reminding me of what Sophie Meredith had said about women living up to a manufactured image of beauty. I asked whether in his view the issues he was talking about were particular to Oldham or were spread across the whole of the UK.

"The unique thing in Oldham is the cultural divide," he said. "It's akin to South Africa in some respects. I can walk in parts of Oldham – Upper Mill, Saddleworth Park – very exclusive, middle class, and not see another brown face. And I can go to Glodwick, a Pakistani area, and not see a white face. My gym is one of the most culturally mixed, cohesive places within the whole town."

"You've got extremes on both sides," he continued. "You've got your skinhead white working underclass, ignorant, racist bigots, using the word 'Paki' left, right and centre, and then you've got your extreme Asian lads. They go to school at Breeze Hill, an all-Asian school, so they see no white people, and then they go back to Glodwick and see no white people and go into their house where they speak in their native tongue. It's only when they come to my gym, where they are meeting white people, which breaks down their misconceptions."

"I think Amir Khan has done more for race relations than millions of pounds worth of state-sponsored multiculturalism," he went on. "The most natural thing is having things in common, having shared frames of reference and, in this instance, it's the boxing."

I asked about the divide between the communities.

"It's a lack of understanding," he said. "If we don't understand something, we fear it; we're hardwired that way from when we lived in caves. And that has been exploited by extremists on both sides. There has been lots of cohesive work and the two secondary schools, one white and one Asian, have joined to form the new academy. It'll take ten years for kids to integrate properly, but it will happen bit by bit."

I reflected on what he had said, how similar the situation he was describing was to issues I had encountered in Belfast, and wondered whether lessons from Northern Ireland could be employed in the rest of the UK to break down social divisions.

We talked on, and Eric told me he didn't want to simply focus our discussion on local issues.

"I'm reading *The Decline and Fall of the Roman Empire*," he told me, "and there are similarities to where Britain is with a massive bureaucratic system. They couldn't afford to maintain theirs, and you can see the same thing happening here. And it's not just happening overnight, it's been the last thirty years. Partly, I think it's a recalibration."

I asked him what he meant by recalibration.

"Recalibration of the world order, perhaps," he explained. "You can see it happening now regarding the Western influence on other countries and world politics."

I asked if he meant power moving east.

"Not just east – look at Brazil," he said.

"What we need to be doing now is managing people's expectations," he continued, "because expectations are going up while our wealth and global position is going down."

I asked what happened when expectations went up and wealth went down.

"Riots," he said with a smile.

"Humbling," he went on after a moment, "we all need humbling. We need to make kids value what we have now. But it's harder now because the capitalist ideals have gone global and are being delivered in a more efficient way by the Chinese through state-sponsored capitalism.

You can't beat them when they're getting into it with a complete disregard for human and environmental rights."

I asked what would happen to the young people he worked with if China and India eclipsed Western economies and the UK had a prolonged period of stagnation or decline.

"It would leave them hopeless," he said, "and you just hope it's not too late to turn the corner. With my children I try to equip them with ideals and morals but, at the same time, they need to be tough – mentally tough, and emotionally tough."

"It was interesting what the Chinese said about not supporting the Greek bailout," he added. "They used the word 'sloth', telling us they weren't going to support our 'slovenly welfare system'."

I asked if China and other emerging economies were in control now.

"Of course they are," he said.

* * * * *

We stepped out of the leisure centre and into bright sunshine, Eric's words about China still echoing in my head. I realised that, while I had been focusing on domestic issues, I had lost sight of the question posed earlier in my journey about the UK's place in the world, which would have a huge impact on the lives of all of the people I had met.

Eric had offered to take me on a tour around Langley in his car, and, as we drove through what was a huge housing estate made up of four thousand homes, we saw Terry Smith, an old friend of Eric's. Terry was loading a van by the side of the road and we pulled in to talk to him. He and Eric started talking about 'meteorite money' and I asked Terry what that meant.

"It's money that starts off big from the government," he said, "but, by the time it gets through every single layer of bureaucracy and arrives in the community it was meant to get to, the vast majority has been burned away."

I said I was surprised that had happened here because it looked like there had been a lot of investment in new housing on the estate.

"There's an old saying," said Terry, "which goes, 'You can put a millionaire in a tent and he'll be alright; you can put a poor man in a mansion and he'll still be poor.' It's not just about bricks and mortar."

It was a beautiful day but there didn't seem to be many people around, so I asked where they all were if they weren't working.

"You've got those that generally go out every day trying to get a job," he said, "you've got those that think 'What's the point?', and you've got those that have always worked because they have been in a trade that their parents have been in…"

"…and then you've got the 'alternative industries', shall we say," Eric added.

"But the problem with that is it's not like the old days," said Terry. "Ten years ago there was loads of stuff coming through the estate, at Easter there were thousands of Easter eggs, in summer, you'd have all the summer clothes, at Christmas all the Christmas stuff, but not any more. The police have got on top of that. These warehouses are reinforced now and they've got technology which stops all that. The only thing left is drugs – that's the only industry the police can't get a grip on."

"It's not all doom and gloom," he went on, "but they have got to give the money to these kids to become entrepreneurs. Thirty years ago you could throw a fence around a patch of land and you had a scrapyard or a car dealership; you can't do that now."

I asked why not.

"Because health and safety stopped it," he said. "Health and safety documentation and everything else meant that all the working-class man used to do is all gone now. So when Lord Sugar is on about where he started, let him fucking try and do it now. I'm not knocking him, it's brilliant what he's done, but when he's on the telly saying 'you can do it now' – you can't because there's too much health and safety."

"But I'll tell you," he went on, "it can be changed round – all the government have got to do is to get the money there, direct, cut the middle stuff out. I remember trying to get a bit of equipment for the lads and I couldn't even get that. A fucking ladder, a bucket and couple of sponges but it was 'We can't give you that,' when they'd just been given seventy-five million pounds for this community."

"But what we do *is* for the community," he went on. "We do gardens for the elderly, we do DIY, painting, decorating. This year we've had twenty-five young people through and nineteen have got work."

"You've got to give people purpose," said Eric, "give them a reason to get up in the morning."

"I tell you what," said Terry, "one of the lads I saw today, Benny, said he'd fallen out with me. I said 'What's up Ben?' and he said 'Even on my days off I can't fucking stay in bed.' That's how much they've got used to getting up in the mornings."

"Break that cycle," said Eric. "Unless people have purpose…"

"…you fucking die like the garden," said Terry.

"Ben said to me, 'Some of the gardens are a right mess,'" he went on, "but the people here, they look like the garden – drained, battered – all hope's gone out of them. When they're sat at the window with no hope, who cares about the fucking garden?"

34

Money, Expectations and Public Sector Cuts in Liverpool and Rhyl

My next stop was Liverpool. I was staying in the Kensington area, and that evening I went for a walk around to get my bearings.

As darkness fell, I walked past a small parade of shops; most of the shutters were down, except for a Chinese takeaway and an off-licence. Further down was another parade with a credit union and a pizza takeaway and a boarded up building with a sign in its window reading 'All items of value have been removed'. I looked into one pub, and there were two staff and no customers. A street light blinked on and off.

In a corner shop, the owner had put up plastic protective guards like a bank, separating him from his customers. To pay, customers had to pass money through a small gap in the plastic, and the owner would pass products through in return. I knew these protective guards were common in Liverpool, but I still wanted to know what the owner thought about being separated from his customers.

"It's safety," he explained. "Sometimes people rob."

I asked whether this shop had been robbed.

"No," he said, "but it's safety."

It made me think about the impact that fear – in this case fear of crime – could have in separating people from one another, so when I saw another off-licence down the road, I went in. Inside the massive, thick door, all the products, as well as the staff, were again cut off by the plastic guard. I asked the young woman behind the counter about it.

"It's for our protection," she said. "All the off licences round here have them. It stops people coming in and helping themselves."

I said it was sad that she was cut off from her customers.

"Yeah," she said, "sometimes I can't hear them."

I said I had meant that she was cut off from people and asked if she felt she lost anything as a result.

"No," she said, "I feel safer. If I were in the back, people could get in and I wouldn't even know."

I asked her if the place had actually been robbed before.

"I'm not too sure," she said.

* * * * *

The next morning I had arranged to meet Paula Nolan, who worked on a project supporting people experiencing unemployment, debt, fuel poverty and domestic abuse in the Kensington area. We started by talking about domestic abuse and she told me she was seeing an increasing number of cases. I asked if she knew why.

"There's no excuse for domestic abuse," she said, "but what we're seeing is an increase of women stating that the perpetrator is using the current economic downturn to legitimise their behaviour. Debt is one of the things that's exacerbating things but it does not cause it."

"You've also got to remember," she added, "that domestic abuse cuts across everything – class, race, you name it. We had a doctor and a pharmacist in recently, for example. We also assist women who've just arrived in this country – where sometimes domestic abuse is culturally more acceptable in their home country but once they get here it's not, so we're going out into the communities to raise awareness, letting women know it's not something they have to accept."

"The only positive trend," she went on, "is that it's treated differently now from the past – it used to be that it was seen as a 'domestic' and left alone – now people don't see it that way, which is good."

"We've got more clients on the other services than we do on

domestic abuse," she continued, "people suffering as a consequence of higher fuel prices, more debt, losing their homes, losing their jobs... There was a point in 2005/6 where things were great – they were advertising for jobs in shop windows, and we could have placed everyone into employment. The kids were getting jobs, and they were looking outside that poverty that they'd been living in for years, but now it's come back, the dark clouds have returned. There are still jobs but they're usually at the lower end – a bit of security work here or there or cleaning jobs in hospitals."

I asked what the consequences of the downturn might be for the people she worked with.

"What we are seeing now," she said, "is it's not one-off debt, it's multiple debt and people are losing their homes more. People are losing their jobs and once you lose your job then you are going to accumulate debt – you can't pay your mortgage, you can't pay the gas and electricity, standing orders, so debt builds up right away."

"A lot of people only need one change in their life to throw them into debt," she went on, "the loss of a job or leaving an abusive relationship, because two earners reduced to one earner equals less money to pay the bills."

"The number of people in fuel poverty is also growing," she said, "and that's not just the unemployed, that's people in work – because fuel is costing so much now."

"Each year," she went on, "we have more winter deaths in this country than they do in Scandinavian countries because people can't afford to heat their homes. It's generally older and more vulnerable people who will die and that's going to happen even more now because they're cutting the grants to support people in that situation. The basic pension is £137.50 for a lone pensioner, and from that you have to pay your water, your gas and your electricity, buy your food and your clothes. It's not enough to do all those things and heat your home adequately. It's dire really."

"Even funding for support projects like ours is going," she went on.

"The city council is having to find another one hundred and fifty million in savings over the next few years, so of course we'll get hit. We'll probably have to cut some of the services we deliver, like during the winter we try to raise money to buy new heaters – that way, when a pensioner's boiler breaks we can give them a heater while we try to raise the money to get them a new boiler. That will have saved lives…"

Before I left, I asked Paula whether her clients held anyone else responsible for the cuts or whether they saw them as an inevitable result of the global economic situation.

"They aren't blaming anyone," she said, "they're just asking for help."

* * * * *

I wanted to get a view from people in Liverpool about benefits and the impact of poverty and public sector cuts before I headed to north Wales, so I went out into Kensington on a bright morning and tried to find people to talk to.

Outside a jobcentre, I found a man and asked what he thought about people who criticised people on benefits.

"Do they think it would be better if we went over to a harsh US-style system?" he said. "Would we really benefit from a large number of substantially poorer people moping around in suddenly much, much worse circumstances?"

"They're also under the impression that you get more money than you actually do," he continued. "I mean, I'm buggered if suddenly a pair of shoes or trousers gets torn – suddenly I'm walking around in torn trousers for two weeks. The people who annoy working people who swan around in their brand new tracksuits or whatever – their houses don't look as nice as their tracksuits. I know guys who spend all their money on motorbikes – they have these gleaming bikes but go to their house and the walls are bare and they just eat beans on toast every day."

Next to him, I met two friends in their late teens, Cheryl and Janie. Janie was deaf, so Cheryl offered to sign for her.

I asked how things were going for them.

"At the moment, not very well," said Cheryl. "We can't find jobs – they say you have to pay your bills, but how can we afford to?"

I asked Janie what she thought.

"She says she keeps looking for jobs," Cheryl said as Janie signed her response. "She puts applications in the whole time and people keep saying no. And she says, with the Disability Living Allowance being reduced, it's just getting harder and harder."

Janie tapped Cheryl on the shoulder and began signing again.

"She says it was OK last year," Cheryl said, "but this year it's getting lower and lower. In the jobcentre they keep saying that we can't have anything but we need that money to live. What are we supposed to do?"

They had to go. Janie signed 'Thank you', Cheryl wished me well and they were gone.

* * * * *

That afternoon, I headed to Rhyl. The sun was going down by the time I arrived but it was still a beautiful afternoon. I walked down to the seafront, and looked out at the offshore wind farm in the distance, the sky above it a mix of purple and orange. Next to me, three couples had started their Friday night early, drinking Lambrini on a wall, but otherwise it was quiet. All the traditional seaside rides had been covered up for the winter, and deckchairs and tables were stacked away.

A man walked past with his dog, a breed I hadn't seen before, and we got talking about it.

"It's a Shar-Pei," he told me, "they're worth a lot of money. I've seen them go for £600, one woman told me they would go for £2,000. They were the guard dogs for the Chinese Empire."

I asked him whether he had bought the dog for protection.

"No," he said, "I just wanted one, and, besides, Rhyl's getting better than what it was – it's one of the most deprived areas in the country and they've thrown a lot of money at it. There's the new shopping precinct, the new cinema, the new park and the new swimming pool. The whole seafront was knocked down and rebuilt, but it's all closed during the winter so there's nothing for the locals to do."

I asked what people did during the winter when it was quiet.

"A lot of the younger ones," he said, "all they do is drink. Summer they've got things to do, things to get up for, but winter they just cause a nuisance."

He and the dog went off on their way, and I looked around. All the buildings on the seafront had their shutters down, and a police notice warned that CCTV was in 24-hour operation. A mural on the seafront showed happy families enjoying their holidays and read 'Rhyl – Sun, Sea and Sand.'

As the sun set, I met a couple on the beach. I asked them what Rhyl was like.

"Diabolical," the man said.

He pointed to the new concrete area between the esplanade and the sea, which housed a number of small shops and offices, a mini-golf course, fairground rides and the new cinema.

"It's just like a concrete jungle," he said. "It's like they've put the beach behind a prison wall. Any local will tell you it's a waste of money – it's a seaside town, you're supposed to be able to see the sea."

I looked at where he was pointing, and realised that there were indeed many parts of the esplanade that would have no view of the sea at all because of the concrete that divided the town from the beach.

"They call it 'the New Drift'," he went on, "but it's just a concrete wall. You used to be able to look out to sea from the paddling pool, but you can't now because it's all surrounded by a concrete wall."

"There's a reason for that, though," his wife said, "the perverts."

"The Sky Tower has gone, too," he went on. "That's another thing they've let go. And they built all these units, but they've never been let all at once."

"Have you been down to the harbour?" he continued. "They've spent millions on the marina and the sea defence wall and they're £1.5m in debt already. They've got to do the sea defence wall because you can't build there until it's defended properly – Asda was coming and a big shopping plaza but it's all on hold now until they work out how they're going to pay for it."

"It's been a very quiet season," his wife said, "but it's been like that everywhere. It's all about money, there's no money around, people are in debt, the government's in debt – that's what it's all about."

They wished me well and went on their way.

I walked along the seafront. The concrete made the sea and the sand virtually invisible for much of the main half-mile stretch of beach along the front of the town. At its highest point, the wall must have been ten feet above the beach, and now two boys played on it, one jumping down on to the beachside path below, winding himself in the process. Further on, there was a man-made pond, concrete turrets, and little shops and office buildings that looked like dolls' houses, giving the whole thing the feel of a massive mini-golf course. Across the road, one of the big shops still had a huge sign above it that read 'WOOLWORTHS', with one of the Os missing.

I walked into town, and at half past four, I saw an amusement arcade on the promenade being closed up. A sign in a bookshop read 'Keep Calm and Buy a Book' and a father yanked his crying toddler son out of McDonald's. A group of boys of perhaps nine or ten congregated around a Subway; one spat on the floor, another simulated sex against a traffic bollard.

Across the road, I spotted a limousine, and went over to talk to the driver, who had just arrived with a group of teenage girls.

"We're still busy in spite of the economy," he said. "Tonight we've got me here, and one of the others has gone to Liverpool. Tomorrow there'll be one or two out in Chester, at least."

"Basically, they're just posh taxis," he went on, "and you have to wear a collar and suit and tie, but otherwise it's just the same. We just take people to Chester for a night out."

I asked why, if they were simply taxis, people paid extra money for them.

"It's the luxury," he said, opening a door and showing me the leather seats, wine cooler and television.

The mother who had hired the limousine for her daughter appeared.

"It's for her thirteenth," she explained. "She wanted a party in the town hall but that was going to be sixty pounds an hour so I just thought this would be cheaper."

Her daughter came over.

"See you at home later, then," the daughter said. "We'll walk back."

She and her friends went off across the road to the cinema.

"They've just gone to see *Twilight*," the mother said. "They'll be back at eight."

I asked if I had heard correctly and they would be walking back.

"Yeah," said the mother, "we only live up the road, so they've just had a drive around in the limo and now they're going to the cinema."

She went on her way. I thought about the limousine and the Shar-Pei and what Eric in Rochdale had said about expectations remaining high even in difficult economic times.

Down the road, in the indoor shopping centre, I met a young man who had just finished his shift at a stationer's and I asked him about Rhyl.

"It's a shithole," he said. "It's just a dump, full of drug addicts and it's full of crime."

I said it looked like a lot of money had been spent on the place.

"But it's not really done much," he said. "All they've done is work on the seafront – there's still more shops closing than opening. It's full of unemployment."

I asked what people who didn't have jobs did.

"Fuck all," he said, "what else can you do? You can't do anything without money."

He wished me luck, and I thought back to what Terry in Rochdale had said about the nice new houses on the Langley estate and no one inside them working, and what Paula and the people in Liverpool had said about the impact of the economic downturn. I thought of all the money that had been spent on Rhyl and wondered how much government funding had been wasted during the years of economic growth and how useful that money would be to the country now. While I felt I had identified some good ideas about building a stronger sense of community in the UK, I knew these would not change the economic situation the country faced. I wanted to find a way in which I could contribute to the big economic questions, but, with two weeks of my journey left, I couldn't see how.

35

Young People and the Rise of New Economies in Bangor

From Rhyl, I headed west along the north Wales coast to Bangor, arriving on a sunny Saturday afternoon, the trees on the hills overlooking the town beautiful in shades of autumn. I had never visited Bangor before, but I knew it was a university town so I thought, as I came towards the end of my journey, it would be a good opportunity to talk to young people about the future. I headed up the hill that overlooked the town to the main university campus, and was immediately struck by the number of East Asian students I saw. I got talking to a couple of female Chinese students and they told me that their university in China had an exchange programme with Bangor, bringing hundreds of students to the town each year.

They walked on, and from the top of the hill I could hear the roars and groans of supporters watching a football match in the valley below. I walked around the main university building, and looked down into the town, and could see the match going on below. I saw a young woman waiting for a friend, so I went over. It turned out she was called Lauren, a waitress from Worcester who was in Bangor visiting a friend for the weekend. She told me she had done well at school but university wasn't for her. I asked why not.

"There's a lot of elitism in my generation," she said, "particularly with the work-education divide. Just because I got straight As, that didn't mean

I felt like I wanted to go to uni, but you're looked down on for that. Some people I know have gone to uni having never done a hard day's work in their entire lives, and they won't for the next three years. They're going to come out with a degree in something pointless, they're not going to be able to get a job because they won't have any work experience but they'll still think I'm the lesser one because I don't have a degree."

"There's this unbelievable pressure to go to university," she continued, "and the amount of people I know who are going to uni saying, 'I don't know if this is what I actually want to do, but I feel like I have to do something.' How mad is that? You're going to have to take out a thirty grand loan for something you might never apply."

I asked, if that was the case, why so many young people were going to university.

"It might have something to do with our parents' generation," she said. "They've wanted the best for us without really knowing what that is. A lot of people I know are terrified of letting their parents down if they didn't go to uni. Don't get me wrong, I'm not saying people shouldn't go but some aren't doing it for the right reasons."

"Degrees are becoming almost meaningless now," she added, "because everyone's got them. I'm not trying to devalue it because you have to work really hard to get one but if there are too many it's just worthless, while at the same time vocational courses are looked down on. It's like I was really into cooking and I said I wanted to do food science, but everyone said 'You can't do that, that's a thick kid's subject.' I ended up doing history and philosophy, but I don't see why that's more important than food."

Her friend arrived, and she wished me luck and went on. I walked through the grounds of the university, hillside paths with rubbish scattered around – a plastic fork, a box of Carlsberg Export, a Coke can, an empty two-litre bottle of cider. On a wall, someone had sprayed the word 'Spliff'. There was a roar from the football stadium and I assumed that Bangor had scored.

I saw a group of college students, aged around seventeen or eighteen, hanging around by a tree so I approached them and told them about the book.

"We're going to be a Third World country, a wasteland" one of the young men said. "It's just going to be people living on the streets – there aren't going to be any jobs."

"There aren't any jobs *now*," another young man said.

"People don't care if they fail in college," said one of the young women, "because they think they're not going to get a job anyway. People are just like 'Fuck it.'"

"In India, there's loads of jobs," another young woman said. "Teachers say you should get any job you can, but people don't want to work in McDonald's."

"My dad had to go and work in Afghanistan," a young man said. "There are no jobs here so he has to go there for months at a time – I hardly see him."

"It's alright," a young woman said, "I'm just going to be a stripper when I'm older – you get good money for that."

I said they all seemed very pessimistic and I asked if anyone felt more optimistic.

"What does optimistic mean?" one of the young women asked.

By the time I had finished with them, the sun had set and the football match had finished. It was a beautiful evening as I looked down over the town.

I headed back up to the library, where all the students going in and out seemed to be East Asian. I got talking to one Chinese student and asked him what Bangor was like as a university.

"Good enough," he said.

I asked him what had brought him to Bangor.

"The English education is good," he said. "Chinese education is good also but the English education has a long history."

I asked what he planned to do after university.

"I will be back to China," he said. "There are more opportunity in China."

I thanked him for his time.

"Cheers," he said, "see you."

On the main road by the campus, I found a store that took up two units right in the heart of the street advertising products from China, Indonesia, Japan, Malaysia, the Philippines, Singapore and Thailand. Next door was a fish and chip takeaway and the Irish bar just up the road advertised Stella for £1.40 a pint from Monday to Thursday.

At the main bar on the university campus, I saw a young man and a young woman having a drink outside, so I went over and asked them about student life.

"It's brilliant," the young man said, "definitely the best time of your life. There's loads to worry about, like money, but people don't worry about their courses."

The young woman agreed.

"We know it's going to get hard," she said, "but there's so much to distract you and, living in halls, you've got friends thirty seconds away. Like tonight, we're going climbing and next year I think we'll both do diving."

I asked whether people talked about the future.

"Obviously the work's going to get much harder," the young man said, "but you've got close friends so quickly – like we only met two months ago, but it seems much longer – so there's lots to look forward to."

"I'm doing a computer course," he went on. "I just want a steady job that allows me to do everything I want to do – diving, climbing and so on. The way I see it, the more time I'm at uni, the longer I'm shielded from the recession. So I'm going to do my degree and then a Master's and hopefully by the time I'm done things will be a bit better."

I said I had been surprised by how many Chinese students I had seen, and how hard they seemed to be working. They looked at each other for a moment.

"They all seem a bit anti-social," said the young woman. "They don't engage in conversation, they keep themselves to themselves. They're all doing accountancy and computer stuff, and, don't get me wrong, they're polite, they're friendly, they smile, but they don't go out of their way to talk to you."

"They definitely work harder and socialise less," said the young man. "It's just the culture, I guess."

"They don't eat much fast food either," said the young woman. "They always cook for themselves."

Inside the bar, there were young men watching the Manchester United-Swansea match on the television, and playing pool. A few young women were in, too, mainly sat at their laptops flitting between Facebook and their studies. A few young men stood at the bar sporting moustaches grown for Movember, the charity initiative where men were sponsored to grow moustaches in November. I found three mature students – Steve, Greg and Gus – having a drink and asked them about university life.

"It's definitely fun," said Steve, "though it's quite hard going on the liver."

They all laughed. I asked if people focused on their work or on drinking.

"Most of the time," said Greg, "it's like 'Oh shit, there's a deadline.' Some people only work hard under pressure."

"I space mine out," said Gus, "during the rare moments of sobriety…"

I asked them what they thought the future held for British students.

"It's pretty fucking black man," said Steve.

"I guess we're all afraid about the future," said Greg. "That's why we're at uni – it puts life on hold for three years."

"On the business course," Steve continued, "the kids are not that interested – they're just doing it for job and promotion opportunities. A lot of people are doing it as the next progression, like they're expected to do it but they don't know why."

"People in this country aren't accountable," said Gus. "If the politicians and bankers aren't held accountable, the apathy just extends. I didn't think it would be like this at uni, but the majority are very apathetic."

It was a feeling I had sensed a lot on my travels and I said to Gus that it seemed to be in stark contrast to the work ethic of the Chinese students at Bangor.

"But that's because they've been brought up in a completely different culture," said Gus. "They actually want to learn. It's an option for us but not for them. They also have to study harder because of the language barrier."

"It's highly valued to have a UK degree," he went on, "but I don't know why – I came here to study hard, but then it's like, 'Why bother when I only need 40 per cent to pass the first year?' I have six hours of seminars and lectures a week – that's a lot of free time and it's hard to get into a regime."

"With the international students," Steve said, "they're walking around with £50 notes in their wallets… China, India – our recession is benefiting them. Look at Corus – overtaken by an Indian company. They're in control now. And if you look at international banking and finance courses, they're full of Asian students."

"One night we got drunk," said Greg, "and we saw a few of them on a bench so we went over to chat to them, just like you would with English students, and straight away they were a bit funny. They clearly had prior stereotypes of what we'd be like."

"They even have their own Chinese-only football games," he added.

"But it's just like the English and the Welsh," said Gus. "I'm in the Welsh halls and they say they don't have a problem with the English but they do keep to their own. The English do that as well – it's just human nature."

Steve told us how he hadn't been introduced to his girlfriend's grandmother yet because he didn't speak Welsh.

"I don't blame them, though," he said. "England kind of deserves it. They just have this innate refusal to learn languages. Whenever I go abroad, I always at least try to learn the basics – hello, goodbye, beer… How can you be a global service industry when we only speak English? In Holland, they speak two or three languages, France, Germany, the same."

I asked why he thought British people didn't learn other languages.
"It's the fucking island mentality," he said, "simple as that."

"And it's just that typical thing," said Gus. "People think, 'Why would I bother?' We just expect other people to learn our language, it's a British arrogance."

I thanked them and headed back to the main road. At Morrison's, the young woman behind me was buying a large bottle of rum and two bottles of lemonade. Many of the people in the queue were clearly students and, as the clock struck seven, I could hear the music from the bars and see people getting ready to go out.

I strolled around for a while, and passed by the library at about ten o'clock. It was closing up, and I saw a Chinese student, who appeared to be the last to leave. We got talking and I said the Chinese students seemed to work harder than their British counterparts. He laughed and nodded.

"We just want the better scores," he said, "the higher achievement for our education, for our lives."

He had to go.

"See you," he said, smiling. "Have a good time."

As I walked home, fireworks were let off in the distance, but it didn't seem like there was much to celebrate: my experience in Bangor encapsulated my growing feeling that, while the UK was struggling, other countries were racing past and I feared that the result would be more of the decline that had so concerned me since I had visited south Wales and Rotherham. As I neared the end of my journey, I realised I had no idea what the national response to the rise of emerging economies should be, but I was clear that it was a question that the country urgently needed to answer.

36

Language, Heritage and Identity in Porthmadog

My next stop was Porthmadog, a small town thirty miles south of Bangor. When I arrived, I noticed immediately that most of the conversations in the high street were in Welsh and flags bearing the cross of St David or the Welsh dragon lined the street. There were Liverpool and Manchester United football strips in the sports shop alongside Welsh rugby union shirts, and a few English voices, but these seemed to be mainly from tourists visiting from England. It seemed an ideal opportunity to follow up on the conversations I had started with the students in Bangor about Welsh and English languages, so I began approaching people to hear what they had to say.

"My wife and her family speak Welsh," one man told me as he waited outside a shop. "I don't speak it but if they're talking about me, I'll understand."

His wife came out of the shop.

"I'm a Welsh speaker," she said. "You've got to keep the language alive – they should teach it in all the schools."

I asked why speaking Welsh was so important.

"Because we're Welsh," she said.

I asked whether she felt schools should also teach English.

"Oh, yes," she said pointedly, "I do think they should also teach international languages."

They moved on, and, around the corner, I met a man from Wrexham who was waiting for a bus and we got talking about independence for Wales.

"When I was younger, I supported it," he told me, "when we had all the industry, when the mines were here. All that's left now is the water, and you can't survive on just selling water. Where's the wealth gone?"

"The people who live here would say yes to independence," he went on. "They're brainwashed to think they would survive. But there's no chance – Scotland has all the money, that's where the oil is. Welsh nationalism is a thing of the past. I'm proud to be Welsh but I'm British first – the four of us are much stronger together."

I asked for his view of people speaking Welsh rather than English.

"People here see Welsh as their first language," he said, "and that's a bad thing. There are youngsters here who don't even do English GCSEs. Imagine someone who can't speak English – they've got no chance. But they're brought up to believe that the English tried to destroy the Welsh language, and they say it's the first language and that's it."

"My neighbour employed someone from this area," he went on, "and this guy couldn't speak proper English. 'Where are the jobs is?' he would say – it was pathetic. You get people called up to the army, not able to talk proper English, and they get the piss taken out of them – it's heartbreaking really."

"It's nice to hear it on the streets," he went on, "but it's got to be a handicap. When I was in school, I was very poor on English and my dad said, 'Don't worry, you're Welsh,' but that's no bloody answer, is it? I didn't even know what a consonant was until I watched *Countdown*."

"This area is about twenty-five years behind us," he continued, "but they're such nice, genuine people. They speak from the heart and that's it – they tell you the truth and there's no bullshit."

"Another thing," he added, "these Welsh people up in court who say they did something wrong because they didn't understand the English signs – it's a load of rubbish, and then we end up spending a fortune having every sign in Welsh. And then, a few weeks ago, people were protesting because a shop had a sign in English and not in Welsh – there was uproar – that's how fanatical they are. It's bloody feeble – we all know Superdrug, don't we?"

He wished me well and I walked on. Further on, I found an Englishman with a dog who had been a regular visitor to the area over the past forty years.

"They love the idea that they're different," he said, "but it's expensive. Every time you get a bill it's in both languages, or the voting forms, pages and pages in English and then in Welsh. But it has changed a lot here – forty years ago, they were setting fire to the houses of the English tourists. Today they accept the tourists as an industry – they still take the mick out of you, but I don't think they mean it maliciously."

"They definitely speak Welsh first," he went on. "I knew a woman who was about ninety; she couldn't speak English – that wasn't uncommon at all. The husbands went to market to trade so they had to learn, but the women stayed at home and had no reason to learn English. Our farmhouse where we park our caravan, their daughter is four and she doesn't speak English. They just say she'll learn it at school."

"Did you hear the story about what happened recently with the council?" he added. "They were opening the new bypass here and the Minister for Transport in Cardiff wrote to the local councillors in English so they boycotted the ceremony. It even made the *Daily Telegraph*. The councillors thought it was disrespectful; they said they should have followed their own Welsh language policy!"

He chuckled to himself and went on his way.

I had some lunch, and opposite the cafe met three young men, Liam, Ryan and Gareth, on their way home from college.

"I'm English," Ryan told me, "but I've lived here all my life. You do get a bit of anti-English – like from the community to my parents. They feel left out because they're English. People didn't talk to me much at little school because I didn't speak Welsh."

"We speak English with him," said Gareth, "but, if it's just me and Liam, we speak Welsh."

"I can't read English or speak it that good," Liam told me. "It's like double Dutch to me."

"Speaking English is helpful," Gareth went on. "You get more chances to go places if you speak it. But it's also important for the English people who move here to learn Welsh, otherwise they'll be left out and it'll be hard to make friends, and the Welsh will say 'Go back to England.' Generally, the English keep themselves to themselves, but if they learnt Welsh it would be different."

I asked them what the future held.

"The Welsh language will go," said Gareth. "The English come to small villages, buy the houses and marry Welsh people, and the Welsh language will be forgotten."

"It's like it says in that poem they teach us in school," Liam said, "what's it called… Colli iaith – it's all about losing the language. We do all these poems in our Welsh lessons – for our GCSEs, we have to remember twelve poems like that."

I asked if they learnt any other languages at school.

"No," he said, "the only languages we need to know round here are Welsh and English."

They wished me well and went on their way.

It was ten to four, and at the bus stop women were greeting their children off the school bus. An ambulance flew past, and I was just able to see it signed 'AMBULANCE – AMBWLANS'.

There was a man still at the bus stop when everyone else had gone so I went over.

"The trouble is that a lot of English people think that British and English are synonymous," he told me, "but they're not. A lot of people round here might say they're British but that's because they've been assimilated into this British nonsense without even realising it. A country without a language is a country without a soul. It makes you who you are. Have you ever met a Frenchman who doesn't speak French, or an Englishman who doesn't speak English?"

"I do think it's important for them to learn English as well," he went on. "It's always good to be able to speak another language, but that doesn't mean you should shaft your own language: 'The slave has to speak the master's language, but the master will never speak the slave's language.' I can't remember where that quote comes from, but it's a good one, isn't it?"

"The English," he continued, "they ruled the world, they even got the Indians to play cricket and drink afternoon tea. They have delusions of grandeur, they still think they run the world and want to meddle with other countries. They say if Hitler had won the war, we'd be speaking German, but for us it's the same with speaking English – it's still a foreign language."

I asked if that was a fair comparison.

"If you do away with somebody's language," he said, "you'll do away with their identity. A union is supposed to be an equal partnership but children were caned at school for speaking Welsh – you look it up."

I said he seemed to feel very strongly about the issue.

"No matter what the country," he said, "identity matters – the Basques have their own language, the Gallicians, the Domarche... Identity, it's all to do with identity. We're a hotchpotch of people from all around the world – it's the language that makes the nation."

* * * * *

That evening, over dinner, I got talking to a woman, Liz Godfrey, and told her about the book and the conversations I had had earlier in the day. She was reading a newspaper and noticed an article about airport expansion in London that she thought might be of interest to me.

"Boris Johnson is saying that China and India are staring us in the face, and we're just not acknowledging it," she said. "We just don't have enough direct flights in and out from emerging economies and they're not going to wait forever."

"All this talk of English and Welsh," she added with a smile. "We should forget that and teach them all Mandarin."

I felt the same sinking feeling I had felt in Greenwich, Rochdale and Bangor – fearing that, once again, by focusing on domestic questions, I had lost sight of the bigger picture. At least in Porthmadog, however, I felt I had learnt an important lesson: where people felt their culture was threatened, they sought protect it, and it was only if communities felt confident in themselves, their identity and their heritage that they could positively look out to the world. More and more, I felt that I wanted to focus my efforts at the end of my travels on building that internal confidence across the country so that other, brighter minds could look out to the world and to the future. But I also knew from my travels that there was a mistrust of political leaders around the country, and I resolved to look in more detail at leadership and how the country dealt with major long-term issues before I finished my journey.

37

Attitudes to Politics and the Environment in Newtown and Welshpool

The next day, I headed south into the heart of Wales and as I passed through Powys, I was struck by the hundreds of signs and placards protesting against a proposed new wind farm in the area. The challenges and compromises of environmental sustainability seemed like a perfect way to look at how the UK dealt with major long-term issues, so when I reached Newtown, a local market town, I decided to try to find out more.

On the edge of the town, I saw a sign for an electric bicycle shop and there I met Jeremy Thorp, the owner, and we talked about his business.

"The people who try the bikes are really enthusiastic," he said, "but, in the main, people are wedded to their cars and it's seen as a retrograde step to go back to the bike. It's getting them to even think about trying it, that's the hard bit."

"They're getting more popular on the continent," he went on, "and in places like China, but we're slow to adopt it here, like everything."

I asked why he felt that was the case.

"It's not something I have a lot of expertise in," he said, "but the British have always liked their independence, whereas on the continent they've always been happier to use public transport. It's also more basic things like people worry a lot about the weather here, but I've been cycling into work for the last year, and you'd be surprised how rarely you get very wet – it's probably only been half a dozen times in the last year."

I asked how people responded when he talked to them about climate change.

"People will listen when you say 'You could save money,'" he said, "but not when you say 'You have to drive your car less' or 'You have to put on an extra jumper rather than heat your home.' The economic pressures at the moment also mean that people are focusing on their own financial situation – there's definitely been a drop in interest in climate change over the past eighteen months."

"It's not that they're not aware of it," he went on, "but I think, as a society, we are just far too busy with other things. I suppose if you have children that's understandable but I still don't see why people with kids aren't more worried about the future."

"The other thing," he continued, "is that, as a nation, we're not very good with numbers, so, for example, you hear lots of people saying that we should be using wave power without understanding that for wave power to replace current power stations would be phenomenally expensive and technologically very difficult. The reality is that you have to do something about demand – people's lifestyles – and understandably the government doesn't want to give that message because it's so unpopular."

I asked whether he felt politicians should show more leadership.

"We can't just leave it to politicians," he said. "They're only representatives of the people – it's the voting public who have to push them to do it."

"What would really help," he went on, "would be if some of the national role models behaved in a responsible way. There seems to be this expectation that if you're important you'll have a certain lifestyle, but if we had leaders who did it differently – less jet-setting and fewer big cars – that would make a big difference. Unfortunately, I think the old adage applies – 'Power corrupts, and absolute power corrupts absolutely.' I think they're decent people and they come in with good principles, but, when they get into office, they start to lose them. It's human nature, unfortunately – we're just fighting human nature all the way."

* * * * *

The next day I headed to the nearby town of Welshpool looking to see whether Jeremy's views on public attitudes to the environment held true. Outside a pub, I met two older men and asked how they felt about the wind farms.

"I don't want them," one told me, "because they're unsightly and they don't work."

I asked him what he thought about climate change.

"I don't think we're having it," he said. "They're just pulling our legs."

I asked him who the 'they' he was referring to were.

"Whoever says it," he said, "the scientists, the government, whoever wants to put these bloody things up."

"This isn't a town now," his friend said, "it's all charity shops. They've got this one-way system – it's the worst thing that's ever happened. And look at the speed of that car, how can people cross a road like that?"

"You want to go shopping," he continued, "and you've got five supermarkets but no clothes shops at all – it's a bloody disgrace."

They moved off, and I approached a woman sitting on a bench to ask for her view on the wind turbines that were planned for the area.

"I know you need energy," she said, "but I wouldn't want them – they'll spoil the countryside."

I asked if there was anyone who could convince her of the need for the wind farm.

"No," she said, "I let things happen and then just go with the rest, unless it's right on my doorstep."

I asked what she would say if a politician stood up and said action was needed.

"You'd have to go along with it," she said. "There's nothing you can do about it anyway. All these things are mapped out – they get people's opinions but they do what they want in the end."

I asked if there were any politicians she did respect.

"No," she said, "they're all the same."

I walked on. Two women looked at shoes and handbags in a shop; staff in the sweetshop restocked its penny sweets. A woman walked past with a shivering Sausage Dog, a squeaky plastic toy in the shape of a rolled up newspaper in its mouth. 'The Doggy News, Kennel Edition', it read. In every window there seemed to be the same sign: 'Say no to Power Plans – People Power, not Power Madness.'

I got talking to a woman looking at one of the signs and asked her what she thought about the wind farms.

"The village I live in is going to have the highest visible impact," she said. "The roads are going to get congested while they put them up, and ecologically they don't make one bit of difference."

I said she seemed focused on not seeing her village damaged.

"I don't want to see *Wales* damaged," she said. "Apart from farming, tourism is the only source of income to Wales now and there are so many places where the beauty is being lost."

I asked if there was anyone who could convince her of the need for action.

"No," she said, "I don't respect politicians."

I walked on and found a man waiting for his wife. I asked him about the proposed wind farm.

"I'm not in favour," he said. "Apart from anything else, from what I've read they're not that energy efficient. I know people say it brings greenhouse gases under control but there must be other forms of renewable energy that people have looked into."

"Why is it that this country has to have all these wind farms?" he went on. "The worst one is China. Why isn't someone stamping on their greenhouse gases? Why do we have to have these massive pylons?"

I asked him if politicians could convince him of the need to act.

"They're all talking a lot of hot air," he said. "If you could bottle it, you wouldn't need any of these wind farms."

"But I'm not very political, I just have opinions," he added, "and I don't trust any of them. They never answer straight questions with straight answers – I'm fed up with them – Glyn Davies, Lembit Opik – they're all the same."

It struck me that most of the distrust of politicians I had encountered was at a national level, but he clearly felt let down by local politicians too. I asked if there was any way in which any politician could win back his trust.

"Do what they promise," he said, "simple as that – make promises, stick to them."

I asked if that applied even if the policies were unpopular.

"You can't please all of the people all of the time," he said. "It's just like taking medicine – sometimes it doesn't taste good but it's going to do you good in the end."

"Look," he went on, "if it has to be, it has to be. I know they've got to be built somewhere, and I know it's like NIMBYs, but maybe it should be solar panels on the roofs. Why can't they do that? I know Britain's not very warm, but wave power... Why isn't that taking off like the wind farms?"

Remembering what Jeremy Thorp had told me, I suggested it was because the wave technology was not yet ready.

"But you can rely on the waves," he said, "you can't rely on the wind. You know you're always going to have waves, but what if we had a couple of years of no wind?"

"I know all the resources will run out one day," he added, "and then we'll be stuffed. We'll have to go back to riding horses – but that wouldn't bother me because I already have one."

"I have to go," he said finally. "The wife will be wondering where I am."

He wished me well and was gone.

I walked on, and met a woman in her early thirties with her baby in a buggy, and we got talking about the book.

"It's all a bit uncertain at the moment, isn't it?" she said. "I don't think anyone knows what's going on, but I've come back here from the city to bring up my son and I find it easy to be apart from it here, where it's the same as it's always been. I know deep down we're all affected at some level and it's my own naivety to pretend that I'm not – but I just concentrate on what's close by and if my little bubble is safe and secure and happy then I don't worry too much."

I asked her what she thought on the debate about wind farms.

"It's a very one-sided argument round here," she said. "It's a beautiful part of the country but a few pylons aren't the end of the world, whereas climate change could be. But some people just see it in very black and white – not everybody's capable of seeing the grey bit in the middle. And some don't care what the big picture might be – they just don't want to see the turbines in front of them. It's the same as I was saying before – their own little bubble."

Down the street, I found two women of about the same age; it turned out one lived in Uganda now, so she referred my question about the wind farm to her friend, who still lived in Welshpool.

"They're very noisy, and the pylons will be very ugly," she said, "and it's the transportation through the town, too – it's a nightmare. They did a dummy run and it was horrendous, all the big trucks. And then the impact on the countryside…"

I asked the woman who lived in Uganda about climate change.

"It's happening there already," she said. "It won't stop raining and everyone says it's more than it did – hardly a day goes by without rain and they're having floods every week."

I asked her whether, having lived in Uganda, she supported renewable energies like wind turbines.

"The thing is they'll have to alter the roundabout," she said, and then looked at her friend nervously, "but in some ways I do agree with them…"

"Yes," her friend interrupted, "just where they don't affect people."

* * * * *

That evening, I headed into a local pub and got talking to Chris Holden, an accountant from Bolton in his twenties, who was in Welshpool on business. We talked about politics.

"My view has been tarnished somewhat by the expenses scandal," he said, "as it has with everyone else. Like there was an MP near me implicated – he came from working-class roots and you think to yourself, 'There's one of our own with his nose in the trough.' That's why people form the view that they're all as bad as each other."

"It was just a total lack of controls on the expenses system," he continued, "and the willingness of those who shouldn't have been willing to exploit it. It transcended all parties and backgrounds – to have those who are charged with upholding the highest standards to be found doing that, it leaves people feeling quite let down. The fact is that, whether you like them or not, their policies have an impact on the country you live in, so you have to have a view on it, but quite a large proportion would say 'To hell with it.'"

"And the thing that gets me," he went on, "is that had somebody not leaked it to the newspapers, it would probably still be going on now. But it's like a lot of things in this country – it usually takes a scandal to get something sorted out. That's a recurring theme whether it's hospital safety or underfunding in the armed forces."

It struck me as an important point that it took scandals or crises to encourage decisions to be made. It seemed to be part of the reason the UK struggled to deal with longer-term issues like its global economic position or climate change.

I asked him if there was anything politicians could do to improve the situation.

"It's like with anything in life," he said. "Trust takes a long time to build up and it can be destroyed in a single action. So the main thing is to build trust up again because, if you don't, people won't believe you, they won't listen to you, they won't take you seriously. If you lose trust, you lose everything."

* * * * *

I had reached the end of my time in Wales, and while I had enjoyed my time there and very much liked the people I had met, my concerns were mounting. For me, the conversations in Welshpool were not simply about the environment – they were about how the UK dealt with difficult decisions, trust in politicians and the ability of people to look beyond their immediate concerns to the country, the wider world and the future. If the conversations I had had were anything to go by, things were not going well and it felt like stronger leadership on the big issues was needed. If politicians were to provide that leadership, it seemed they needed to quickly rebuild their tarnished reputations, but I still did not understand why people were not demanding more change to a status quo they seemed so unhappy with.

38

Attitudes to Change in Nottingham and Birmingham

As I headed to Nottingham, my first stop back in England, I was on the last stretch of my journey, beginning to think about the country's future but still concerned about the way I had seen difficult long-term issues like environmental sustainability approached in modern Britain.

I walked into the centre of Nottingham and passed a shop that had a great deal of the wartime 'Keep Calm and Carry On' memorabilia in its window. I had seen the memorabilia a number of times on my journey, and heard 'Keep Calm and Carry On' quoted as a mantra a few times during my interviews, so I decided to go inside.

The shop was busy, and the music playing was of another era: 'Living Doll', 'My Guy', 'Dancing in the Street'. The characters in the books and toys on sale were of a different age too: Paddington Bear, Roland Rat, the Wombles, Basil Brush, Bagpuss. Wrapping paper bearing the images of the Mr Men was on sale too.

I asked the manager about the 'Keep Calm and Carry On' memorabilia.

"Because of all the stresses and strains this country is having, it's really taken off," he said. "One thing that really unites people, whether they're Scottish, English, Welsh, whatever – is saying up yours to everyone, we're going to keep going."

He wished me well with the book and I headed up into the main square, where protestors from the Occupy movement had set up camp beside the Christmas market and the fairground rides. By the time I reached them, the sun had gone down and it was bitterly cold. The camp still had two volunteers at the front so I went over and told them I had a few questions. They huddled for a moment and then went inside and brought a spokesman out. I asked him about the campaign.

"The main focus is the culture of greed at the top of the world," he said. "One per cent of this world controls 90 per cent of our resources on this planet and the wounds from their culture of greed and carelessness are deep. It tends to be bankers, greedy bankers – their behaviour is beyond cruel, it's almost inhuman. At school, I was taught to lead by example, but their example is greed and, as a result, people are dying. People like us naturally react to this so we're talking to the public and getting them to see what's going on, as a lot of people aren't looking very hard at the moment."

"I don't blame them," he added, reminding me of what Jeremy Thorp in Newtown had said about people's reactions to climate change, "that's just natural – people live in a nine to five environment and they just try to feed their families."

I asked what the public reaction had been to their campaign.

"We get a few people who are staunchly against us but we also get support," he said, "particularly from the elderly. The more we talk to people, the more they get us."

"They're talking about taking seven billion off welfare," he went on, "and that's going to come from sickness and invalidity benefits, and yet one of the big mobile phone companies has an outstanding tax bill of six billion pounds. If I don't pay tax, they threaten me with jail, but one company, if they paid their tax bill, it would completely negate the need for cuts – that's not very fair, is it?"

"Recent research suggests the FTSE 100 company director salaries have increased by almost 50 per cent in the last year," he went on, "an average of £2.27 million per person, and that's not including bonuses that can be £5 million a year. These are their austerity measures, this is them 'leading by example'."

"It's completely amoral," he continued. "The charities which monitor this put out a report saying they fully expect two hundred dead this winter because of their cuts – that's not putting people through hardship, that's killing people."

It was exactly the same figure that Paula, the debt advisor in Liverpool, had given me.

"All the homeless shelters are going," he added. "A Polish guy died just down there. They can't get his body home because it's going to cost ten thousand pounds to transport him. That might be an aside but I just want to show you that people are literally dying in the street. There's going to be a lot of blood on the hands of the people drinking from their champagne flutes laughing about what they've done."

I asked him how long the camp would be there for.

"Indefinitely," he said. "We started with four tents, and now we have thirty-five. Even as this winter gets harsher, they keep coming."

I asked him finally whether he himself would be there indefinitely.

"I've been here since the start," he said, "and I'm in it for the long haul. I've got two kids who I don't get to see and a job which I've had to turn down contracts for. This is too important; things need to change."

He headed back into the camp to warm himself against the freezing cold. Next to me, a man had stopped to look at the camp so I asked him what he thought.

"I don't understand what their point is," he said. "They don't actually tell you. If they tried to make it clearer there might be a bit of sympathy for them. There must be more practical ways to do what they're trying to because no one's taking any notice."

His wife appeared.

"They need to be clearer about what they'd do differently," she said. "That's the main thing, from my point of view."

They continued on and I had to go as well but I resolved to find out more about how people responded to the Occupy movement when I went to Birmingham the next day.

* * * * *

That evening, I stayed with Matt and Jacqui Burke and their four sons in their home on the edge of Nottingham. When I arrived, the house was full of noise – Owen had come back from football training, Dylan had arrived back from playing on his scooter, Mackenzie was kicking a ball about, and Ewan, the baby, was crying. Matt and Jacqui fed them, helped Owen and Dylan with their homework and one by one put them to bed. They watched *I'm a Celebrity, Get Me out of Here* and went to bed themselves at ten o'clock.

They were all up again before seven, and Matt and Jacqui were packing lunchboxes, changing nappies and getting themselves ready for the day ahead. Matt got his first client call at half past seven as he gave me a lift into town and, when he had finished, we talked about Dylan, who had been complaining about the lack of porridge in the house.

"I try to get it," Matt explained, "but we're too busy to keep track of everything."

I thought of the Occupy protestors moving into a camp in the middle of Nottingham – it didn't seem a realistic option for people like Matt and Jacqui.

* * * * *

When I arrived in Birmingham, I decided to go straight over to the Occupy camp, a group of tents in Paradise Square, a few hundred yards from the city centre, and ask people walking by what they thought. I started with two women who were passing.

"I work in the building opposite," one of them told me. "I don't really know what it's about."

"They've been there for weeks now," said her friend. "They need to get on with it – get a job."

I was surprised by the bitterness of her reaction, which was contrary to my overwhelmingly positive experience of British people throughout my travels, but as I talked to other people walking by I heard similarly negative reactions. Others were less bitter but were simply dismissive of the movement.

"I think they're wasting their time," one young man who was walking past with his girlfriend told me. "I understand why they're doing it but, to me, they're not achieving anything. The government's going to do whatever they want – whatever we protest it's not going to change anything."

"Come on," said his girlfriend, pulling him away, "I'm freezing."

Behind them, I met a computer specialist walking past and asked him what he thought.

"I just think it's funny seeing them in their tents made by cheap Chinese labour," he said, "and do they have mobile phones? Because all these things are driven by profit and wouldn't have happened without globalisation."

I asked whether he had any sympathy for the protestors.

"I'm an absolute cynic," he said. "The big issues, they're not going to change, so I think I might as well get on and live the best life that I can and contribute what I can to the people that I care about. That's all you can do. If you try to think you can do everything, you'll end up doing nothing, so I'm positive, but that might just be a 'British' attitude to carry on regardless."

I said it seemed he thought the Occupy protestors were wasting their time.

"Yeah," he said, "but that's just my opinion. If that's the best weapon they've got available and they want to use it, go for your life. They're not hurting anyone, and actually I like the far ends of the spectrum – but more for my amusement than thinking anything's going to actually change."

He said he had to get back to work, and was gone.

I went into the camp to talk to the protestors and met two of them, Ian and Anthony. I told them that some people had seemed sympathetic to what Occupy were saying, but didn't feel their approach was the right one.

"If there's an acceptance that what we're standing for is right," Ian said, "then that's a question for them as much as it's a question for me. I'm answering it my way – how do they answer it? That's for them. You can only be responsible for what you do."

"People who do this," he went on, "they're generally out of the system or there's a personal cost, at least an economic cost, and that type of sacrifice, most people are not prepared to make, or they can't make very easily because of commitments. This is more of a cry out for people to talk, to get together and to see if we can work together. We're saying 'OK, we don't know how to do it, this is part of an evolutionary process'."

I thought back to Matt and Jacqui, and suggested that theirs was quite a complex message to get across to very busy people.

"They're in consumer mode," said Anthony, "but the fact is we're not against anything, we just know that something's not right."

"People are disempowered, disenfranchised, disenchanted – pick your word," Ian said. "It's all put down on them from above, so they look at the political system as hopeless, whereas we're looking *outside* of the political system. They tend in their heads to think 'Are they going to form a party?' but Occupy is explicitly non-hierarchical, so it's like the concepts we're talking about don't exist in their minds yet. So you may say 'They're busy, they need soundbites' but I don't feel an overwhelming burden to provide solutions; we just know something's wrong."

I suggested that it could be difficult for people to hear someone say that the UK faced a serious problem without suggesting a response.

"If you go back to feudal times," Ian said, "people didn't know about representative democracy, they just knew that they should be campaigning for better rights, and then new forms developed out of it. The thing that empowers me is the simple elementary, fundamental principle that you should care about the kid across the road."

"I see an equanimity in people that scares the hell out of me," he went on, "because they know something's wrong, they know that they don't have a solution, and they often know that they act inhumanely, but I don't see any emotional response."

As I left them, I used my mobile phone to look up a word Ian had used to describe people's failure to act in the face of the inhumanity of the world – equanimity. The definition was calmness and composure in the face of a difficult situation, which sounded very much like 'keeping calm and carrying on'. I wondered whether that most British of mantras was why there hadn't been more clamour for change in the situations people felt uncomfortable with and whether the reason Occupy caused such negative responses was that they challenged that way of coping with the problems of the world. I decided to look further into that question before I ended my journey.

39

Consumerism in Birmingham

I was staying in Moseley, an affluent suburb of south Birmingham, and the next morning, a Saturday, I went down to the farmers' market, the views of the Occupy protestors still on my mind. Around me, people were buying fresh farm produce, a brass band was playing Christmas carols and people were handing out 'I love Moseley' badges.

I found two men in their late twenties, Dom and Andy, looking at the stalls and got talking to them.

"It doesn't look good at the moment," Dom said. "I'm not that affected by it but, realistically, the economy is just shot and there's a subsection of society which is screwed, the newly qualified young people and the poor."

"But, then again," he went on, "look around – it's full here and it'll be the same at the German market and the Bullring... This is only affecting certain people and, unless we're careful, we'll create a massive underclass and there'll be more social unrest, rioting and stuff."

I asked what they did in response to the problems the UK faced.

"Not a lot," Andy said. "I'm in quite a stable job; we're not really impacted by the recession. I'm an accountant, and in a horrible way it's quite good for business."

"Maybe you should do more," said Dom.

Andy laughed.

"Yeah..." he said, unconvincingly.

I asked Dom how he responded.

"Just carry on really," he said, "until it affects you, and then you can't do anything, anyway. But it is quite frightening. If I lose my job, I'd be screwed."

I asked whether there was more he could do.

"But you don't know what you can do," he said. "We don't have that much of a say, you feel like your vote is worthless…"

He drifted off, and Andy said they had to go.

Behind them the Christmas band played 'Oh Come All Ye Faithful', and I got talking to a woman and her husband.

"We're going to hell in a handcart," she said. "We're all doomed."

"I'm just feeling a bit pessimistic," she added after a moment. "I think it feels like a phoney war, like it hasn't really started yet. The gap's widening and I'm pleased to see people camping outside St Paul's. I'm not sure what I want to happen but I know I don't like the enormous inequality and being ruled by millionaires."

"But that's no change from the way it was before," said her husband. "It's just that the technology has changed. What is different now is that we are more cheek by jowl with people who are vastly better off and the people who have nothing. Tile Cross, Shard End – there's a complete lack of hope, crime…"

"I try to resist entrenching myself," said his wife, "but what worries me is that bad news feeds the level of fear. If it's too awful, I limit what I read about it."

"I just do what I can," she went on. "Like this year I've volunteered to do Christmas at a homeless shelter. If I were younger, I'd be on the steps at St Paul's. Now I just want to engage with people in a positive way and not accept the scaremongering."

"I just don't read the paper any more," her husband added.

They went on their way and so did I. At the gate to the central patch of grass where much of the market was based, flowers were tied to a fence with a card that read: 'To my darling husband, I miss you so much.'

I got talking to an Asian man walking around the market and asked him what the future held.

"More than likely," he said, "our standard of living is going to go down and there's going to be more hostility to people who are not native white people. It used to be the Irish, now it's the Muslims. In the seventies it was the National Front, now it's the English Defence League – extremism resides in every person."

"Come on," said his wife, "you could be here all day."

"You have to understand people," he told me as she pulled him away. "Everyone breathes, everyone has a family, we're all the same if you just take two minutes to get to know them."

* * * * *

I headed into the centre of Birmingham where the Bullring, the main shopping centre, was as packed as Dom had suggested it would be.

"I can't believe how many people there are," I heard a young woman say to her friend. "I thought there was supposed to be a recession on."

I bought a baked potato for lunch and chatted to the couple who owned the stall.

"It's Christmas shoppers," the husband told me. "Last weekend was even bigger, you couldn't see the pavement."

"I don't know where they get the money from," said his wife. "It's like Children in Need raked in twenty-six million – where did that come from?"

Around me, people weren't just shopping, they were also enjoying the German market, drinking beer and chatting, and things felt happy.

By the market, I found a woman waiting for her husband. I asked her how she felt things were going in the UK.

"I haven't really thought about it," she said. "I do think we're spending more money than we've got. I mean look at this."

She waved her arm at the thousands of people milling around.

"People are very worried about redundancy," she went on, "but then you've got Christmas and the expectations get bigger and bigger each year – we're not really focused on the right things."

"It's mad," she went on, looking at the people with their shopping bags. "It's frightening the amount of money they're spending. But you don't feel like you have any choice. You'd like a different lifestyle but you still end up spending all your money buying things. It's just unrealistic expectations, we expect to have everything. This is what we do now as a society, we go shopping – it's like America."

"But look at me," she added, showing me the Selfridges bag in her hand. "I look at myself in the mirror and I think 'Hmmm'... I'm part of it, to be sure. It's like going to work – you pay someone to look after your child and you could just stay at home and build your relationship with your child – the only difference would be I couldn't afford to go out to Selfridges."

"There was a programme called *The Good Life*," she added, "and sometimes I think we should just buy some chickens, grow some vegetables, just drop out of it and see if that was more satisfying."

Her husband called and they had to go. They wished me well and went on. I looked around; a man wore a T-shirt which read: 'No drugs, no gangs, drink milk'. There were many Movember moustaches in the throng of people and at a poster stall I saw three posters in a row, all in the same design and typeface: 'Keep calm and carry on', 'Keep calm and have a cuppa' and 'Wake up and smell the coffee'.

I met three women drinking mulled wine and asked them what they thought about how busy the shops were.

"It's funny you should ask," one said, "because we were just saying that people are drinking and enjoying themselves and spending money and yet all you hear in the media is recession."

I asked what she thought that was about.

"I think there's a pressure," she said. "You hear about people who get into debt over Christmas and spend the year paying it off. I'd never do that myself but I'm from a different generation. There's a greater sense of entitlement now. And people start their working life with debt because they all go to university so it becomes the norm."

"It's young people I feel sorry for," she added, "because their expectations are more and their opportunities are less."

She turned to her friends.

"Last weekend, Ian bought the papers and I refused to read them. It's all doom and gloom and you just think, 'What's the point of reading it?'"

"The world is so greedy," she went on, turning back to me. "I was quite heartened by the Occupy movement – we moan a lot but don't do anything so it's good that they're making this point. It's like banks, there just seems to be no accountability – they caused a lot of this recession and they're still getting big bonuses. We work for a local council and we have to tell people their services are being cut – their needs haven't changed but we can't afford to help them any more. Carers, adults with learning difficulties, pensioners – how are they going to cope?"

I asked what she thought would happen in the UK during this difficult period.

"I don't know," she said, "because we're not so strong now. We were poorer but we were more supportive. People live next door to each other and don't know each other. When we went to Norfolk on holiday, it amazed us how many honesty boxes there were – where we live, they'd steal the money and the apples and the table…"

I thanked them and let them get back to their drinks. Back inside the shopping centre, I saw a woman surrounded by shopping bags, so I went over and asked her why so many people were shopping.

"No idea," she said. "Christmas is coming up and people are just thinking 'To hell with it.' It probably goes on credit cards and then they spend the next six months trying to pay it off."

"The unfortunate thing in Birmingham is people get their priorities wrong," she went on. "It's like, the more gold you've got, the more important you are – but yet the fridge is empty."

The shopping centre was closing, but as I made my way for the exit I met a man from Dudley and asked him why he felt the Bullring was so busy.

"Christmas is the main reason," he said. "There's definitely a pressure, especially if you've got children – they see it on the telly, or it's 'what so and so has got'. I suppose a lot of it is also comfort shopping – I think we all need that when the times are hard."

"You don't want to disappoint people around you," he went on. "People work hard all year round – it's supposed to be a happy process, but there's a lot of pressure if you can't afford it. It's sad that you've got to express your affection that way but you do find yourself doing it – it's not so much keeping up with the Joneses but the kids do talk in the playground."

I asked him if he thought things would change.

"Yeah," he said, "I think it'll get worse. I don't think you can go back – Christmas will never be simple any more."

His wife kicked him and gestured that it was time to go, and as they left I reflected that all day I had met people who seemed to feel utterly powerless.

* * * * *

That evening, I headed back to Moseley and found a pub with an open fire roaring and a warm and friendly atmosphere. I bought a drink and sat down near the fire, thinking back over the past few days: Eric Noi's words about expectations still rising seemingly borne out in Rhyl and Birmingham; a bad relationship between the public and political leaders brought into sharp focus in mid Wales; the Occupy movement challenging the very British principle of 'keep calm and carry on' but encountering a sense of powerlessness and apathy amongst the people they were trying to convince; and, in the background, the fear that changes in the world economy could make the economic situation the UK faced even more challenging in the future.

Next to me a man was reading a book and after a moment he looked up from it.

"I have to put it down," he said with a smile. "It's so good that I'm going through it too fast."

I told him about my own book and the questions around change I had been exploring in recent days.

"I don't think day-to-day life has changed that much in Britain," he said, still smiling. "This pub would have been very much the same thirty or forty years ago."

I asked if people thought much about the future.

"I'm not convinced they do," he said, "stiff upper lip and all that. It's like I'll be at the West Brom game tomorrow – now there, in the Black Country, there's no industry at all. But everyone carries on – go to the football, moan about West Brom's defence, then talk about the racing, the same conversation you've always had. The more things change, the more they stay the same."

"There's a line from a song," he said, smiling again. "I can't remember its name but it goes something like 'live in the short term and hope for the best'. I can't speak for everyone else but I think that's what a lot of people do – I know that's what I do."

I thought of my conversations in recent days, and asked him if he ever felt that simply keeping calm, carrying on and hoping for the best was sufficient.

"Yeah," he said, his smile disappearing for the first time and his voice hardening a little, "but how's that going to change? It's like the Occupy people, I'm not sure what they want, but fair play to them for saying something's wrong. But then you get the feeling like the government don't have a clue what to do – people who are paid six figure sums to figure this stuff out. I just think this country is drifting a bit."

The word 'drifting' seemed to capture the national situation perfectly. I asked him what the answer was and he laughed.

"If I did know I wouldn't be here," he said. "I haven't got a fucking clue – I don't think anyone has. Ask me in a few hours when I've had a few more pints."

He went back to reading his book; a woman came over and her dogs jumped up on the sofa next to me. The conversations and laughter continued as people warmed themselves in front of the fire. It was a happy place, but I was really worried: the man reading the book believed that the country was drifting but didn't know what to do, and from my travels I felt that no one else did either. Many people seemed to be coping by keeping calm and carrying on, looking after themselves and their families or not reading the newspapers, but I feared this was not going to suffice given the challenges the country faced. I was now convinced that the UK needed stronger leadership from people who could combine words with actions, and that could only mean politicians.

40

The Future in Coventry and Oxford

As I entered the final leg of my journey, I wanted to focus my questions on the future. I started in Coventry, planning to head down from there to Oxford and finally to my last stop, Slough.

It was grey but mild in the centre of Coventry. As I walked away from the train station, I found a woman huddled under the awning of a theatre near a bus stop and I asked her what she felt the future held for the UK.

"Not a lot," she said. "All the jobs are going – it doesn't feel like there is a future, does it? It's quite upsetting, the things we had that the kids are never going to have."

"We've got no work," she went on, "no factories like we used to. To be honest, I feel sorry for the youngsters. When my daughter went to university, she didn't have to pay. But now my grandchildren are going to struggle to afford it."

I asked her how she personally responded to everything that was happening.

"I try to forget about it, don't listen," she said. "I try to do my best, keep my head above water, I don't owe anyone anything. I've worked all my life, come from parents who've worked all their lives. So you just plod on."

Her friend came over.

"When we were kids," she said, "men could leave one job on Friday and start a new one on Monday. But now... My nephew's done a degree, and by no fault of his own, he's not in a job he wants to do and he's got a twenty-seven thousand pound bill round his neck."

"It's a bit early in the morning for this," she added, "but it's a bloody shame."

They had to go. One patted me on the shoulder and the other said "Good luck, merry Christmas, and a happy new year."

A man in his fifties walked past and I asked him what the future held.

"I couldn't tell you, mate," he said, "uncertain really. This used to be a great centre of manufacturing but the things that made it prosperous have all gone – watch-making, car-making… Jaguar's still got a design centre here but that's owned by an Indian company so whether that'll end up abroad we don't know. Maybe there'll be a new breed of electric car which we could produce, or wind turbines or solar, but then again maybe they'll make it abroad…"

"That's the thirty-six," he said, spotting his bus. I thanked him and he hopped aboard.

I walked into the pedestrianised centre of the town and found a woman sitting on a bench smoking. I asked her what she felt the future held.

"Hopefully, we'll pick up," she said, "and there'll be more jobs for everybody. At the moment, we've got people with degrees doing shop work – my daughter's one of them – it can't be right."

I asked her what she personally did in response to all the challenges the country faced.

"Just get on with it," she said. "I'm going through cancer; you've just got to stick your heels in. You'll be a long time dead so you need to live, that's my motto."

I wished her luck with her treatment, and she wished me luck with the book.

I went into Coventry's indoor market. A wet floor sign fell over and people walked past it for a couple of minutes until a market official came along and picked it up.

I walked on and met an Asian stallholder. He didn't seem to have many customers so I asked him what he felt the future held.

"It looks really bad for the next generation," he said. "It's a recession and all the money's going to Afghanistan and Iraq."

"It's to do with jobs," he continued. "Everything from A to Z stands still, the kids have nothing to look forward to, no way they can afford a house, student fees – they're not happy at all."

"I'm feeling the pinch," he went on. "I'm hardly making anything – it's just surviving at the moment. The country is going downhill – like America – lots of Iraq people, Afghanistan people coming here. We've got to support them, but that will create problems when local people don't have jobs – they'll blame people like me, even though I've been here fifty years…"

"Foreigners seem to get housing before the English people," he added, "and then the EDL gets going. England's a small island, it can only take so much – the government's got to do something otherwise innocent people will get hurt."

"By trade, I'm a textile technician," he continued. "Leicester used to be full of textiles but now it's all abroad. The manufacturing's all gone, because we just said we'd get it cheaper from abroad. But charity starts at home. Before you give anything abroad, we should look after ourselves first, you know what I mean?"

I asked him how he responded to the challenges of the world.

"What can you do?" he said. "Just work hard and pray to God that things go right. I want to work, pay my bills, but it's worrying, you know?"

I thanked him for his time.

"It's OK, boss," he said, gesturing to his stall with no customers nearby. "As you can see I'm not doing anything else."

* * * * *

I headed to Oxford, keen to look at the country's future from a global perspective, rather than looking solely at domestic issues. It was a cold, sunny day, and the pedestrian centre was busy. I found a woman in her forties and asked her for her view.

"Britain's always been strong, resilient, prominent and well respected," she said, "and I don't think that'll change. We're always there at the forefront of efforts around conflict resolution. As a nation, we take control; we don't shy away from it. Take somewhere like Norway, we're not insular like them – we like to take a lead."

"We're only an island at the end of the day," she continued, "and we moan too easily. I actually think we're quite strong. We've got internal issues and life's tough in terms of money, but we're survivors and we'll deal with whatever we have to deal with."

She wished me well and went on. Behind her I met a young couple and asked them what the UK's future looked like. They paused, looked at each other and laughed.

"I struggle with that," the man said finally. "The times are so uncertain that I can't even see six months into the future. I just finished PPE and I must admit it doesn't look good from an economic perspective."

I asked about what the UK's future global role might be.

"I think we're going to have to accept that we're not going to be such a big player," he said. "China and India are growing and, in time, they'll start asking why we're still on the UN Security Council."

"I guess people won't like that," he went on. "We still see ourselves as 'Great' Britain and remember the Empire, but it's happening already so we'll just have to accept being more on a par with everyone else."

"But I don't know what I'm talking about," he added. "I'm just making this up as I go along."

They wished me luck and went off on their way.

On the bench next to where they had been standing, I found a woman having a cigarette break and I asked her what the future held.

"It's all doom and gloom at the moment," she said. "I try not to watch the news or read the newspaper – it just makes you gloomy. I'd rather read a good book. It's a bit of ostrich syndrome, head in the sand."

I asked about the UK's global position.

"I think we're going to fall behind," she said. "It's too expensive here – like Twinings Tea, they've buggered off – not sure where they've gone but I know they've left."

I asked what the UK's role would be in the future.

"Arse-kissers to the Americans," she said, and laughed to herself, "but then it's bloody expensive there, too, so maybe we've been arse-kissing the wrong people."

"Let's hope it gets better," she added, heading back inside, "if they can find the fairy with the magic wand."

I walked on, and found a man carrying a baby in a sling.

"Our place in the world is definitely diminishing," he said. "We're isolated in Europe and too dependent on America. And then when America goes to war, we tend to go along with it. Due to our Empire, we've entrenched ourselves and lost sight of who we are. They say on the news we've lost our national identity and they're right."

"If you look at it," he went on, "we've become less important so people are less reliant on us. Take the euro crisis, we keep trying to get involved and the French and the Germans keep telling us to butt out. I'm not an advocate of the euro but my concern is that there'll be a two-tier Europe and we'll be on the outside."

As it got later and the sun went down, people began to swell into the centre of the city, where the Christmas lights were due to be switched on that evening. By one of the Christmas fairground rides, I found two female politics students waiting for a friend, and, when I asked about the UK's future global position, they launched into the question.

"I think it'll be reduced," one said. "Britain needs to accept the fact that we're not a major player in international affairs but we still have a lot to offer in terms of being an old country with a quiet dignity, nobility and pride."

"And a bit of shame, too…" her friend added.

"It's the older brother style of politics," the first went on. "Learning from our mistakes in terms of colonialism means we've got a lot to teach the world."

"I don't think we should go down the big brother route," her friend said, "because it echoes the colonialism of the past, but we can help shape developing countries to develop in a green way. But I'm optimistic – not in a kind of nationalistic, 'we're great' kind of way – a cautious optimism. Scientifically, we're pretty cutting edge. We've also got creativity and, in theory, we've got an education system that encourages that…"

"…though the cuts to higher education don't exactly help our position in terms of global leadership on education," her friend added.

The young man they had been waiting for arrived and they went off together.

As I made my way towards the station, headed for Slough, there was a buzz around as it was announced that Roger Bannister was shortly due to switch on the Christmas lights.

"Roger Bannister," I heard a young man say, "who's he?"

Behind him, I found two young women, students at the university, and asked them what they thought the future held for the country.

"I don't know," said one, "I have no idea. At the moment the future for me is trying to get this bag open."

She wrestled with the catch on her handbag, and eventually prised it open.

"I can tell you about the future of biology," the other said, and then turned to her friend. "You're a historian – doesn't history tell you the future?"

"That's what we say," the historian said, "but we only use it to say I told you so."

"I think we're going to be overtaken," she said finally, "but we are just a very small country and we have no industry so I think we have to get used to that."

"Somebody told me," said the biologist, "that if the law changes all the banks will move and we'll not be a big economic power any more."

"But if the banks went," said the historian, "we wouldn't be so reliant on London and that'd be better."

I asked her if she was worried that it might have a negative impact on the British economy.

"No," she said, "because the rich will leave and the rest of us will just stay the same."

A friend of theirs, a young man in his early twenties, came over.

"He knows about this stuff," the historian said. I explained what we were discussing.

"Essentially," he said, "everyone has to live within their means. It's just not that sustainable the way we're living right now."

I asked him who he felt should be talking to people about living within their means.

"That's a difficult one," he said, "because the government know it's going to be unpopular. I guess the drive has to come from people themselves seeing that they've been spending too much, but while the government dictates it, nothing will happen."

"There's just a culture that we deserve this and we deserve that..." the historian said.

I asked if she felt that herself.

"I don't feel it's my right," she said, "but if I want something, my parents will generally give it to me."

41

The End of the Journey in Slough

It was the last day of my journey, a Saturday, and I had come to Slough, a fairly typical British town, to get some final thoughts from its residents. It was a late morning and around me in the pedestrian centre, two young women walked hand in hand, a man and a woman ate KFC out of a box, and McDonald's was packed with white, black, South and East Asian families. Outside, a mother gave her daughter in a pram a Happy Meal. A boy in a hood bounced a tennis ball against the wall of Poundland. Many shops had Christmas sales on, and, in the sky above, I could hear the rush of planes coming in and out of Heathrow.

I headed into the shopping centre and met a woman, Cheryl, who was promoting an education centre.

"It's quite depressing at the moment," she said. "I'm an optimist but a lot of things have gone wrong in the past and I think we're going to take a while to come to terms with them."

"But I don't want to be negative," she continued. "Slough is quite a diverse area and I think, if we can learn to work together rather than against each other, we've got so much to offer as a country. There's some amazing people out there and if we can learn not to judge them, then the future will be OK."

"That's the optimist in me," she added with a smile.

I let her get on and stepped outside. Just as it turned midday, the sun poked out from behind a cloud. I looked around and saw a woman with lots of shopping bags sitting on a bench. I asked her what she thought about the future.

"Hard times I think," she said, "probably for the next ten years. You've got to worry about China and India, Germany and France – they all seem to be doing better than us."

I asked her if she had any idea of what the UK should do in response.

"I don't know," she said. "I don't know what the answer is. I don't think we should have gone into Europe; I don't think we should be told what to do by the French and the Germans."

"We've got no industry," she continued. "France and Germany – their companies get all the contracts. Like that contract we lost with the trains – Bombardier – that wouldn't have happened in any other country. We just let people walk all over us."

I thought back to the man from the Bombardier factory I had met in London three months earlier. It felt a long time ago. I reflected that, in those early days, there had been a lot of high emotion – the frustration of the factory workers, the fear and anger about immigration in Essex and Suffolk, the recriminations in the wake of the riots. As my journey had gone on, it felt like anger had been replaced by apathy, powerlessness and sadness.

"And I tell you what else," she continued, "I've lived here all my life but I can safely say this will be one of the last times I come into Slough. It's all just charity shops, even Marks and Spencer is just full of reject stock."

I asked her if there were any positive things she could say.

"For me, there's not a better country in the world," she said, "the countryside, the British people are lovely – I wouldn't live anywhere else – this is my country and I'm very proud of it really."

"The whole world has developed because of us," she continued. "They wouldn't be where they are now if it wasn't for us. Our scientists and inventors are the best, and yet we're being bullied into doing things by other countries."

I asked if there were any examples she could give of that bullying.

"I just think Winston Churchill would be turning in his grave," she said.

I asked whether she would like to go back to the way things were in Churchill's time.

"You have to move with the times," she said. "We have to use the technology but some basic rules from the past would be good too. There are good things that are happening now so we need a bit of both."

Her husband appeared, and I asked him what he thought the future held.

"Not a lot," he said. "I knew Slough when it was just a straight town and it was bloody beautiful. Just look at it now."

"It's very difficult," he went on. "People don't look to the future because there's not a lot for them, and everybody just seems to be arguing amongst each other."

I asked him about the global position.

"China's rattling its sabres in the Pacific," he said. "It's a bit of a ruthless country, and I don't think America is strong enough against it now…"

"We've retired," he went on, "and thank God we have because the people who are at work haven't got a lot to look forward to – unless you're in government with their pensions… And don't get me started on the Human Rights Act – I believe in justice but it's not the same as human rights…"

He smiled.

"I'm going to have to go home and think about this," he said, "because I just don't know what's going to happen."

He shook my hand and they were gone.

I walked on for a while. It was a busy Saturday afternoon, and people seemed to want to get their shopping done and get home rather than stop and talk. Eventually I found a man who was waiting for his family. I asked him what he felt the future held for the country.

"The way it's going, not a great amount," he said. "It's really screwed up at the moment and the government's not doing us a lot of favours."

He sighed.

"Sending all these forces to Afghanistan," he went on after a moment, "it's a dead loss, they're never going to win – all they're being used for is a turkey shoot. All these wars are wasted, and they wonder why people get up in arms."

I asked if he had anything more positive to say.

"Nothing whatsoever," he said, "it's a total loss."

I asked what he thought about the British people.

"Oh, the people are good," he said. "They're my people."

His family appeared and he wished me well. I walked around for a while and eventually found a couple from Nottingham who were in Slough visiting friends.

"It's initially doom and gloom until we escape this Eurozone thing," the husband said, "but I'm hopeful for the future – we're Britain, we have to be."

I asked what they thought about China, India and other emerging economies.

"I don't think China will overtake us," he said. "Everything they do is shoddy. India may not either – they've got too many people, not enough roads. They've got the money but they haven't got the infrastructure. I go there on business so I see it."

"The problem is that we've got far too many kids coming out of schools without the basic skills," he went on. "It's apprenticeships that are lacking now – skills would be passed down but we've missed two generations of engineers and we'll never get that back."

I asked him what he thought we should do, and he thought about it for a long time.

"I've no faith in any of the political parties," he said finally, "so I just don't know."

They went on, wishing me well, and I found a woman standing nearby and told her I was doing some research for my book.

"I don't read books," she said.

I said that I just wanted to know what she thought about the future.

"Not a lot," she said. "You've just got to take every day as it comes."
I asked if she ever thought taking each day as it came wasn't enough.

"Yeah," she said sharply, "but what are we going to do, and who's going to suggest it? No one knows what to do."

I had pushed her too hard, and she moved on.

I approached another man and asked him about the future. He sighed.

"I'm sixty-seven now," he said, "I could pop my clogs any minute. I think the young people are still OK, still on track, though you still get your villains as you always did. People are generally kind, considerate – I think the future is OK."

"We're still a leading nation," he continued. "We've come this far and we're still a force to be reckoned with. I know we've lost our manufacturing base but we always find something new to do. China and India are having their heyday now, but there's going to come a time when China is going to feel the force of the working classes all wanting the trappings of middle-class life. India has very intelligent people, but it might only last thirty or forty years because you've got to have cheap labour to keep on top."

"I do believe that we're still the financial centre," he went on. "China and India are our working class, our workers – see all these pound shops – it's all from China. Their day will come – when you're sixty-seven, China will suffer a huge downfall."

"The thing that frightens me is the climate," he added. "I don't think it's hyped up, but I think we'll get there with it. The only thing that would wipe us out is a meteorite, but we'll all be on a new planet by then – and there'll be a little Great Britain up there too."

I walked on, looking to find someone to whom I could give the last word. Finally, I found a young man, Jesse Dodoo, who was on a break from his job in the shopping centre. I asked him what he felt the future held.

"Well, unfortunately," he said, "I'm in the eighteen to twenty-four bracket, so the immediate future looks quite tricky… Quite devastating, in fact – fewer jobs, lower prospects, the cost of housing... Thankfully I've finished university so I saved myself the nine grand hike, but it still looks quite bleak unfortunately..."

I asked him how he personally responded to the difficult situation people of his age faced.

"You just have to ride it," he said. "It's not burying your head in the sand, but what else can you do? There have been riots, there have been protests, there have been strikes and nothing changes. You've just got to find yourself a job, secure it, work as many hours as you can to provide for your family. Just stay calm and carry on."

I asked him whether it was sufficient to carry on in a time of such great uncertainty.

"We can only go by what we've been told," he said. "Those up top are saying we're in a load of debt, so what can we do as people to change that? We've got our hands tied. It's not a town problem, or a problem for one group; it's a national problem, so there's not much we as people can do."

"And, besides," he added with a smile, "I think that's what makes us so special, the whole British culture of getting on with it. We can be OK if we work together to see each other through this..."

He wished me luck and headed back inside. As he left, I reflected that although, like Jesse, I felt the British people were special, just getting on with it did not feel sufficient for the challenges we faced. I felt we needed to work to build a stronger society, and that was where I wanted to focus my efforts, but I also felt we needed much stronger leadership to face an uncertain future.

As I walked back towards the station and the end of my journey, it all flooded back: a pub with men drinking heavily inside; a jeweller with a sign that read 'I love you: Say it better this Christmas with half price gifts'; a group of friends greeting each other warmly outside a coffee shop; a mother and daughter eating sandwiches from brown paper bags; farmers selling produce direct from their stalls; the image of an impossibly beautiful woman in a perfume advert; and, on the Christmas merry-go-round, children of all backgrounds smiling, laughing and enjoying the ride, the clouds behind them pink and wispy in the setting winter sun.

Conclusion

I had travelled for a hundred days, meeting over a thousand people along the way, and I could not begin my conclusion in any other way than by saying how special they were. Hidden beneath nervousness, modesty and, occasionally, bravado, I found more kindness than I could ever have expected. Most of the people I approached were complete strangers but I could count on one hand the number of times I experienced discourtesy or hostility; indeed, some of my most positive experiences were with people whose paths I would not normally have crossed and who, in other circumstances, I might have feared. By far and away the most common words people said to me wherever I went were 'Good luck'.

Most of the people I approached were initially wary, but, when it became clear that I wasn't trying to sell them anything, they loosened up and let me into their lives, even if only for a moment. I felt privileged to have had that opportunity because, in the vast majority of cases, I found decent people doing their best in often difficult circumstances. There was much to like about them – their quirks, their mannerisms, their sense of humour – but, most of all, I admired their ability to cope with whatever life threw at them, epitomised by the woman in Coventry who was fighting cancer: "You need to stick your heels in," she told me. "You'll be a long time dead so you need to live."

On my travels, I also came across established national institutions like the Salvation Army and the RNLI and newer local groups – the Belfast Friendship Club, the Burton community cafe – all working in their own way to make the country stronger. While I travelled, both Children in Need and the Royal British Legion's Poppy Appeal had bumper years, between them raising over £64million during an economic downturn. The generosity of the British people, both to me and to each other, was humbling and transcended age, gender, ethnicity and class. I came home feeling that, having had the chance to get to know my fellow Britons better, I liked, respected and trusted them more than when I set off. I could not pay them a greater compliment than that.

Yet in spite of returning more confident in those around me, I also ended my journey more concerned about British society: in many places, and not just those of high deprivation, I found fear and prejudice, often amongst those same people who had shown me kindness and respect. While in some parts of the country it seemed as though relative prosperity and government investment had papered over the cracks, I could see how easily those feelings could become more intense and aggressive if the economy declined further and the impact of public sector cuts grew. In a small number of places, violence, disillusionment and despair already seemed to be the norm, with some residents clearly feeling they had nothing to live for or to lose.

In parts, the UK also felt like a divided society. Although religion raised the strongest feelings in the people I met, class seemed to me a far more divisive factor in terms of opportunity and quality of life. As I travelled, I came to see that class in modern Britain was about more than just money and power; it was also about the opportunities and attributes needed to get on and succeed – knowing the right things to say in a job interview, support networks to provide advice and to open doors, and developed personal qualities such as nous, self-confidence and ambition. The country I saw on my travels might not have had such rigid social structures as in the past but many of the people I met did not feel this had translated into greater opportunities for them. This belief seemed to have limited their ambition and undermined their confidence and in so doing had become a self-fulfilling prophesy.

Another big division I found was between those keen to remain part of the UK and those seeking separation from it. Before I had set off on my travels, the media focus around the future of the Union was on the upcoming vote on Scottish independence, but the prospect of a Catholic majority in Northern Ireland – set to become a reality within the next twenty years but hardly discussed – seemed as big a challenge to the status quo. As I travelled, I came to see that even if people felt a separate identity from Britain, it did not necessarily mean they wanted political independence. Nevertheless I sensed that these pressures meant that, within my lifetime, the way the UK was constituted would change significantly.

For most of the people I met, however, the issues were more immediate: keeping a job, getting through university, finding a way to pay the bills. But I also found a more subtle layer of concerns relating to the way people felt about themselves and those around them in modern Britain: self-image in an age where fewer men could demonstrate their masculinity through manual work and where women (and girls) judged themselves against the unreal 'beauty' of photo-shopped images; identity in a multicultural society, a particular issue for some in the 'indigenous' population of England and Wales who felt their culture was under threat; and a sense of alienation from the country that people saw portrayed in the media.

The most consistent concern I found, however, was the feeling that, for all the huge social, economic and technological strides forward in British society, too much had been lost along the way: a sense of community, shared values, mutual respect, trust. My first reaction when I encountered this feeling was to dismiss it as nostalgia, but as I heard it again and again from people of all ages, classes and corners of the country, I came to see that the feeling of loss was real and very painful. That sense of loss seemed to reflect not only a belief that the UK's best days had passed but also great unease about life in a rapidly changing society where there no longer seemed to be many role models, leaders and institutions to rely on. It felt like talking about the past was the only way some people could articulate how much they were struggling in this unstructured, uncertain present.

Some people, of course, were thriving in modern Britain. Many seemed to live in communities where there was a sense that the best days lay ahead: migrant communities in London, or the Catholic community in Northern Ireland, for example, in contrast to many white working-class communities in England, Scotland and Wales or the Protestant majority in Northern Ireland. Others who were thriving were working in industries that were clearly booming – such as social media – and seemed to be savvy enough make the most of the less-ordered, more technology-based society that others were finding very difficult to navigate.

Amongst the many people I met who were unsettled or uneasy in modern Britain, I found a sense of powerlessness to respond to situations they were struggling with. There is a cliché that the Brits like to complain but the people I met weren't complaining, they were getting on with things – 'keeping calm and carrying on' – because, it seemed, they did not know what else to do. From those dependent on Shetland's oil revenues to shoppers in Birmingham and Milford Haven, I found people accepting situations that they were both unhappy with and to some extent perpetuating. Many seemed to have resigned themselves to unsatisfactory circumstances over which they felt they had no control and chosen instead to withdraw into smaller personal networks, focusing on doing their best for themselves and their families and trying to avoid watching the news. Some seemed to have let go altogether, eating and drinking like there was no tomorrow.

Deep down, however, I felt that everyone I met knew that they couldn't really escape what was happening in the world beyond them. As I travelled, the economic downturn was beginning to bite and the potential for this slump to be exacerbated by the Eurozone crisis was the focus of media attention. In the background, however, loomed a potentially bigger long-term challenge: the rise of emerging economies, growing rapidly as the UK and other Western countries struggled.

Towards the end of my journey, my conversations led me to wonder whether what the country was going through was not simply a temporary downturn, but rather an adjustment in its global economic position, a clear threat to its much cherished international status and a potentially significant step on the road to a markedly different role in the world. When I asked people about these issues, I found confusion and few ideas on how to respond: it was as though the rise of emerging economies had found their way on to the 'too difficult' pile, sitting alongside climate change as issues that people felt were simply too big and too complicated for them to influence.

This problem with dealing with major, long-term issues seemed to be compounded by the worsening relationship between the public and politicians. If the most common thing people said to me on my travels was 'Good luck', the second most common was 'They're all as bad as each other', a view that seemed consistent across genders, classes, ethnicities and ages. Whether this view was fair or MPs were being used as scapegoats for Britain's problems, the fact that it was so commonly held was clearly damaging. There was a perception that MPs' behaviour was symptomatic of a moral malaise across the whole of society, and that this in some way justified others breaking Britain's rules. At the same time, there seemed to be a risk that, as the legitimacy of those charged with looking at the big picture was eroded, the country would drift without strong national leadership at a time when it was clearly badly needed.

And so a journey that had started with high emotion and extreme feeling in the aftermath of the 2011 riots ended with the quiet sadness of decent people struggling to respond to the modern world, their relationship with those who could have been leading the way seriously undermined. I came home concerned that, while we all, myself included, were focused on our domestic concerns, the world beyond was passing us by, and I feared that the end result would be decline, accepted sadly but without a fight by people determined to 'keep calm and carry on'. I had seen decline on my travels – with its own unique despair linked to fading memories of better times – and had felt hints of it throughout my journey, crystallised in regular references to a better past. I did not want the feeling that the nation's best days had passed to spread any further and so I returned from my travels determined to use what I had learnt to play my part in strengthening British society so that it could look to the future with greater energy and optimism.

* * * * *

I am well aware of the imperfections of my study but remain convinced that the concerns it captures are real and deeply felt. Each reader will interpret what they have read in their own way, but, for my own part, I hope that the stories of the people I met will serve as a call for stronger political leadership on the issues they raised. While most of what I heard about politicians on my travels was negative, I came back convinced that, deep down, given the great anxiety that people feel, they would hugely value strong leaders guiding a national response. Such leadership can only come from those with the power and the mandate to affect real change at a national level, and for all their faults that has to mean politicians.

Honest, direct communication with people about our national position would seem the best place to start: from my conversations, I believe that the majority of us accept that the world has changed, that the UK is not as powerful as it was and that difficult years lie ahead. The questions that remain unanswered are about the kind of country we want to build, what our place in the world should be and how we are going to get there. If our leaders cannot answer these questions with a vision for the future that can compete in our national consciousness with the myths and memories of the past then we should not be surprised if we keep looking backwards and find ourselves drifting as a result. If, however, they can answer that question convincingly, I believe they can win back the trust and respect of the British people and earn the right to be called leaders once again.

At the same time, I believe that British society will need to be strengthened if we are to focus on the bigger picture without the distraction and pain of internal division. Here I hope that we, the people, will look in the mirror rather than at politicians. How our society functions is determined by the choices we make every day, how we behave towards one another, our ability, as one young man I met in Hackney put it, 'to walk in each other's shoes'. We face difficult circumstances that can feel overwhelming, particularly as so much seems beyond our control; but we *can* control how we respond to those circumstances and the contribution to society that we choose to make.

For my own part, I have chosen to use the lessons I learnt on my travels to found a new charitable trust aimed at helping to build a stronger sense of community in the UK. While the four nations are very different and should be treated as such, wherever I went a feeling of trust in and responsibility to one another lay at the heart of what the people I met felt had been lost. Based on my experience, however, I believe that sense of community can be restored. My confidence comes from the most powerful lesson I take from my journey: that in spite of all the changes in our society and the challenges we face, the kindness and decency of the British people lives on.

On my travels, I also picked up some valuable lessons on the types of initiative that the new trust might support to harness that kindness and decency and to build a stronger society. First, projects bringing people together, building social bonds, fostering trust and breaking down barriers between individuals and communities; and second, initiatives that enable people to help each other to navigate their way in an increasingly complex, difficult world, building the skills, networks and personal attributes needed to get through and to thrive. Small but important initiatives such as these could foster a greater sense of community and citizenship that might not make our future any more certain, but would help us to face it together. To find out more and get involved, visit: www.thecommunitytrust.org.uk

Acknowledgements

A huge number of people have helped in the writing of this book. First, those who were willing to give up their time for interviews or to give me a bed for the night while I travelled, many of whom also offered help on the book editing when I returned home: Ronke Adenle, Alec Anderson, Jean Anderson, Les Anderson, Matthew Anderson, Issac Andrews, Haroona Ashraf, Shabaz Ashraf, Zain Ashraf, Zubair Ashraf, Dave Aukett, Molly Aukett, Val Ayling, Andrew Bamford, James Bamford, Patricia Bamford, Ruth Barratt, Richard Benn, Cheryl Brace, John Briner, Molly Brooks, Ewan Burke, Dylan Burke, Jacqui Burke, Mackenzie Burke, Matt Burke, Owen Burke, Joel Braniff, Maggie Braniff, Richard Braniff, Peter Brennan, Ian Candy, Tracey Candy, Ian Clements, Sheri Clements, Bea Costello, Gillian Costello, Terry Costello, Mauricio Cortez, Alan Courtney, Ann Courtney, Laura Courtney, Lester Cram, Valerie Cram, Stacey Cram, Jim Deery, Anne Devin and the young people at Edge Hill Youth Club, John Dinnen, Jatinder Dhillon, Jesse Dodoo, Gavin Emmett, John Ewington, Sarah Ewington, Cheryl Falder, Martin Falder, Josh Feldberg, Sylvia Finnemore, Julie French, Alex Fyfe, Breidge Gadd, Keshav Gaikwad, Uel Gillan, Liz Gillan, Lotte Glob, Andy Grimes, Steve Grimes, Liz Godfrey, Val Handley, Mohamoud Hassan, Alex Hawkins, Karen Hawkins, Jane Hayman, John Hayman, Mike Herbert, Chris Holden, Breedagh Hughes, Ameen Hussain, David Jones, Dawn Jones, Joe Jones, Sharon Jones, Kosta Koroni, Vanessa Lee, Oli Mansell, Imelda McGhee, Declan McKee, Lisa Mellor, Sophie Meredith, Janie Metcalfe, Brian Metcalfe, Mary Meyrick, Chris Minshull, Stephanie Mitchell and everyone at the Belfast

Friendship Club, Paul Moore-Bridger, Crescencia Nga Che, Eric Noi, Paula Nolan, Lauren O'Donoghue, Kingsley Oji, Laura Peters, Avais Qureshi, Paul Rhodes, Christine Riley, Jake Robey, Jane Robey, Sam Robey, Steve Robey, Dennis Rogan, Cameron Roxan, Abdi-Aziz Suleiman, Alex Smith, Terry Smith, Gerald Solinas, James Stewart, Irene Taylor and everyone at Kensington City Church, Laura Thompson, Janice Thornton, Jeremy Thorp, Ben Thurley and the young people at Clayfields House, Chris Vance, Jess Vance, Maurice Vassie, Raphael Warner, Colin Westgate, Shoqo Warsame, Duncan Withall and the Bideford street pastor team, Howard Williamson, Robin Wilson, Walter Wolfe, Karin Woodley, Keya Woodley, Melissa Wright, Guuleed Yaasin. I would also like to thank those who agreed to be interviewed but wished to remain anonymous. They know who they are and I hope they know how grateful I am to them.

I would also like to thank all of those friends and family who have helped in the subsequent development of the book, providing invaluable feedback and advice: Peter Hennessy, Peter Riddell and Olivia Seligman; Lori Heaford; Emma Birchall, Ruth Cox, Laurence Erikson, Danielle Evans, Emma Klapsia, Joe Kenyon, Maia Liddell, Katie McCrory, Maja Melendez, Rob Neal, Jamie Nicolaides, Paddy O'Dea, Kevin O'Gorman, Gina Page, Jennifer Painter, Ranil Pilimatalawa, Simon Surtees-Goodall, Alice Tomei, Helen Warrell, Dave Weir, Nick Wigmore; Louise, Ben, Jake, Dave, Mum and Dad.

Finally, and perhaps most importantly, I would like to thank those strangers, over a thousand in number, who gave me their time and let me record their views. Many of them may never remember talking to me, but I still thank them for making this book what it is.